# Universals of human thought

# UNIVERSALS OF HUMAN THOUGHT

*Some African evidence*

EDITED BY

## BARBARA LLOYD
*Reader in Social Psychology, University of Sussex*

## JOHN GAY
*Social Analyst, Ministry of Agriculture, Maseru, Lethoso*

CAMBRIDGE UNIVERSITY PRESS

*Cambridge*
*London   New York   New Rochelle*
*Melbourne   Sydney*

Published by the Press Syndicate of the University of Cambridge
The Pitt Building, Trumpington Street, Cambridge CB2 1RP
32 East 57th Street, New York, NY 10022, USA
296 Beaconsfield Parade, Middle Park, Melbourne 3206, Australia

First published 1981

Printed in Great Britain at the
University Press, Cambridge

*British Library Cataloguing in Publication Data*
Universals of human thought.
1. Perception – Congresses
2. Universals (Philosophy) – Congresses
I. Lloyd, Barbara Bloom
II. Gay, John
153.7′36   BF311   79-41471
ISBN 0 521 22953 7 hard covers
ISBN 0 521 29818 0 paperback

*To Michael Ogbolu Okonji,*
*pioneering psychologist of Africa*

# Contents

vii

# Preface

This volume has developed from a conference on 'universals of human thought' with special reference to African evidence held by the African Studies Centre of the University of Cambridge at Clare Hall, 14 and 15 April 1975. The original suggestion for a lecture series on cognitive studies had come from Sandy Robertson, the Director of the Centre. He had put these ideas to John Gay who was spending the year 1974–5 as a visiting fellow of the Centre and of Clare Hall, Cambridge.

Impetus for organizing the proceedings around the problem of universals had come from discussions between Barbara Lloyd and John Gay about issues left unresolved in her paper on the quest for universals presented at the Decennial meeting of the British Association for Social Anthropology at Oxford in July 1973. The original terms of reference were extended to include archaeology and literature as well as anthropology, psychology and linguistics. Jerome Bruner chaired the two-day meetings and provided an integrative summary at the final session.

The participants undertook revisions of their papers in the light of the proceedings. After reading the revised chapters and edited conference discussion Ernest Gellner prepared a general philosophical introduction. While we have had time to reflect and improve our original contributions the pleasure of the conference has been over-taken by two sad events. In September 1975 Michael Ogbolu Okonji, one of the conference participants, died suddenly. We are fortunate to have an appreciation of Okonji, the man and scholar, written by Herman Witkin, one of Okonji's intellectual fathers. But before the production of this book was completed Witkin died suddenly in July 1979 after a brief illness. Our volume thus marks the untimely passing of two men who contributed importantly to our understanding of cognitive universals.

We wish to thank all of those who sustained us in making the conference a reality and in making its substance a readable book. In Cambridge we received help from the African Studies Centre, its Director, Sandy Robertson and his secretary, Margaret Cooter, the fellows and staff of Clare Hall and Jeremy Mynott and his assistants at the Cambridge University Press. Judith Jenkins compiled the indexes, secretarial help was provided at Sussex University by Nicola Gillham, Betty Hayde and Doreen Mitten and we were also fortunate in being able to call upon the cartographic skills of Chris Heaps. Finally we would like to thank our contributors who came to Cambridge for the conference at short notice and afterwards worked diligently to prepare their papers for publication.

*Barbara Lloyd*
*John Gay*

*July 1979*

# Michael Ogbolu Okonji: African psychologist[1]

*Herman A. Witkin*

Although he died at a tragically early age, Okonji had already produced a considerable body of empirical and theoretical work. That contribution is on record and can thus exert its appropriate impact on psychology.

The real meaning of Okonji's loss to the field is of another kind. At the time of his death he was clearly growing as a psychologist. An 'agenda', for himself and for African psychology, was already evident in general outline in his research and other activities, and appeared to be taking on a more definite form. Had he had the time to crystallize that emerging agenda, and to act on it, his impact on the development of African psychology is likely to have been even greater than it has been. Himself an African, steeped in African traditions and experiences, and sensitive to their potentially unique impact on psychological development, he was able to bring an African perspective to his conception in the way only someone indigenous to the scene possibly could. In a period when there are so few psychologists who, in their own lives, have shared directly in the African experience, any reduction in that small company can be ill afforded. The loss of Okonji from that small group is, for several reasons, especially serious: he was theoretical minded; he had qualities of

[1] **Herman A. Witkin**
With great sadness we report the death of Herman A. Witkin while his tribute to Okonji was in press.

Professor Witkin received his PhD from New York University in 1939, taught at Brooklyn College from 1940 to 1952, served as Professor in the Department of Psychiatry of the State University of New York Downstate Medical Center from 1952 to 1971 and came to Educational Testing Service in Princeton, New Jersey in 1971. In 1976 he was appointed Distinguished Research Scientist at Educational Testing Service where he remained until his death on 8 July 1979.

He was a world-renowned investigator of cognitive styles as integrative processes in personality development. He authored numerous books and articles on a variety of scientific issues and is included among the 100 most cited authors in the *Social Sciences Citation Index*. His tribute to Okonji was among the last of these publications.

*Donald R. Goodenough*

leadership, both in conceptual and practical matters; his scholarship in psychology was very broad and deep; and his contact with Western psychology and psychologists was extensive and comfortable. So it is because he died when his emerging conception of African psychology seemed to be moving toward fruition, and because the small company of African psychologists was deprived of one of its best members and a potentially outstanding leader, that we feel a particular loss in the untimely death of Okonji.

Okonji's experience and training were broad and diverse. He was an Igbo from a traditional background, and a family of very modest means, making especially impressive the intellectual distance he managed to traverse in so short a life. For some time he worked for Shell Nigeria. His academic career began in sociology, which he studied at the University of Ghana. From there he went to Strathclyde, Scotland, where, working under Gustav Jahoda, with whom he earned his PhD in 1968, he shifted to psychology, in fact cross-cultural psychology. His first academic post was as Lecturer in Psychology at Makerere University, in Uganda. He remained there until 1972, when he left to become Lecturer in Psychology at the University of Zambia in Lusaka. In 1973, he moved to the University of Lagos in Nigeria as Senior Lecturer. Shortly before his death, he was made Associate Professor at that institution. During this brief academic career Okonji showed himself to be a fine teacher and productive investigator. His promise as a psychologist was quickly recognized beyond Africa. This was evident in his participation in many international meetings and conferences and in his relations with a number of psychologists around the world.

It was in fact when he visited me in Princeton in 1974 that I came to know him well, although we had corresponded in the preceding years. Our time together during that visit made it very evident that here was a first-rate scientist, a scholar who was very knowledgeable about the psychological literature, eager to learn as much as he could from others, yet critical and independent-minded in charting his own course. In the matter of scholarship, one of his purposes in coming to Princeton was to read papers available there which would be helpful for the review he was preparing of the cross-cultural literature on psychological differentiation. In the months following he frequently wrote for copies of additional papers. Beyond adding to my respect for him as a scientist, he impressed me, during his visit, as a really fine, warm, and substantial human being.

Okonji's work was diverse, but there are themes which flow

through it and bind it together, features which characterize its conduct, and areas of recurrent interest.

First, he was theoretically orientated, concerned both with the critical examination of particular theoretical systems and with tests of their propositions. Another feature of Okonji's work, already mentioned, was his concern with the unique influences of the African context on psychological development and functioning. With his interest in broad theoretical frameworks and psychological universals on the one hand, and the influence of specific situational contexts on the other, it need not be surprising that Okonji's work was both intracultural and cross-cultural. Much of his intracultural research reflected his concern with problems of education, with the hope that the research might help deal with these problems in practical ways. Finally, the empirical work Okonji did quite consistently bears the trademark of a really good and meticulous methodologist who was well informed about the field in which he was engaged.

Each of these aspects of Okonji's work merit further comment. Because of the importance of his Africanist stance in so much of what he did, that is a good place to begin. That stance is best described in his own words (Okonji 1975a):

In Africa, as in all other human groups or societies, the scientific enterprise is rooted in the prevalent World view, the systems of beliefs and values. African approaches to the study and understanding of human behavior are shaped by the African's view of the nature of the Universe and man's position in it as well as the systems of beliefs and values. It is true that there are some variations in African culture and ecologies, hence the need for caution in generalizing about the whole continent. But while caution is useful to guard against extreme sweeping generalizations about Africa, my personal impression in my travels through Western, Eastern and Central Africa is that African cultures are more alike than we are even prepared to accept. (p. 297)

It is noteworthy that while seeking to develop a psychological perspective which reflected the African setting, Okonji did not regard Western psychology as a source of danger to such an enterprise which had to be guarded against. This is not surprising since he received his graduate training in the West. In fact, Okonji seemed quite eager to learn as much as he could about Western psychology's theories and methods for his work in the African setting. At the same time he kept a critical eye on their relevance and appropriateness to that setting and sought to maintain the distance he felt necessary to allow achievement of the independent African position he was seeking to formulate. By not seeing Western psychology as a threat to the African enterprise, it was possible for Okonji to maintain congenial, colleaguely relations with Western psychologists. This situation greatly facilitated communication, to the benefit of the field at large. Indeed, he seemed to be looking toward the eventual integration of what came out of the African work with concepts and findings in Western psychology, in order to achieve a psychology which is free of Western cultural biases and which has universal applicability.

A paper Okonji presented at a symposium at the Kingston meetings of the IACCP, 'African approaches to the study of be- haviour' (1974a) expresses his African orientation very cogently. The basic position Okonji takes in this paper is that non-Western peoples, no less than Western peoples, study and try to identify the behaviour of others within their group, as part of their need to predict and control the behaviour of these people. In making this basic point, he notes:

So far it has been taken for granted that the science of psychology is an esoteric Western invention beyond the grasp of other people (there are even people who still maintain that psychology is too abstract and complicated a business for Africans and Africa). Yet we do know that the ability to predict future behavior is indispensable for the survival of any group of people. (p. 1)[2]

To make his point that non-Westerners 'have a psychology' which mirrors their group's existence, Okonji presents a sensitive, descrip- tive set of what he calls 'ethnographic notes' on the Igbo of Nigeria, and on several other African groups. The focus in these accounts is primarily on cosmology, especially the religious belief systems and values of these groups. These accounts, though brief, make fascinating reading. Following their presentation, Okonji goes on to consider the 'tools' Africans use in their approaches to the study of each other's behaviour. Naturalistic observation is plausibly described as the main one. Another is physique watching, which derives from the categories of physical typologies and stereotypes, relating physical characteristics to behaviour, which many Africans have developed. Still another particularly fascinating approach is role-playing, in which the intention or veracity of a child or adult is checked through the use of a contrived situation which might, for example, make it possible for the person being 'checked' to be caught in the act of

[2] This statement was in the paper Okonji presented at the Kingston conference, but was not included in the shortened version published in the proceedings of the conference.

doing something of which he had been suspected. Yet another approach is the use of personal, family and clan case history.

What Okonji sought to do in this examination of ethnographic settings, and of the approaches people use in trying to understand each other in order to conduct their relationships, was to start with behaviours in their naturally-occurring context and then to identify methods of studying these behaviours which are appropriate to them. Such a sequence is quite different from the more commonly followed one of importing Western approaches to the study of non-Western behaviours.

This perspective on the study of behaviour, and the attention he drew in some of his empirical reports (e.g. Okonji 1970) to the need for more carefully worked out taxonomies of Western tasks taken over into non-Western cultures, encourage the speculation that Okonji might have made more use of tests devised for their indigenous appropriateness, to complement his predominant use of tests of Western origin – in other words, to have followed both an emic and etic approach.

Okonji's focus on the African scene carried with it a strong commitment to using the knowledge about African psychology and behaviour on behalf of Africa's practical problems, particularly in the area of education. Interestingly, Okonji saw a strategic political reason for doing applied work, aside from the payoff such work might have for problems of everyday living. Thus he wrote (Okonji, in press):

It has been suggested that it may be premature to become applied-oriented at this stage of the history of psychology in the developing countries. Yet, a psychology which is still associated with metaphysical and philosophical disciplines runs the risk of acquiring the image of an abstruse and irrelevant discipline unless it can be made to appear concerned with some of the immediate and pressing problems of society. Since most activists in the field of cross-cultural psychology are foreigners in the countries where they do this research, the whole enterprise may be seen as an aspect of neocolonialist exploitation of the developing parts of the world. Worse still, cross-cultural psychology may come to be seen as a European-masterminded plot to study and understand people in non-Western societies for the sake of showing how inferior they are, thereby justifying racism and racist oppression.

Beyond expressing these ideological concerns, Okonji did a good deal of research on cognitive variables (mainly from the Piagetian tradition) relevant to education which might ultimately be helpful in increasing the number of technologically trained people in Africa. These studies had an intracultural focus, and used as subjects children of different ages, educational experiences and socio-economic background. In one instance a Western group was included as well, but in most cases the results obtained with the indigenous groups he studied were looked at against extant knowledge about the behaviour of Western children in similar situations. The cognitive function which received particular attention in these studies was classificatory behaviour (Okonji 1968, 1971a, 1974b). Other functions examined included understanding of geometry (Okonji 1971b) and auditory-visual integration (Okonji 1975b). In comparing the results for his indigenous groups to data from Western studies, Okonji sought to identify what may be 'special' to the cognitive operations of his African children, and eventually useful in maximizing their learning. It is worth noting, parenthetically, that in some of these papers on cognitive functioning universals in behaviour continued to intrigue Okonji.

Okonji's concerns with practical applications were not limited to his empirical work alone. As we see later, it was also an important focus in his thinking about theoretical issues and systems. And it took him into the public arena as well. Mundy-Castle (1975), in a memorial statement on Okonji, notes that Okonji gave radio talks and wrote popular articles on such themes as 'African personality' and 'Psychological causes of civil war'.

We turn now to what has been another major feature of Okonji's work and thought: his theoretical-mindedness. Two theoretical frameworks, Piagetian theory and differentiation theory (especially its field dependence-independence cognitive-style component), were of particular interest to him throughout his career. These two conceptions guided his very first research, carried out for his doctoral dissertation on cultural variables in cognition (Okonji 1968, 1969). For Okonji there were important similarities between these two conceptions and they shared characteristics which drew his interest to them. He saw both as developmental in nature, with a particular emphasis on differentiation; their stance was an organismic one; they seemed to lend themselves to use across cultures; they offered opportunities for pursuing his continuing interest in universals in behaviour, which he approached with an eye for the moderating influence of situational factors to which his concerns as an Africanist led him; they were 'big' theories (he apparently felt comfortable with such theories), which offered leads for examining diverse facets of behaviour in their interrelationships and with regard to their origins; and they had potential for fruitful application to problems of education, which was so important to him. But his interest in these two approaches went beyond charting parallels between them. He had already pointed out in his dissertation, written as early as 1968, opportunities for bringing them together and the possible advantages of doing so:

For both the notions of the development of cognitive style and Piaget's theory of cognitive development make their central process that of ego-differentiation or ego-decentring. But Piaget failed to make adequate allowance for variations in socialization practices across cultures in spite of all its influences in both the rate and pattern of cognitive growth. It is the writer's view that a full appreciation of the implications of the concept of cognitive style and applying them to the Piagetian model of intellectual development will enable it to cope with problems of intertask consistency and variations in patterns of growth across cultures that have cropped up from time to time in the literature. (p. 181)

In both these insights, Okonji was ahead of his time, and a very large number of studies have substantively confirmed the first of them. (See Huteau, in press, for a recent review of the literature relating performance on Piagetian tasks to individual differences in psychological differentiation.) Okonji himself (Okonji & Olagbaiye 1974, 1975) contributed to that literature a number of years later, thus putting his conception of the interrelation between the two theoretical frameworks to empirical test. This study showed, among Nigerian children, an impressively high relation between field dependence-independence and performance on the Piaget & Inhelder 3-mountain task. In a paper completed just before his death (Okonji, in press) he commented on the potential value of bringing these two conceptions together in the cross-cultural arena in particular. 'If these two theoretical approaches can be demonstrated to be closely linked in cross-cultural studies,' he wrote, 'then the way will have been paved for a unified organismic theory of development.' This evidence of a continuing interest in the relation between Piagetian and differentiation theories, his proposal on the possible benefit to be gained by pursuing that relation in the cross-cultural arena, and the empirical work he did on that relation late in his career, makes it possible that this is one of the lines of work he might have continued.

In addition to his study with Olagbaiye just cited, from his dissertation onwards Okonji did a number of studies on Piagetian variables in children (Okonji 1968, 1971a, b, 1974b). As noted when these studies were cited earlier, though primarily intracultural, they attended to Western findings on record for the sake of identifying cognitive operations in African children which might enter into how such children learn.

In the case of differentiation theory, here again Okonji conducted empirical studies, but in addition he wrote papers of a conceptual nature, including his contribution to the present volume, and an extended review of the cross-cultural literature on differentiation (Okonji, 1980). We can imagine that several features of differentiation theory – that it is concerned with formal psychological properties which are more likely to be similar across individuals and groups than are content properties, and yet the expressions of these formal properties are influenced by concrete prevailing conditions – may have made it attractive to someone like Okonji who was intrigued by universals and at the same time concerned with how seeming universals are moderated by the African setting.

Considering first his empirical work, Okonji's dissertation research (1968, 1969) focused particularly on rural/urban differences in extent of field dependence-independence among Nigerians. His expectations here were based on proposals from the original Western-based theory on the role of child-rearing practices in the development of cognitive style. Other hypotheses he considered came from proposals in the Western conception about sex differences in cognitive style and self-consistency in performance across cognitive-style tasks.

Although a risky enterprise, it is tempting to seek continuities in Okonji's work over time. In speculating about the bases of the partial confirmation he found of his expectation of greater field dependence among his rural than among his urban subjects, Okonji (1969) points out that though he emphasized the contributions of differences in child-rearing practices to this outcome, other influences may have played a role as well; and he calls for research on the contribution of each of the components of what is in effect a complexly integrated assembly to the development of cognitive styles. Perhaps in pursuit of this directive, Okonji subsequently conducted a study (1973) in which he examined mother–child interactions in relation to children's cognitive style, taking the very desirable methodological step of interviewing mothers and making direct observations of actual mother–child interactions. One of the problems Okonji ran into, however, came precisely from contextual factors and/or data characteristics specific to the setting in which he worked. Scores for variables derived from both methods showed an exceedingly restricted range. While the bases of this lack of range is not clear, it inevitably had an adverse effect on the possibility of obtaining significant correlations between these scores and other measures.

Okonji's comprehensive review of the cross-cultural literature on psychological differentiation, which he finished drafting just before his death (Okonji, 1980), gave him an opportunity to examine differentiation theory and its empirical underpinning, from a cross-culture perspective. Okonji came out of his examination of that literature with what, on the whole, is an essentially positive view of the general validity of most of the postulates of differentiation theory and its potential for use in other cultures. Thus he wrote: 'Considering the conglomeration of tests and experimental situations used in these studies one is amazed that so many results seem to be saying the same things have been obtained.' At the same time he pointed out lacunae and areas of vagueness in the conception; and he identified places where things may be different, conceptually and empirically, in non-Western settings than in the West, suggesting directions of enquiry for documenting these differences and their possible sources. He saw the job ahead in this way: 'We recognize from empirical observation and anecdotal evidence...that the concept of style in cognitive functioning may be applicable to non-Western peoples, yet we do need studies which will detail and clarify the ways in which these styles are conceptualized in different cultural groups.' Whether he might have taken such further steps himself, it is of course not possible to say.

Because Okonji's review was conducted from the vantage point of someone outside the culture in which differentiation theory grew up, his views about the usefulness of the theory and its accompanying methodologies in the cross-culture enterprise, and his critical commentaries merit serious attention.

It has been possible to spell out what Okonji accomplished in his lifetime, and to conjecture about where he seemed to be heading in what would ordinarily have been a still long span of working time ahead. As to what he might have accomplished had he lived, that can be no more than guesswork. Because he was already a fine and productive psychologist, it is reasonable to believe that he would have gone on to grow and accomplish much. His commitment to an African psychology, joined with his activist stance and his concern with theory, make it also reasonable to believe that he would have done his part in, and perhaps given leadership to the development of an African psychology which had legitimacy in its own right and connecting pathways to general psychology. But these are all in the realm of what might have been. There can be no doubt, however, that he helped give impetus to a development which will be carried forward by his colleagues and successors, in part because historic forces compel it. In this sense, we may say, in keeping with the ancient Greek wisdom, 'No voice is wholly lost that is the voice of many men', that Okonji left a mark on psychology which will continue to be felt.

## References

Huteau, M. (in press) 'Dépendance-indépendance à l'égard du champ et développement de la pensée opératoire', *Les Archives de Psychologie*

Mundy-Castle, A. C. (1975) 'In memoriam: Michael Ogbolu Okonji (1936–1975)', *International Journal of Psychology* 10, 297–8

Okonji, M. O. (1968) 'Cultural variables in cognition', Unpublished PhD thesis, University of Strathclyde, Glasgow

—— (1969) 'Differential effects of rural and urban upbringing on the development of cognitive styles', *International Journal of Psychology* 4, 293–305

—— (1970) 'The effect of special training on the classificatory behaviour of some Nigerian Ibo children', *British Journal of Educational Psychology* 40, 21–6

—— (1971a) 'A cross-cultural study of the effects of familiarity on classificatory behaviour', *Journal of Cross-Cultural Psychology* 2, 39–49

—— (1971b) 'Culture and children's understanding of geometry', *International Journal of Psychology* 6, 121–8

—— (1973) 'Child-rearing and the development of cognitive style in Uganda', Pre-publication draft of a monograph to be published by the University of Lagos Press

—— (1974a) 'African approaches to the study of behavior', Paper presented at the 2nd Conference of the International Association for Cross-Cultural Psychology, Queen's University, Kingston, Ontario, August

—— (1974b) 'The development of logical thinking in preschool Zambian children: classification', *Journal of Genetic Psychology* 125, 247–55

—— (1975a) 'African approaches to the study of behaviour', in Berry, J. W. & Lonner, W. J. (eds.) *Applied cross-cultural psychology.* Amsterdam: Swets & Zeitlinger

—— (1975b) 'Socio-economic background, race and auditory-visual integration in children', in Dawson, J. L. M. & Lonner, W. J. (eds.), *Readings in cross-cultural psychology.* Hong Kong University Press

—— & Olagbaiye, O. O. (1974) 'Egocentrism and psychological differentiation: a cross-cultural perspective', Paper presented at the 2nd

Conference of the International Association for Cross-Cultural Psychology, Queen's University, Kingston, Ontario, August
—— & Olagbaiye, O. O. (1975) 'Brief reports: field dependence and the coordination of perspectives', *Developmental Psychology* 4, 520
—— 'Psychological differentiation', in the present volume
—— (1980) 'Cognitive styles across cultures', in Warren, N. (ed.) *Studies in cross-cultural psychology* 2. London: Academic Press
'In memoriam: Michael Ogbolu Okonji: 1936–1975', *Journal of Cross-Cultural Psychology*, 1975, 6, 389

# Contributors

JEROME BRUNER has been Watts Professor of Experimental Psychology at the University of Oxford and has taught at Harvard University. He has undertaken research on social, developmental and cognitive psychology in the United States, England and Senegal.

BERNARD COMRIE is Associate Professor of Linguistics at the University of Southern California and was previously Lecturer in Linguistics at the University of Cambridge. He has studied language universals and language typology, drawing evidence from a variety of linguistic groups. His special interest at present is the syntactic typology of the non-Slavic languages of the Soviet Union.

PIERRE DASEN is a Research Fellow in the Faculty of Psychology and Educational Science at the University of Geneva. He has done research in cross-cultural psychology, with particular emphasis on Piagetian psychology, in the Ivory Coast, Kenya, the Seychelles, Canada and Australia.

RUTH FINNEGAN is Senior Lecturer in Comparative Social Institutions at the Open University and has recently taught in the School of Social and Economic Development in the University of the South Pacific, Fiji. She has done research in oral poetry and folklore in Sierra Leone and the South Pacific.

ROLAND FLETCHER is Lecturer in the Department of Anthropology at the University of Sydney in Australia. He has carried out research in settlement patterns in Malta, Ghana, Crete and Egypt.

MEYER FORTES is the Emeritus William Wyse Professor of Social Anthropology at the University of Cambridge. His research among the Tallensi of Northern Ghana has included, on the basis of his original training as a psychologist at University College, London, studies of perception and cognition.

JOHN GAY is a rural sociologist for the Ministry of Agriculture in Lesotho and is currently studying cognitive and affective aspects of farming among rural Basotho. He has taught at Cuttington College in Liberia and done research on cognition among the Kpelle of Liberia.

ERNEST GELLNER is Professor of Philosophy (with special reference to Sociology) at the London School of Economics. He has published work on many topics in philosophy, social theory, and anthropology.

GUSTAV JAHODA is Professor of Psychology at the University of Strathclyde, and has taught at the University of Ghana. He has undertaken research on perceptual development as influenced by environmental factors and the development of social concepts in several African countries.

NIGEL LEMON is Principal Lecturer and Head of the School of Social Sciences at Sunderland Polytechnic and has been Lecturer at the University of Dar es Salaam, Tanzania. His research interests include bilingualism, attitudes and socio-legal applications of psychology.

BARBARA LLOYD is Reader in Social Psychology at the University of Sussex. She has studied socialization among the Gusii in Kenya and the Yoruba of Nigeria. Since 1968 she has studied cognitive development in English and in Yoruba children.

OGBOLU OKONJI was Associate Professor in Psychology at the University of Lagos at the time he died. He had taught at Makerere University in Uganda and the University of Zambia. His research interests were in the area of cognitive development.

# General introduction: relativism and universals

*Ernest Gellner*

A spectre haunts human thought: relativism. If truth has many faces, then not one of them deserves trust or respect. Happily, there is a remedy: human universals. They are the holy water with which the spectre can be exorcized. But, of course, before we can use human universals to dispel the threat of cognitive anarchy, which would otherwise engulf us, we must first *find* them. And so, the new hunt for the Holy Grail is on.

A sensitive reader with a yearning for an overall plot might well conclude that this, or something like it, is what confers underlying unity and philosophic aim to the volume, or to the intellectual endeavour of which it is the expression. He may well be right, though it is wrong to be dogmatic in interpreting the intellectual undercurrents of other men's thought.

The essays which constitute this volume are contributed by experts in various fields, and a general introduction cannot usefully pursue them in their specialized regions; any attempt to do so would inevitably be superficial. But what it may do, with some hope at least of rendering a useful service, is to seek for and examine critically the underlying plot.

The underlying and interconnected issues, as I see them are these: just what is the problem of relativism, or rather, what *are* the problems of relativism? How are they related to the issues of human uniqueness or the existence of human universals? What are the general features of explanation of human conduct which are pertinent to this? What are the influential themes in recent thought which provide the terms and assumptions in which they are likely to formulate both questions and answers?

There are (at least) two problems, but those two problems are absolutely fundamental: is there but one kind of man, or are there many? Is there but one world, or are there many? These two

1

questions are *not* identical; but they are not unconnected either. But it is quite wrong to identify or confuse the two questions, as is sometimes done. The second problem – one world or many – can also be formulated as: are there many truths or one?

The papers in this volume do not, on the whole, sharply separate these two issues. By and large, they concentrate on the first question. The preoccupation with the issue of human or social 'universals' is in effect a concern with whether there is but one kind of man, or whether there are many kinds of men; or alternatively, what shared features unite all men or all human societies. There are exceptions to this approach, as in the discussion of Aristotelian and Cartesian styles of conceptualization of space and methods of measuring cognitive development, but nevertheless, it is the unity of *man*, rather than the unity of *worlds*, which is in the foreground of the discussion. Yet behind this, one senses a concern with relativism.

The two issues are of course intimately connected, as indeed is visible from the occasions at which the discussion strays from one to the other: if man is not one but many, then will not each kind of man also make his own kind of world, and if so, how can we choose amongst them? What happens then to the uniqueness and objectivity of truth? Our moral intuitions tend to impel us in different directions at this point. Liberalism, tolerance, pluralism, incline many to find pleasure in the idea of a multiplicity of men and visions; but the equally reputable and enlightened desire for objectivity and universality leads to a desire that at least the world and truth be but one, and not many. (The tolerant endorsement of human diversity becomes very tangled if one realizes that very many past and alien visions have themselves in turn been internally exclusive, intolerant and ethnocentric; so that if we, in our tolerant way, endorse *them*, we thereby also endorse or encourage intolerance at second hand. This might be called the dilemma of the liberal intellectual.) By contrast, extreme leftists are sometimes addicted to the thesis of the plasticity or malleability of man. This tends, especially in the case of Marxists, to form part of a polemic against the alleged habit of their opponents of turning the conceptual artifacts of one particular social order into a human universal, so as to discourage any questioning of that social order.

The pursuit of universals, of the unity of man, is also on occasion inspired by the desire to underwrite the brotherhood and equality of man. Whether indeed our values are or should be so directly at the mercy of scholarly findings may well be doubted. I do not anticipate that on the day of the publication of a generative grammar of colloquial Bongo-Bongo, definitely establishing the absolute unique-ness of Bongo-Bongo syntax, I shall promptly conclude that the discriminatory measures imposed on the Bongo-Bongo by hostile authorities are henceforth justified.

But it is, I believe, profoundly significant that by and large, whilst the ultimate motive of the enquiry may be the establishment of an unitary world, the method employed is the pursuit of the unity of *man*. Yet the unity of the world seems at the same time tacitly *assumed* within the enquiry, as providing the framework within which it is carried on (even though one also senses the tacit hope that it will also in turn be demonstrated, *through* the unity of man).

I believe this to be significant twice over. It tells us something about the current intellectual climate: we are fairly sure about which world we inhabit, and that there is but one, though we are much less sure about the foundations of this conviction, or its precise definition. We flirt with relativism, which we then try to refute by showing mankind to be one, by means of an enquiry nevertheless carried on within a unitary, unrelative world. . . . We are less sure about the unity of man, or precisely what it would mean. This also constitutes a clue, to my mind, concerning the only solution to which the problem of relativism is really susceptible.

Relativism is basically a doctrine in the theory of knowledge: it asserts that there is no unique truth, no unique objective reality. What we naively suppose to be such is but the product – exclusively, or in some proportion, which varies with the particular form the relativism takes – of the cognitive apparatus of the individual, community, age or whatever. (Relativisms differ in many respects, including the identification of the units to which the relativity is meant to apply.) If this is inherently and necessarily so, then perhaps no sense attaches to speaking about a unique, absolute or objective truth, but only of a truth or reality relative to the unit or cognitive apparatus in question. Notoriously, there is no room for the assertion of relativism itself, in a world in which relativism is true. The previous sentences have sketched out a world; but if they did succeed in painting a relativist world, do they not at the same time willy-nilly say something absolute about it ? This difficulty should not be overstressed. It does not inhibit our intuitive capacity for visualizing a relativist world; and to use this difficulty as a reason for treating the fear of relativism as groundless, seems to me facile and superficial. Despite all the problems which attach to articulating the idea of a plurality of worlds and truths, intuitively this notion does make sense, and I believe this intuition to be justified.

Note however that such relativism is perfectly compatible with the existence of any number of, so to speak, *de facto* or contingent human 'universals'. In a world unbounded by any unique truth, it might still be the case, by accident, that all human languages had a certain grammatical structure, that chromatic perception was identical in all cultures, that all societies proscribed certain relations as incestuous, etc., etc. *A priori* one would perhaps have less reason in such a world to expect that these universals or constants should obtain. This is so because *one* reason, but one reason only, for this expectation would be absent in a 'relative' world: this reason being the direct constraint by objective truth. 'Objective truth' being absent, it could no longer constrain anyone. But *other* constraints could still operate.

If, on the other hand, in objective and unique truth, or in independent reality, colours 'really' are such and such, and if certain types of relationships 'really' are wrong and incestuous, etc., then, *in as far as* the human mind also apprehends the unique and rational truth, it will be canalized into a unique, universal and constant mould. Diversity of perception or opinion could then only spring from the presence of *error*. But truth is only one factor influencing the mind, amongst other possible ones, and incidentally not always a powerful one: so despite the uniqueness of truth, some societies might still be under the sway of chromatic, moral or other error. In fact, societies have often believed this about each other, and sometimes about their own past.

On the other hand, whilst not necessarily led to a unique position by Reason – which notoriously holds but a feeble sway over the human spirit – men might *still* be led to a unique position which was *not* the 'right' one, by *other* and possibly less praiseworthy factors. There might be non-rational constraints of a neurological, social or other kind, compelling mankind to remain within some moral, linguistic or other universal, even though objectively this single path was not unique – or possibly not even correct at all.

So it is conceivable that relativism be true, and yet human universals obtain; and equally, it is possible that relativism be false, and yet no universals obtain (or only trivial ones). . . . There seems nothing at least intuitively or *prima facie* absurd about a uniquely determined universe, available in principle for cognition in one correct form only; but one such that, within it, inside such a metaphysically well-favoured and attractive universe, it should so happen that grammatical, conceptual, kinship, moral etc. systems were so highly variegated, that comparative grammarians, anthropologists etc. had to despair of ever finding any universal traits. A God outside this universe would know how its variegated sub-systems all successfully operated within one total system, without any one of them embracing the totality and without any being mutually translatable. In as far as this diversity extended to all aspects of life, things might indeed become very difficult. First of all, if the cognitive equipment of cultures varies so much in such a unique-truth universe, it follows that all their cultures (with at most one exception) must be cognitively in error, at least in some measure; and their inability to grasp the *others* must make them, at best, incomplete. There is nothing absurd, or at least nothing unusual, in such a supposition. More difficult still, if the cognitive equipment of societies differs radically, there may be some difficulty in the practice of intercultural anthropology *at all*, for obvious reasons.

It is an interesting fact about the world we actually live in that no anthropologist, to my knowledge, has come back from a field trip with the following report: *their* concepts are *so* alien that it is impossible to describe their land tenure, their kinship system, their ritual. . . . As far as I know, there is no record of such a total admission of failure. Perhaps sanctions applied by anthropology departments are too severe? Perhaps such anthropological failures do not present their theses, or even report back from field work at all. This doesn't prove, of course, that it has never occurred; and if it had occurred, it would not prove that it was due to the inherent inaccessibility of the material, as opposed to the deficiencies of the particular investigator. What one does quite often hear is admissions of partial failure of comprehension: 'I simply cannot imagine what the so-and-so, a West African tribe, mean when they speak of washing their souls'; 'I thought I knew the Himalayan hill folk well, having lived amongst them for a considerable time, but when a death occurred in the family, I saw from their reactions that I did not understand anything'; etc. Such partial incomprehensions are common, but they have not, to my knowledge, prevented the drawing-up of an account of at least large parts of the social life, language, etc., of the community in question. I have heard an anthropologist who had come back from a but recently discovered group in New Guinea say that they really were 'very very distant' in their way of thinking, and implying that the strenuousness of his effort had had to be much greater than on his other field experiences with 'closer' cultural communities; but he did not report *failure*.

I think all this is significant, and indicates something (at worst, it could indicate complacency and a misguided supposition that we understand when in fact we do not); but, on the often rather *a priori* reasoning of relativist philosophers, who start out from doctrines such as the ultimacy and self-sufficiency of 'forms of life', we might have expected such failure to be much more common. It is *success* in explaining culture A in the language of culture B which is, in the light of such a philosophy, really puzzling. Yet shelves groan with the weight of such books.

So, the truth of the matter seems to me this: the issues of relativism, and that of the existence of human universals, are *not* one and the same issue. The problem of relativism is whether there is one and one only world, in the end; whether all the divergent visions of reality can in the end be shown (leaving out cases when they are simply mistaken) to be diverse aspects of one and the same objective world, whose diversity can itself be explained in terms of the properties or laws of that world. There are some reasonably persuasive, if not formally compelling, reasons for holding the belief in such unique reality.

But this not the same question as that concerning whether or not man is one and unique, whether in basic features, humanity is internally alike, and perhaps also externally unique (whether all men are alike, and unlike everything non-human). Not only are the two questions about whether there is one world and whether all men are alike, not identical, but the widely diffused assumption that a positive answer to the first depends on a positive answer to the second, seems to me quite mistaken. In my view, the reasons for which will be given, the reverse relationship obtains: the positive answer to the first hinges on a negative answer to the second. The uniqueness of the world hinges on the diversity, the non-universality of man. There is one world only, there are many men; and just because there are many kinds of men, there is one world. For the unique world is the achievement of *some* men only; and had men and cultures not been diversified, the single world might never have emerged, for social forms would not have differed enough to hit on this special one; and all this is of the essence of the thing. But this paradoxical claim requires clarification and defence.

It is, as stated, a striking feature of the explorations – one is tempted to say, flirtations – with the idea of the diversity of man, of radical differentiation in the human conceptual or other equipment, that it is carried out in the context of *one unitary world*. The assumption, if it becomes conscious and explicit as a result of challenge, can, I suppose, be defended as follows: but what else do you wish us to do? Where else, other than in the shared and assumed common world of the scientific and scholarly tradition in which we were trained, do you want us to carry out our investigation into the Diversity of Men? This doesn't mean that we necessarily grant that shared world more than a kind of interim status. If our researches lead us to conclude that man is irreducibly diverse, and that each kind of man has his own kind of world, then we shall accept and endorse that kind of plurality of men, visions, worlds, and refuse to endow the unique world, within which our enquiries were initially conducted, with any kind of special status. It was the door through which we entered the many-chambered mansion, but once safely within it, we see that it is not an unique or privileged door. This ladder we may throw away when we have ascended. . . .

Perhaps such an attitude is possible. But I doubt it. I believe that our attachment to the unique world, within which alone the enquiries into the diversity of man and hence the diversity of his visions is carried out, is far deeper and more significant than that.It is not *a* world; it is *the* world.

Before discussing why this should be so, it may be essential to consider, as briefly and schematically as possible, what this world – *the* world – is like: what are its general traits?

This one privileged world is a public and symmetrical world: symmetrical in that it contains within itself no privileged places, times, individuals or groups, which would be allowed to exempt cognitive claims from testing or scrutiny. On the contrary, all claims and all evidence are deemed to be ultimately equal: some of course are treated with respect due to past distinction, and some with derision; in intellectual matters as in social, equality is far from complete. But an idea is an idea for a' that: and their status differentiation is not absolute, total and eternal. Reality is not ranked and stratified in dignity and availability for scrutiny, as it is in other and more traditional kinds of vision. Amongst civilized members of the republic of the mind, it is recognized that in principle no idea is so silly as not to deserve any hearing at all, and none so elevated as to be exempt from discussion. All must submit to the same base-line of evidence. Quite literally, this means that nothing is sacred. Decent cognitive comportment, the observance of proper epistemological rules, cast a secularized world as their own inescapable shadow. Evidence in turn is broken up into small packages, and is not allowed exemption from scrutiny. Practice may not fully live up to this ideal, but it does not altogether violate it either.

Equality of ultimate civic rights of all ideas and evidence, so to speak, is not the only feature of this shared and unique world of ours. It also has traits which seem to attach more directly to the stuff of the world rather than to the ideas about it (though this distinction may itself be questioned). What are these substantive traits? A kind of orderliness of behaviour: it is assumed that like causes will have like effects, thereby making generalization and theory-building possible. This feature used to be given names such as the Regularity of Nature or the Principle of Sufficient Reason, and no doubt others.

The orderliness of the world is also assumed to be systematic: not only are there regularities to be discovered, but these also form a system, such that, if we are successful in our enquiries, the more specific regularities turn out in the end to be corollaries of more general ones. Ideally, the system might even one day turn out to possess an apex, an all-embracing theory. In the meantime, the fragments of it which we do possess seem to point towards such an apex, and seem to urge us on in the pursuit of it.

What reasons have we to believe in such a world – and in its unique validity – over and above the contingent and in itself plainly inconclusive and indeed suspect fact that it happens to be the vision within which, at least in office hours, most of us think and work? This is the one world, *within which* we enquire whether mankind is unitary. Yet it is itself the world of *some* men only (including *us*). Is it more than just our vision, is it the account of how things actually are? And if so, why?

There is of course no non-circular way of establishing this Single World or Unique Truth. (Other visions validate themselves by their own rules, and will not play according to ours. Hence any move which eliminates them, also breaks their rules, and is consequently question-begging.) But there are at least partially non-question-begging ways of supporting this position, and these are probably all we can ever have. *If* it were the case that there existed a number of centres of consciousness or knowledge, each as it were plugged into a different cosmic programme, which in turn remained unrelated to each other, then that would be that, and there would be nothing we could do about it. (I leave aside the intriguing question whether in such a universe, the above sentence would not nevertheless contain a unique *and* all-embracing truth, relating the centres and their experiences to each other precisely by the assertion that they are not congruent.) But that does not seem to be our world. What reasons can we adduce in support of such a conviction?

There are two converging arguments, the epistemological and the sociological. They need to be sketched out briefly.

(a) *The epistemological.* Here we start out with the minimum of assumptions, so as to beg no questions. Initially *anything* may be true. We ask: How can we pick out the correct option of belief, seeing that we have no prior indication of what it may be? The answer is contained in the epistemological tradition which has accompanied the rise of modern science, at first to help it along, and later so as to explain its miraculous success.

The answer is, in rough outline: eliminate all self-maintaining circular belief systems. As the main device of self-maintaining systems is the package-deal principle, which brings about the self-maintaining circle of ideas, break up information into as many parts as possible, and scrutinize each item separately. This breaks up the circles and destroys the self-maintenance. At the same time, nevertheless assume the regularity of nature, the systematic nature of the world, not because it is demonstrable, but because anything which eludes such a principle also eludes real knowledge; *if* cumulative and communicable knowledge is to be possible at all, then the principle of orderliness must also apply to it.... The inherently idiosyncratic has no place in a corpus of knowledge. Unsymmetrical, idiosyncratic explanations are worthless – they are not explanations. Unconvertible currencies are not suitable for trade, and ungeneralizable explanations are useless for a practical and cumulative body of knowledge. If like conditions did *not* produce like effects, then the experimental accumulation of knowledge would have no point and would not be feasible. Only theories built on the assumption of symmetry and orderliness can be negotiated and applied. Material not amenable to treatment within this assumption is worthless, and must either be re-interpreted or discarded.

In brief: the atomization of information and the orderly systematization of explanation are imperative. Neither of them is established except as a *precondition* of having real knowledge at all. But, *ex hypothesi*, they do generate a unique world, one subject to a unique set of laws only. Information is atomized and thus obliged to shed excessive and covert theoretical loading; and theories are systematized and thus incoherences and putative idiosyncrasy are eventually eliminated.

(b) *The sociological.* In our actual and shared world, diverse cultures, though not sharing their beliefs, nevertheless seem to have little trouble in communicating with each other. The world contains many communities, but they visibly inhabit the same world and compete within it. Some are cognitively stagnant, and a few are even regressive; some, on the other hand, possess enormous and indeed growing cognitive wealth, which is so to speak validated by works as well as faith: its implementation leads to very powerful technology. There is a near-universal consensus about this, in deeds rather than in words: those who do not possess this knowledge and technology endeavour to emulate and acquire it.

As it happens, the cognitively cumulative and powerful communities apply, in their serious intellectual life, an epistemology roughly of the kind singled out previously in the specification of the epistemological argument. Powerful technology is based on a science which in turn seems to observe the rules of an information-atomizing enquiry, and of symmetrical and orderly theory-construction.

The epistemological argument is abstract and, on its own, shares all the weaknesses of abstract arguments. The history of thought must contain countless specimens of abstract arguments which sound plausible enough but which either failed to carry conviction or were eventually shown to be false or both. The sociological argument on the other hand is crude and pragmatic to the point of meretricious opportunism.

Moreover the conjunction of the two is extremely inelegant. The epistemological one deliberately starts from scratch with the absolute minimum of assumptions, whilst the sociological one makes itself a present of the world which we think we live in, of our shared and often unexamined views of what is going on in it, and incidentally of some rather crass earthy values prevailing in it. Thus, a totally impractical abstraction, an argument beyond all contexts, excogitated in a putative 'cosmic exile', is fused with a meretriciously crude and all-too-wordly consideration based on greed for wealth and scramble for power. What strange bedfellows! – but they do point one and the same way, and jointly constitute the grounds we have for choosing and accepting the unique world we think and live in.

Thus, for all the inelegance of their juxtaposition, the incongruity of this bizarre marriage of convenience, and for all their great faults taken singly, this conjunction and its two elements are the best we have, the most we shall probably ever have, and they do, in fact, jointly carry conviction and – I am myself tempted to add – rightly so. But perhaps that adds nothing (other than complacency) to the preceding statement.

But if it be accepted that it is by this kind of reasoning that we have attained a Single World and Unique Truth, then the somewhat paradoxical conclusion follows that a Single World, and Single Man, do *not* go together at all. On the contrary: for the particular thought style which alone generated this unique, converging, cumulative world, as the object of human cognition, was *not* universally dispersed amongst men. On the contrary, it was but one tradition amongst many, and a very untypical one. It prevailed, *and* we hold it to be valid. Within it, and on its terms, we carry out investigations into the other visions which were once its rivals. *It* provides the single context, within which we investigate and interpret all other visions. We do not hold it to be valid only because it has prevailed, but the fact that it generates a kind of technology which helps its adherents to prevail also indisputably constitutes *a* consideration.

This position differs from pragmatism in a number of important ways. For one thing, practical success is but one consideration, as indicated. This view asserts that a given vision is valid *and* therefore is practically effective, but it does not identify validity and effectiveness. There is in fact no reason to suppose that effective science does increase the survival-prospect of the species which carries it. The self-destruction of humanity, through nuclear or other war or ecological disaster, is perfectly possible and perhaps probable in the post-scientific age, whereas previously mankind did not possess the power to destroy itself, and, owing to its dispersal, was virtually certain not to face destruction by any outside force. So if truth were equated with that which increases the probability of survival, then science would certainly be untrue.

But perhaps philosophically the most significant and profound difference hinges on the fact that pragmatism, like various related strands in the evolutionist and Hegelian thought styles, believed the true cognitive vision, or rather practices, to be something ever-present in history (including, for pragmatism, *biological* history), only becoming ever more effective and manifest with the progress of time. In one famous formulation of this kind of view, the amoeba and Einstein use the same method, which is the key to all real knowledge (namely, trial and error). On the view which is here advocated, and presented as the (only) way in which we have overcome relativism, or can ever do so, this is not so at all: the correct vision or cognitive style appears at *a* definite point in time, and thus introduces a radical *dis*continuity in history. Just as it is not universal in space – it characterizes *some* men, not *all* men – so it is also not universal in time. Pragmatists and Hegelians believed in a kind of Permanent Revolution; the valid thought-style or its underlying ultimate principle was confirmed by eternal repetition, and its authority reinforced by such reiteration. On the present view, no such reiteration occurs to underwrite the One True Vision. This difference is the crucial difference between the nineteenth- and twentieth-century philosophical uses of history. The twentieth-century version has not yet been properly formulated philosophically.

So the Singleness of Man is *not* required for the Uniqueness of the World or of Truth. These were initially carried only by an eccentric minority, and they are not underwritten either by human universality or by permanence in time. This vision is underwritten – if valid at all, as I hold it to be – in quite a different manner which was briefly sketched out.

So the universality of a single model of man, so to speak, is not required for the philosophical purpose (the overcoming of relativism) for which it is, I suspect, often introduced. But, whether or not required for this end, it also has an inherent intrinsic interest, and deserves consideration for its own sake. So, what is the state of play with respect to the Universality of a Single Human Model?

There are (at least) two ways of approaching this: first, by asking whether there are manifest and, if you like, surface similarities in men; and secondly whether there are underlying identities or similarities in explanatory principle or mechanism. Furthermore, of course, each of these questions can be asked separately for various aspects of human activity and experience, and the answers may vary from field to field.[1]

A proper survey of the phenomena in each field could only be carried out by competent specialists in that field, and the contributions to this volume do indeed endeavour to initiate just that. Nonetheless, it may be useful for a non-specialist to give a general impressionistic

---

[1] Cf. for example an excellent survey of this problem in connection with the perception and conceptualization of colour: *Voir et Nommer les Couleurs*, Laboratoire d'Ethnologie et de Sociologie Comparative, Nanterre: Serge Tornay, 1978.

overview of what the findings suggest, when such surveys are completed.

In fields such as sensory sensibility and motor performance, differences do exist but are not very striking or extensive. It appears harder to locate them than it is to locate intercultural or inter-ethnic similarities in these fields. Moreover, when they do occur, it seems quite reasonable to expect differences to be explained by the impact of, for example, climatic or social environment on basically similar underlying physiological equipment. So, differences are not striking, and furthermore, they tend to become eliminated at the next explanatory level. To put this in another way: men seem to move and act in pretty much the same world and with much the same physical equipment.

Truly enormous intercultural differences, on the other hand, occur in certain other areas, where societies, as one is tempted to say, are free to indulge their fantasy: mythology, cosmology, metaphysics, and in some measure, in social, political, ritual organization. The profound and radical differences in world vision between sophisticated cultures are reasonably evident: when they translate their doctrines in each other's language, the resulting translations sometimes sound very odd indeed. Yet the translations are widely recognized as reasonably accurate by bilingual or bicultural persons. In this area, the view that the oddity enters only through mistranslation, is implausible and difficult to sustain.

The situation is somewhat different and complex when it comes to identifying and interpreting the 'world-view' of 'primitive' peoples, i.e. those which have no script and no clerical class to codify that view. Here, the interpretation and systematization is carried out by outsiders (or those who were trained by outsiders), and the view that the oddity lies in the translation, and not in the view translated, acquires some plausibility. In what sense, for instance, can a tribesman who is no theologian, and whose society does not have theologians, be credited with a theology which seems implicit to the outsider in his ritual or myths? This question is highly pertinent to the once fashionable attribution of a distinctive 'primitive mentality' to populations living in simple societies; but it is equally pertinent to the more recent revival of the attribution to them of the scientific and experimental spirit. The issue is open and methodologically difficult. Just how different one finds the savage, seems to hinge largely on whether one goes by what he *does* (which is not strange – he acts in the same world as we do, and in a similar way), or by what he says (very odd by most translations), or by functionalist interpretations of what he says (not odd after all), or whether in the end one is swayed by the thought that though odd the statement is context-bound in ritual (hence also not odd). And yet, its impact on him in the ritual hinges on it sounding odd *to him as well*, if interpreted in parallel with daily ordinary statements – and so it is odd after all. As far as I can see, you can pick and choose as to which of these levels of sophistication you select as your resting-place, and hence which conclusion you reach.

So to sum up: minor and so to speak explicable differences at sensory and motor level; very great differences at the level of self-conscious, codified civilization with codified criteria of valid belief – though interestingly a very good measure of translatability exists at the same time, which facilitates the highlighting of this divergence. (Translatability does not seem to mean agreement.) There are all kinds of 'translatability,' (e.g. 'they say such-and-such, combining what seem to be equivalents of such-and-such notions in our language, in a way which makes no sense to us but does appear to make sense to them'). In between these extremes, dealing with societies which do not themselves codify their own views, one is not clear what one should say: the answer appears to hinge on just how *we* codify *their* views for them.

But the really significant difference is between what may be called validation systems: the procedures and principles employed for extending and deciding the acceptance of new items. Primitive societies do not codify these, and they can only be extracted from their practice, which need not be consistent. Literacy, by creating a norm outside custom, or rather, providing the means for stabilizing such a norm, is supremely important. In the end, however, it is the establishment and institutional underpinning of the *one* outstanding cumulative cognitive style, atomistic and symmetrical, which produces the really decisive parting of the ways. It is then that the practice of *some* men finally generates *one* world.

Such, roughly, are the intersocial differences at the phenomenological or descriptive level. What about the explanatory or structural level?

The Chomskian theory of language may serve as a useful baseline, precisely because it is so very clear on the issue both of the universality and uniqueness of man. If that theory is correct, then human linguistic competence is explained by an innate equipment which is identical in all men, but which is not shared by any other organism. The argument for the identity of this equipment is simple and important: the evidence available to language-learning children is so very fragmentary and feeble that the transition from it to internalizing the complex grammatical rules involved in the generation of an indefinite class of utterances, as employed by mature language-users, constitute a truly tremendous leap. But infants of any genetic background appear able to make this transition to whatever language they are exposed to: hence not only *is* there a tremendous leap, inexplicable without hidden (innate) aid, but it also appears to be the *same* leap which is made by all mankind. If a hidden key (which is not seen, but which is inferred from our amazing linguistic competence), opens a multitude of doors, we may conclude that the locks are identical.

The theory claims the leap is towards one and the same underlying linguistic structure. Hence the acquisition of familiarity with the *idiosyncratic* traits of individual languages must somehow be explicable as a consequence of the reiterated use of the same shared innate principles, as identical bricks can be used to erect different structures, or alternatively, as something requiring only very small and hence perhaps less mysterious 'leaps', which might consequently be explicable without any recourse to the assumption of special innate linguistic equipment. To a non-specialist, this seems a difficult programme: the idiosyncratic aspects of languages *also* seem most complex, over and above the complexities which they share, and the prospects of explaining them all in the manner indicated, dubious. I doubt whether the argument for innate equipment loses its force even with the *tiniest* 'leaps'. But we can leave that problem with structural linguists. Our present use of this theory is a kind of yardstick, and does not actually require that theory to be true or demonstrated.

Whilst postulating a pan-human shared mechanism as the explanation of human linguistic competence, the theory at the same time insists on the radical discontinuity between human language and animal systems of communication. Thus, on this theory, in the field of linguistic phenomena, *one* mechanism explains all men, and *nothing* but men. The situation can be represented diagrammatically (Fig. 1.1), where horizontal shading covers humanity, and vertical shading is that which is covered by the theory.

If B indicates the apex or genus, so to speak, covering all living or biological phenomena, and H and L cover human and linguistic phenomena respectively, then the areas covered by H and L are

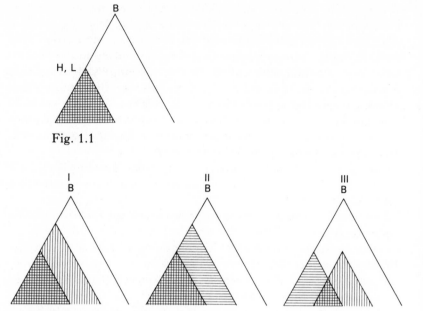

Fig. 1.1

Fig. 1.2

congruent, and jointly constitute a single segment of the biological. More simply: the class of men and that of proper language-users are the same class.

The thesis of the uniqueness of man, or of the existence of 'human universals', presumably means that such a congruence does hold, in the fields of linguistic and other behaviour. Schematically, it means that if, once again horizontal shading covers humanity, and vertical shading cover the field of application of some explanatory theory, then one might require that situations should not arise which can be schematized as in Fig. 1.2.

But it seems obvious that non-congruence of type I *does* occur: mankind obviously shares physiological mechanisms with other organisms. One's inclination is to say that these mechanisms explain aspects of behaviour which are not characteristically or distinctively human. But if only behaviour which is 'distinctively human' needs to be explained by distinctively human explanatory mechanisms, then the uniqueness-hypothesis clearly risks becoming tautological.

Non-congruence of type II raises more complex issues, as does type III. In a sense, it is obvious that explanatory mechanisms or structures of type II also occur. Suppose a political anthropologist or a political scientist develops a theory of all possible forms of political organization, by isolating the elements which go into state-formation, and then deducing all the possible forms generated by their various combinations. This theory – if the elements had been correctly isolated and the manner of their possible combinations correctly described – would constitute an explanation of possible political forms, but clearly would not cover societies too small or too decentralized to have a state at all. Would such a theory contradict the 'human universals' thesis?

Similar considerations apply to non-congruence III. It is quite possible that some explanatory mechanisms or principles are applicable both in *some* human societies and *some* non-human ones (say primates, or insects). Does this contradict the 'human universals' thesis?

Once again, this thesis risks becoming tautological or trivial, if it is reduced to the mere assertion that there are *some* (unspecified) human explanatory universals in some fields, covering all mankind, but without excluding the possibility of important *specific* explanations for *some* men only in other fields. What presumably those who uphold the idea of 'universals' mean, is that in important fields (politics, kinship, economy, mythology, ritual – either in all, or perhaps more modestly just in some of them) – identical principles do operate for all human societies; and if the uniqueness of man is added to universality, that they operate only in human societies. What would be the evidence for or against such a view?

Partly, this will turn out once again to be a matter of definition, in a number of ways. If some organizational principles only apply to, say, societies endowed with agriculture, or to societies above a certain size, then nevertheless pre-agrarian or small societies can be incorporated in the scheme, if the absence of a certain factor or variable (e.g. agriculture, size) is itself included as one possible variant in the range of situations 'generated' by the elements in the theory.

In brief, in as far as theories endeavour to unify, the question about the unity of mankind, at the explanatory level, risks having a trivial answer, an affirmation which simply reflects our theoretical aspiration towards unitary explanation.

Nevertheless, I suspect that those who assert the unity-of-mankind thesis have a non-trivial point in mind, and one which hinges on the distinction between genetic and social explanation; what is asserted is that social forms are so to speak indifferent to the individual human material which is fed into it. Just as any man could have been brought up in any language, so also no social formation depends on the *genetic* specificity of the men composing it. There is a good deal of evidence to support such a supposition: the diversity of human performance appears to depend on socio-cultural factors to an incomparably greater degree than it does on individual genetic equipment. The regions of the world which produced most of the innovations which lie at the base of modern industrial civilization, for instance, were themselves cultural backwaters a fairly small number of generations earlier, and yet it is unlikely that their 'gene pool' changed radically. (If anything, one might suspect that mediaeval clerical and monastic celibacy may have caused it to degenerate.)

At the same time, the argument requires refinement. Genetic equipment imposes a ceiling on performance, even if socio-cultural factors are crucial within that ceiling; and a community with a higher average ceiling would presumably have a different range of possible performances from one with a lower ceiling. A community artificially recruited, say, from physics professors, would presumably, in the next generation, have a different range of possible performance from a randomly selected one, even if the two new populations were given similar training.

In other words, if some potentialities are genetically limited (or rather, if the limitations are not distributed with absolute evenness), as indeed is plausible, and if communities were recruited so as to accentuate such uneven distribution, we could *then* possibly have a so to speak non-universalistic sociology. This doesn't however appear to be the world we actually live in. Whilst there is no reason to suppose that the genetic ceiling is absolutely even and flat all over humanity, any more than anything else is distributed with total evenness, (such an assumption is terribly unplausible), yet the differences in performance by the same and genetically continuous community at different times are *so* much greater than are the differences between individuals which may be attributed to differences in inherent equipment, that for most problems it would seem bad strategy to seek genetic explanations. It seems to me extremely unlikely, moreover, that such genetic unevenness as may exist, correlates at all with the historic performance of communities. The two things are probably often related *inversely*. For instance: some gene pools must be richer than others in potential great footballers. But is there the slightest likelihood that the point of high concentration of such talent, is *also* the area where football historically emerged? The same argument applies to other cultural achievements. But it would be wrong to treat any interest in genetic preconditions as logically absurd.

Those who exclude it moreover make what could be called the Continuity Assumption, which has at least two aspects: that, although the genetic ceiling can be assumed to vary, and that its distribution need not be even, any more than the land surface of the earth is totally flat, nevertheless, it only varies statistically and the unevennesses are not very extreme. If, for instance, a given social performance requires the presence of some individuals with special talents, i.e. with a high ceiling with respect to some specific kind of performance, then the *numbers* required to ensure that some such individuals are found, will not vary very much in different human populations. If a given social performance requires the presence of, say five people of unusual mathematical potential, the population size required so that it should contain five such persons, *may* vary in different parts of the world, but probably does not vary very much.

The second aspect of the continuity thesis is this: that although human performance or individual ceilings vary, they vary in degree rather than in kind. The difference between the ability to speak at all and to use language like Shakespeare is great and important, but it is in some sense much less radical than the difference between having and not having the potential of speech at all. Not all men are Shakespeares, but all sane healthy men have the power of speech. The genetic precondition of social forms consists of the former kind of potential rather than the latter.

Neither aspect of the Continuity Thesis has been formulated with any precision; and perhaps it would be in principle impossible to do so. What precisely is, in general, the difference between a difference in degree and in kind? Nevertheless, despite this imprecision there *is* something like a natural interpretation of the Continuity Thesis; and it is also reasonable to suppose that it holds true. In other words, the existence of explanatory schemata which apply to some human societies only, if such schemata exist at all, need not be attributed to the non-universality of some human *element*, but only to the specificity of some forms of social *organization*, which however remain open to all human populations in similar circumstances.

These, as far as I can see, are the ideas or issues which underline the question about 'human universals'. The issue can be advanced as it has been in this volume, but it can hardly be settled. But to recapitulate:

The problems of relativism and that of the existence of human universals are *not* identical.

The doctrine of 'human universals' is often tacitly conjoined with that of the uniqueness of man: the claim is not only that the essentially human *is* present in all of us, but also that it is *not* present in anything else.

Universality at the phenomenological level is highly questionable or trivial. At the explanatory level, the notion is complex and obscure.

The solution of the problem of relativism does not hinge on the establishment of human universals. If it has a solution, it lies elsewhere.

Relativism is about the existence of One World: and the conceptual unification of the world is, precisely, the work of one particular style of thought, which is not universal amongst men, but is culturally specific.

But this in turn does not actually subvert the Universality Thesis: for although the conceptual unification of the world does have specific socio-historic roots, it is evidently accessible to all men, and is in fact now being diffused generally.

Science needs one world. It does not need one kind of man within it. But one *kind* of man did make the single world. His historical situation may have been unique, his basic constitution was *not*. The single world seems to be gradually adopted by all of them, and appears manifestly accessible to all men.

# Part 1

---

# Perception

# Editorial introduction to part 1

The authors of the four papers in this section take as problematic the diversity of spatial interpretations of the world, a world they themselves assume to be single and plain to see. They do not question that pictures represent external realities in the world (Fortes) and can be interpreted two- or three-dimensionally (Jahoda), or that settlements are built (Fletcher) and space mapped (Gay) in ways that suit the needs of their inhabitants. Gellner's observations on this point in the General Introduction are well taken, but his questions are not the questions of these papers.

The intention of the papers is to show how the act of perception imposes order on the raw materials of experience. Not only are the sense impressions structured in a lawful way so as to give them intellectual coherence, but also the very materials themselves – the world 'out there' – are recognized so as to make the lawful ordering of experience an easier task. A series of successive approximations bring the mental and physical representations of this external world into line with each other.

Each society achieves this goal in its own way, and the authors try to show how the approach to the interpretation of space taken by a society can be explained as allowing a useful adaptation to the demands both of nature and of culture. The one objective world is dealt with in an opportunist way, to use Bruner's term, as each culture interprets its spatial framework. Fortes shows how Tallensi children of the 1930s, having never before used or even seen pencil and paper, were able within a day to represent trees, animals and people in ways sensible to their culture. Jahoda shows that, whereas the ability to recognize depth in a two-dimensional picture is probably universal, the demands of a culture can lead the viewer to ignore the depth cues. Fletcher shows how settlements are constructed in contemporary Ghana and ancient Egypt in such a way as to make sense out of the physical setting. Gay relates spatial organization to both physical experience and abstract classification systems.

A further point is that there are diverse ways of ordering experience, even within a particular culture, depending on the particular needs. Tallensi children can fill space in a decorative or representative way (Fortes). Pictures can be interpreted two- or three-dimensionally (Jahoda). Structures can be built according to the more restrictive perceptual demands of house interiors or the more generous allowances for deviation of exteriors (Fletcher). Cartesian maps and tree diagrams can be used to represent space (Gay).

The authors thus point to what Bruner in his concluding Review and Prospectus calls process universals, underlying the diversities within the societies which they study. People make marks on paper which they identify with familiar objects, the more so as the drawers discover ways to improve their products. Manipulation of objects which are represented in pictures allows viewers to move more rapidly toward a common way of understanding the pictures than mere passive observation. Builders of houses appear to use tacit rules in order to make the houses habitable. Certain ways of mapping space alone seem to be used, and these are generalized to encompass the description of realms other than space in ways which are formally isomorphic across cultures. In general, it is the isomorphisms, the formal descriptions of the processes, which are held in common.

The authors thus see the people they study as members of one human race, observing one external world. They differ widely in specific behaviour, but at the level of competence, they are at least in principle capable of all the types of spatial perception described in the papers. As a result, to use Fortes' comment in the general discussion after the presentation of the papers at the Cambridge conference, universals are not binding. They are present, but they don't condemn their users to remain forever within a certain cultural frame. Bruner phrased it as a kind of opportunism, whereby people use what fits. If there is a tablet of universals, he says it must be printed on very soft stone. Cultural diversity is thus not a rigid diversity, but is the result of varied responses to circumstances, using the available models as heuristic devices in a permanent learning process.

# 2    Pictorial perception and the problem of universals

*Gustav Jahoda*

Perception must figure prominently among universals of human behaviour, since it underlies all our modes of adaptation to the environment. It is a process whereby we extract information from the surrounding world; hence learning and cognition are ultimately subordinate to perception. If human groups differed substantially in their perceptual functioning, this would have considerable repercussions on most other psychological processes, which should be readily observable. In fact nobody has seriously suggested that there are sizeable variations in perception across human groups, and the exceptions are only apparent. For instance, when Lévy-Bruhl wrote 'les primitifs ne perçoivent rien comme nous' he was not referring to perception in the strict sense, but merely to beliefs or emotional dispositions associated with the objects perceived. There is no empirical evidence whatsoever for systematic cross-cultural differences in perceiving the natural world.

When we talk about cross-cultural differences, therefore, the focus is on what has been called 'indirect perception'. One area of interest here is that of geometric illusions, and it might be mentioned in passing that the well-known study of Segall, Campbell & Herskovits (1966) rests on a universalist postulate: namely that varying environmental learning experiences affecting a common perceptual system produce predictable variations in illusion susceptibility. The other main concern is with pictorial representation, which can be subdivided into the perception of objects in pictures and pictorial depth perception.

## Pictorial recognition

Perception of objects in pictures is perhaps a good example of the problem of universals, indicating that 'universal' cannot be equated with 'genetically determined' except in the trivial sense that the

25

development of any skill presupposes an appropriate genetic potential. Learning is probably involved in most, if not all, psychological universals and is therefore not a distinguishing characteristic as such. The critical issue is whether or not the environmental conditions necessary and sufficient for such learning are present in every human culture. As far as the perception of objects in pictures is concerned there have in the past been numerous, though mainly anecdotal reports suggesting that there were cultures where people could not recognize objects from pictures. This led Segall, Campbell & Herskovits (1966) to the view that photographs can be regarded as an arbitrary convention that has to be learnt. The evidence was marshalled more systematically by Miller (1973) who concluded that 'the ability to perceive anything in a pictorial representation requires some experience with pictures in order to acquire the set that pictures can represent more than a flat surface' (p. 148). This would imply that recognition of pictorial objects is not a universal.

On the other hand it should be pointed out that the views quoted are based on somewhat questionable evidence. The only well-controlled psychological study in a culture where no pictures exist is that of Deregowski, Muldrow & Muldrow (1972), conducted among a remote Ethiopian tribe. The finding was that even these people were able, albeit sometimes with difficulty, to make sense of pictures. Moreover, there is the well-known work of Hochberg & Brooks (1962) in which a child, deprived of pictures until the age of 19 months, was then able to identify at least seventeen out of twenty-one pictorially represented objects. Hence the authors concluded that there must be *some* native ability for pictorial recognition, so that it is the deficiencies reported for some cultures which required special explanation.

In the hope of throwing further light on this problem, a study was designed which took advantage of natural settings in which there was a minimum of pictorial material in order to replicate the Hochberg & Brooks work with larger samples (Jahoda *et al.* 1977). The main study was carried out in four remote rural Ghanaian villages and an additional sample was tested in a rural area in Zimbabwe–Rhodesia. The subjects in the first part of the experiment were forty-six children aged about 3, younger ones being too shy in the presence of strangers to allow testing. A preliminary task with actual objects was given to ensure that the children were familiar with the names. Subsequently they were presented with sets of randomly placed photographs of similar objects and on being given a name were required to pick out the appropriate picture. The overall success rate was 86 per cent correct, which owing to the strictness of the criteria applied is a conservative estimate.

The second part of the study, confined to Ghana, involved direct comparison between children differing radically in their exposure to pictures. One group of children coming mostly from relatively westernized homes attended a model nursery school lavishly equipped with pictures and picture books. The other group had parents with little or no education, and no child attended a nursery school. Since the procedure was simpler, merely asking the children to select a photograph from an array depicting a named object, it was possible to use somewhat younger children. The mean percentages of correct responses were 73 for the nursery school sample and 71 for the others – almost precisely the same. There was thus no indication that a sharp contrast in richness of pictorial environment has any descernible effect.

The outcome of this work is in line with the findings of Hochberg & Brooks (1962), lending further support to the view that pictorial object recognition is a human universal little affected by cultural variations.

## Pictorial depth perception

At one time the simple question was believed to be whether or not everybody can understand pictures. However, the issue has become complicated by the realization that people who can recognize pictorial objects may nevertheless be unable to grasp the representation of depth in pictures. People exhibiting this behaviour are conventionally called 2D perceivers, as opposed to 3D ones able to make use of depth cues. The discovery of this is due to Hudson, who stumbled on it when using a projective technique with Bantu factory workers. Many of their responses seemed bizarre, until he realized that they made psychological sense if it was assumed that the perceiver was ignoring the depth cues in the pictures.

Hudson then constructed a test for pictorial depth perception, named after him, and applied this to a number of black and white South African samples of varying educational and occupational levels. Fig. 2.1 shows that part of the test which has been most frequently used in subsequent studies. Subjects in the original study were asked three questions: (i) What do you see? (ii) What is the man doing? (iii) Which is nearest to the man, elephant or antelope?

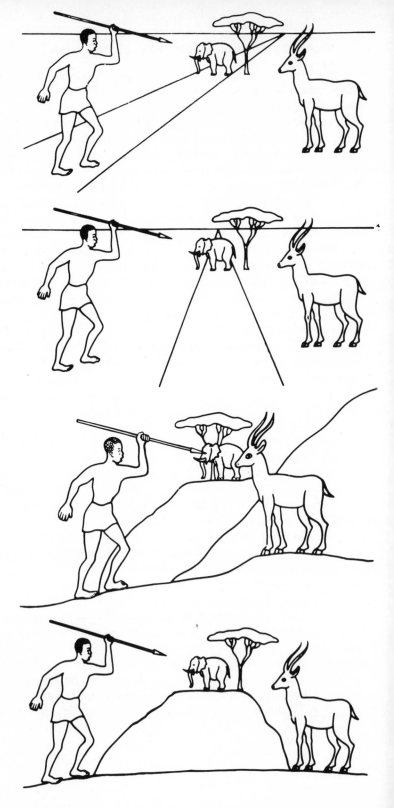

Fig. 2.1

Answers to questions (ii) and (iii) were used in scoring, though I might mention that there seemed to be some lack of clarity about the exact way scores were arrived at.

It is not possible, nor necessary, to give all of Hudson's results in detail, and so I shall describe only the salient features. Adult illiterate black subjects were entirely 2D responders and, in Hudson's words, 'saw the pictures flat'. The same was true to a slightly lesser extent of adult black samples with only primary education and, it is important to note, a sample of white labourers from an isolated forest settlement. This finding, as Hudson stressed, precludes any simple ethnic/genetic determinant.

Nearly three-quarters of white school children at the top of primary school were 3D responders, as compared with about one-third of somewhat older black pupils. The surprising finding was that only about half the black high school students and graduate teachers performed 3D on the Hudson test.

In discussing the implications of these findings, Hudson (1960) suggested that intelligence and education independently influenced depth perception, but in the case of whites only. Subsequently (1967) the emphasis was slightly changed allowing some effect of education for blacks also. But in his own words: 'formal schooling in the normal course is not the principal determinant in pictorial perception. Informal instruction in the home and habitual exposure to pictures play a much larger role' (p. 95).

Hudson's work led to a number of other investigators carrying out similar work in other parts of Africa, using his material. These include Holmes (1963), Mundy-Castle (1966), Kilbride, Robbins & Freeman (1968), and their findings are generally referred to as though they directly confirmed Hudson's work. Thus this whole area of research has entered the textbooks in a greatly oversimplified and often distorted manner. It can be shown that one of the supposed replications (Holmes 1963) is methodologically so defective that it must be discounted; others cannot be directly compared with Hudson's original study (Jahoda & McGurk 1974b). One study on which I intend to comment is that of Mundy-Castle (1966); and I propose to do this in some more detail, since he worked in Ghana where part of our own research was carried out with a closely similar sample. Mundy-Castle tested 122 children aged between 5 and 10 with the four pictures shown (Fig. 2.1). His method of scoring was clearly defined, and may have been more stringent than that employed by Hudson. At any rate, out of these 122 children, only one girl, aged

8, gave 3D responses to all four cards, all others being characterized as 2D. It is not feasible to compare this result directly with Hudson's findings, since he had not tested any black children below the age of 14. Mundy-Castle interpreted his results as supporting Hudson's contention that 'cultural stimulus' (by which he means home environment) as opposed to schools is critical for the development of pictorial depth perception. It is worth observing that the single 3D girl was curiously enough the daughter of an illiterate rural farmer!

When I first read the report of Mundy-Castle's study I felt somewhat doubtful. I had worked for a number of years with Ghanaian children, and was aware that they sometimes experienced difficulties in handling certain types of spatial-perceptual relations. However, when using pictures with them I had never noticed any gross inability to understand pictorial depth. Just about that time I came across the work of Deregowski (1968), which suggested an approach that might help resolve this puzzle. He had developed an alternative mode of getting at depth perception, in the form of a construction test. Briefly, he presented Zambian schoolboys and domestic servants with test stimuli consisting of drawings that could be interpreted either two- or three-dimensionally. Following a preliminary practice in the use of construction materials, subjects were instructed to build what they saw on the picture. Deregowski also administered the standard Hudson test to the same sample. Subjects who gave different responses to the two tests responded significantly more often 3D to the construction test. While this divergence may have been somewhat exaggerated by Deregowski's very generous scoring method on the construction test, it could also be argued that this was justified on the grounds that the construction called for skills to which the subjects were unaccustomed. In any case this work indicated the potential value of attempts to assess pictorial depth perception by means other than the Hudson test.

From my own experience of using the Hudson test with African subjects, I felt that one of its major drawbacks was excessive reliance on verbal communication. My impression was that it might function to some extent as a kind of projective test, responses being based on elements other than those directly portrayed in the pictures. For instance, Mundy-Castle quoted one child as saying that the man had to kill the elephant first, otherwise it would kill him. There have recently been some replications of work with the Hudson test, employing modified versions (Omari & Cook 1972; Omari & Mac-Gintie 1974): however, these fail to overcome the basic problem of the predominantly verbal interaction between experimenter and subject. The aim was therefore to develop a new kind of approach which minimized this risk and, like Deregowski's construction test, relied mainly on performance; moreover, the performance should not require any special skills. Together with a colleague, Harry McGurk, I embarked on a lengthy series of explorations from which a new test finally emerged (Jahoda & McGurk 1974c). This was first perfected in Scotland, and later used in several cross-cultural investigations.

The basic principle is simple. The child is first presented with pictures of pairs of figures located on a single plane in the foreground. These might be two adults (large), two children (small) or one adult and one child, their positions varying right or left. In front of the subjects is a response board, and four schematic wooden figures like chessmen, two large and two smaller ones, only two-thirds of the height of the large ones. Subjects are told that these represent women and girls, and questioned to ensure that they understand which is which ('hand me two women; a woman and a girl', etc.). It should be noted that terms denoting size like 'small' or 'large' are never used at any stage of the procedure. Subjects are then trained to select the correct pair and place it on the response board in positions conforming to those in the pictures. Before proceeding to the actual test sets it is explained to the subject that the figures would now be located at other positions, and they are made to rehearse these on the response board with the wooden dolls.

Then follows the test series, and Fig. 2.2 shows a few examples from one particular version of the test. Fig. 2.2a contains an adult in the foreground and a child in the background; this is a neutral picture since no subjects, even 2D ones, experience any difficulty. In Fig. 2.2b there are two adults; their objective size differs, so that 2D subjects will choose a woman and a girl. Lastly, in 2.2c there is a child in the foreground and an adult in the background; note that the objective size of both is the same, so that 2D responders will identify them either as two girls or as two women.

It can be seen that, in addition to size, the procedure also involved systematic variation of perspective cues to depth, whose separate effect will be considered later. Here it should be pointed out that it is possible to derive two distinct scores from the responses. One is based on the number of correct size judgements (expressed of course in terms of women and girls), and this is the one with which I shall be concerned at present. The other relates to correct spatial location of the figures.

Fig. 2.2

The first study to be described (Jahoda & McGurk 1974b) was a comparative one using this version of the test with samples of sixty Glasgow and sixty Ghanaian children in the classes Primary 2, 4 and 6. Mean ages in Glasgow were $6\frac{1}{2}$, $8\frac{1}{2}$ and $10\frac{1}{2}$, and in Ghana 7, 10 and 12, with fairly wide variations. It was amount of schooling rather than

Fig. 2.2 cont.

age which was therefore constant. The Scottish children came from a school whose catchment area was mainly semi-skilled working class. The Ghanaian children were from the village primary school attached to the University of Ghana at Legon. This village houses junior workers originating from all parts of the country and including clerks, porters, stewards and labourers. One major reason for choosing it was not only that the population was roughly equivalent to that tested by Mundy-Castle, but also that another study using the Hudson test had been done there three years previously (Ofori 1970).

All children were administered in alternating sequence the version of the new 3D test just described and the published version of the Hudson test. The questioning in the Hudson test was shortened slightly, since some of the questions could only be adequately answered by sophisticated adults, e.g. 'how do you know that the buck can see the man?' In responding to such questions children just confabulate laboriously and rapport is spoilt.

Now for the results, shown in Fig. 2.3. Consider first the Hudson data on the right. The level of performance of all three Ghanaian groups is significantly below chance. The two younger groups of Scottish children were about chance level, while the oldest rose significantly above it. Analysis of variance of both sets of scores shows a highly significant cultural difference and a significant age trend. Turning from statistical to substantive significance, it seems to me

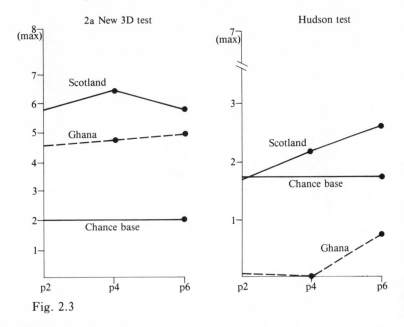

Fig. 2.3

that the striking fact is that the Scottish children also make a rather poor showing on the Hudson test.

Let us look now at the new 3D test: here every one of the mean scores, Ghanaian as well as Scottish, was very significantly above chance ($P < 0.001$). Analysis of variance again showed a significant cultural difference, but no age trend. Although there is a significant difference between the cultures, in absolute terms it is rather moderate.

It is apparent from the graph that all subjects performed much better on the new 3D test; the visual contrast could be greater were it not for the fact that the scale for the Hudson test is relatively expanded. The extent of the difference can be conveyed in another way: if one takes the overall mean score of all subjects and expresses it as a percentage of the possible maximum score, then this would be 67 per cent for the new 3D test as against a mere 18 per cent for the Hudson test.

In order to determine whether these results merely reflect differences in the absolute level of difficulty represented by the two measures, and also to facilitate interpretation of the age trend apparent in the Hudson test data, a small group of Scottish adults was tested. Half of these (eight) were in unskilled occupations (janitor, cleaner), the other half had some further education (technician, secretary). The corresponding percentages of maximum scores were 69 for the new test and 72 for the Hudson test – in fact they were closely similar. Note than on neither of the tests did European adults uniformly attain the maximum score; on both measures scores differed according to education level, though owing to the small numbers this fell short of significance.

In the light of the above, the age trend visible in the Hudson test data and absent from the new 3D test (Fig. 2.3) can also be meaningfully interpreted. The perceptual skills assessed by the new 3D test are acquired relatively early and there is little further improvement beyond the beginning stages of the primary school period. Success on the Hudson task, however, requires some inferential skill and is dependent to a considerable degree upon verbal understanding. These abilities are poorly developed during the primary school period and there is much scope for later improvement.

Turning now to the differences between the African and Scottish samples, the data confirm that African children have some difficulty with pictorial depth perception and tend to lag behind European children in this. On the other hand, the difference between them is relatively small compared not only with the origin but also with the chance base; in fact, only a single one of the Ghanaian children obtained a score of less than three times the standard error above chance with the new 3D test! In other words, given appropriate conditions practically all the Ghanaian children were capable in varying degrees of responding to depth cues in pictures; this was true even of the youngest age group tested, namely Primary 2.

While this study shows quite clearly that Hudson's work greatly overestimated the difficulties experienced by African children in 3D perception, the fact remains that overall they performed at a significantly lower level than Scottish children. Hence Hudson's argument about the difference being due to cultural deprivation, specifically a lesser exposure to pictorial material in the home environment, could still be valid. However, one should recall in this connection Donald Campbell's important methodological dictum that differences between two natural groups are uninterpretable. It therefore becomes necessary to look at more than two groups, and this was done in another series of investigations which I shall briefly describe.

In this series of studies the method was the same, but the stimulus material consisted of more realistic coloured pictures, as shown in

Fig. 2.4

Fig. 2.4. In relation to the previously described study the size variable, i.e. whether the children select the correct figures corresponding to those in the pictures, was considered. Here I should like to introduce the second variable, which we call 'space'. This refers to children's ability to understand and reproduce the spatial relationships depicted. Since one figure on the test pictures was always in the foreground and the other in the background, this meant that they had to place the dolls on the response board along the appropriate diagonal. They were carefully prepared for this during the training session, when a variety of possible placements always including several diagonal ones were rehearsed. Young children usually found this difficult, the most common error being that of aligning the dolls horizontally.

The samples tested were as follows:

*Glasgow*: working class children, mainly from a semi-skilled background.

*Zimbabwe-Rhodesian Africans*: children of low socio-economic status from rural villages and a small township near Salisbury (mostly Shona). In many cases ages could not be reliably ascertained, hence the data will be presented according to years of schooling.

*Hong Kong (urban)*: children drawn from a large school catering mainly for middle class and lower middle class families.

*Hong Kong (boat)*: these 'boat children' are so called because they spent most of their lives on junks. Their parents have only recently been persuaded to send them to school on land. These children do not start school until 7, and some even later.

From the point of view of cultural background, especially in terms of exposure to pictures before school, these samples vary widely. Both Glaswegian and Hong Kong urban children have a rich pictorial environment; that of Zimbabwe-Rhodesian Africans is extremely poor, with Hong Kong boat children intermediate. In the course of their schooling all these children encounter illustrated textbooks and have pictures in their classrooms.

Let me turn to the findings, beginning with common trends. The first concerns the effect of perspective cues. The more cues there are, the better the performance in the *size* aspect of depth perception; and this is not surprising. The next result is non-obvious, but equally lawful across these cultures. Namely, the more depth cues there are, the *poorer* the performance on the *spatial* variable. This is an interesting problem, which we have tried to interpret in terms of frame-of-reference hypotheses consistent with Piaget's account of spatial development; but I cannot pursue this here (Jahoda & McGurk 1974c). At any rate, the effect of the cues is the same for all samples, collapsed over ages.

Going on now to the developmental changes in the various cultures, these are presented graphically for the size variable in Fig. 2.5. Consider first of all only the two Hong Kong samples, ignoring for the moment Glasgow and Zimbabwe–Rhodesia. Taken in isolation the Hong Kong data tend to support Hudson's view about the predominant influence of cultural environment in terms of degree of exposure to pictures. In the case of both Hong Kong samples most of the learning about pictorial depth had taken place in the home environment, before the children ever went to school. The additional learning that took place as a result of education was modest – the Hong Kong age trends fail to reach significance. Lastly, as would be expected on the 'pictorial deprivation hypothesis', boat children performed significantly less well than urban ones.

Let us now turn from Hong Kong to Glasgow and Zimbabwe–Rhodesia. Here again the results do not contradict the importance of what might be called the 'pictorial environment'. Most of the learning by Glasgow children has occurred before they get to school; and even though the performance of unschooled African children was comparatively very poor, it is still well above chance level. But here

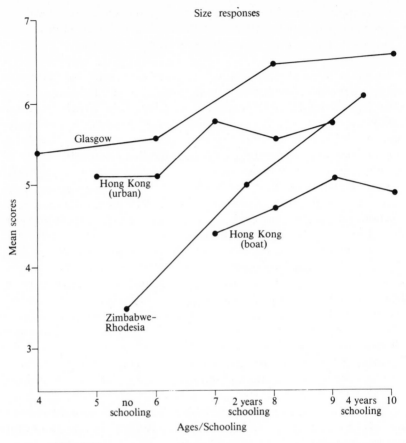

Fig. 2.5

the similarity ends. For with Glasgow children there is significant improvement during the school years, and for the African children the impact of schooling was dramatic – after four years they have practically caught up with Glasgow children.

If one looks at the whole array of data for all four groups, any simple explanatory scheme breaks down. Not only does the effect of schooling appear to vary from slight to extremely powerful, but the overall ordering of the cultural groups does not appear to correspond to the comparative richness of their pictorial environment. Thus Hong Kong boat children are outdistanced by Zimbabwe-Rhodesian Africans, whose pictorial background is poorer. I should also like

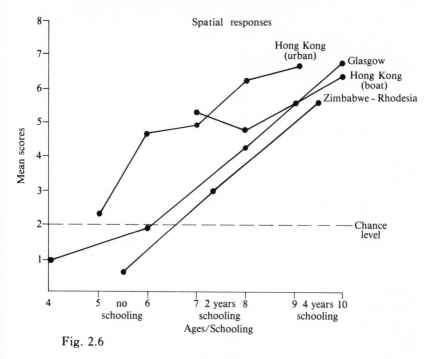

Fig. 2.6

to remind you of the findings comparing Glasgow with Ghanaian children, employing a somewhat different version of the method. In that study no strong schooling effect was detected in either sample. It is evident, therefore, that from all these findings about children's ability to make correct size judgements on the basis of depth cues in pictures, no clear pattern of environmental determinants emerges. Both the culturally determined degree of exposure to pictures and the amount of formal schooling appear to be involved; but in such a complex interaction, and with the likely addition of other unknown factors, that they cannot be disentangled in the kind of study we carried out.

Now I wish to go on to the second aspect of data, concerning children's ability to understand the spatial relationships depicted. In Fig. 2.6 one encounters quite a different pattern of considerable uniformity. All the younger children, whether or not at school, start at or below the chance level. They then progress fairly regularly to an almost faultless performance after the age of about 9 or 10. This progression, it should be stressed, takes place *irrespective of culture of schooling.* Note in this connection that the Hong Kong boat children, at their late entry into school, immediately perform as well as the other children with two or more years of schooling. It should also be mentioned that the Ghanaian data not shown exhibit almost exactly the same pattern. There are of course minor variations that cannot be readily understood, e.g. the rate of correct responding by the younger Hong Kong urban children is significantly higher than that of Glasgow ones. Yet on the whole, there are strong grounds for holding that one is dealing with a clear-cut maturational pattern largely independent of environmental factors.

### Further studies

More recent investigations have used variations on the Hudson test (e.g. Opolot 1976) or devised alternative measures. Thus Olson (1975) devised a new approach suitable for very young children and was able to demonstrate that American children can handle depth cues from the age of $3\frac{1}{2}$ and perhaps earlier. Leach (1977), working in Zimbabwe–Rhodesia, constructed a new picture test and applied this to a sample of Shona children; it would seem that these children produced an even higher proportion of correct pictorial depth responses than those studied by Jahoda & McGurk (1974a). These and other researches indicate the extent to which the actual levels of performance appear to depend on the particular methods used.

Jahoda and colleagues (1976) carried out an extensive classroom study of secondary school pupils' ability to utilize pictorial information in learning. Samples were obtained in Scotland, India and several African countries – Ghana, Kenya and Zambia. The material consisted partly of pictures of simple objects and partly of more complex representations requiring an understanding of pictorial depth. It emerged from two separate experiments that information take-up was equally efficient for both types of material in all the various countries. This suggests that as far as those who reach secondary school are concerned, cultural differences in handling 3D representations in pictures have become negligible. Such a view might appear to conflict with the findings of Nicholson & Seddon (1977) working with Nigerian secondary school pupils, who concluded that the ability of their subjects to understand depth relations in pictures was relatively poor. However, their stimulus material was highly abstract, consisting of cuboid and hexagonal frameworks; moreover, these stimuli could be said to have suffered from a certain amount of ambiguity in as much as they could be regarded as being to some extent reversible like a Necker cube. Nevertheless, the discrepancy once again brings home the point that findings in such a sphere should only be considered in the context of the method used.

## Implications for psychological 'universals'

The main lesson to be learnt from this account is probably that questions regarding universals are always relative to the given state of knowledge. In logical, though not strict chronological sequence the first issue was whether 'understanding pictures' could be regarded as such. When the global entity 'understanding pictures' came to be broken down into pictorial object recognition and pictorial depth perception, the evidence increasingly indicated that the former is likely to be a universal. This does of course not mean that pictorial object recognition needs to be regarded as some kind of innate ability. One merely has to assume that learning accurate perception of physical objects in ordinary life, characteristic of all normal humans, transfers readily to 2D representations. Where people are unaccustomed to dealing with 2D, they may experience difficulties at the outset as shown by Deregowski, Muldrow & Muldrow (1972); but there is also evidence that a relatively modest amount of informal training can bring about very rapid improvement (Forge 1970).

On the other hand pictorial depth perception turned out not to be a straightforward entity, but seems to involve a number of component skills whose nature remains as yet somewhat unclear. As long as that is the case, researchers will apply their own notions or guesses regarding the critical attributes and will operationalize the concept accordingly. This accounts for the method-linked variations in the outcomes of different studies, but this fact does not in itself preclude the involvement of undetected universals. The reason is that practically all complex behaviour is to some extent affected by cultural learning, so that universals are not readily detected by simple observation but have to be laboriously winkled out; a famous example of this is the work of Ekman (1973) on facial expressions of emotions, in which he showed the presence of both universals and culturally determined 'display rules'. Like the brilliant studies of Rosch (1977) on categories, such universals can be fairly closely related to biological aspects of man, thereby providing a more solid basis. There seems to be no ready means of establishing such relationships in the sphere of 'indirect perception' dealt with here, which is why there is so much trial-and-error groping.

One helpful clue is provided by the comparisons of developmental trends, though it must be done cautiously in view of the numerous potential pitfalls described by Wohlwill (1973). When one pursues this clue with the material obtained in the present study, it looks as though one of the two component skills analyzed, namely the ability to understand *simple* spatial relationships depicted, might at least tentatively be regarded as a candidate for 'universal' status. On the other hand the ability to make inferences about size–distance relationships on the basis of monocular cues seems unlikely to qualify as a universal. The reason is the considerable divergence of results from studies using the same method, indicating that apart from variations in the richness of the pictorial environment a number of other as yet unidentified cultural factors are probably involved.

It will have been noted that the fundamental criterion for a psychological universal adopted here is invariance across both cultures and methods. Such a formulation immediately raises the question of how rigidly 'invariance' ought to be defined. Given an unavoidable minimum of error variance due partly to imperfections of method and partly to cultural factors presumably unrelated to the main dependent variable (e.g. the relative ease of establishing rapport with the subjects) there will always remain *some* differences. When one deals with absolute levels of performance this problem is insoluble, and any decision is bound to be arbitrary. No such problem arises when one can specify *relationships* whose direction can be specified in advance, and which remain consistent across cultures. In the present case the inverse relationship between number of depth cues and accuracy of spatial responses was only discovered *ex post* and therefore cannot be used to support any claim of universality. Only when an adequate theoretical understanding of the processes involved has been achieved, followed by further successful testing of the resulting prediction, would the spatial performance be firmly established as a universal.

The presumption I am putting forward here is that a type of behaviour or a psychological process cannot be regarded as a universal unless there is powerful evidence to that effect. Since it might be thought that this is labouring the obvious, it is worth noting that the opposite view is quite common as an implicit assumption and is sometimes stated quite explicitly. As regards the former, psychologists conducting studies in the industrialized cultures where the bulk of such work is done are apt to take it for granted that their results would replicate anywhere else in the world. This seems to me a rash assumption, and the textbooks contain theoretical statements or generalizations which, on internal evidence alone, could not be universal. In contrast with such unwitting acceptance of universals there are others who make a judgement of this kind with their eyes open, one of the most articulate being Triandis whose carefully argued position deserves quoting in some detail:

By universal is meant a psychological process or relationship which occurs in all cultures. This statement must be interpreted liberally, however, since it implies that *any* evidence that the relationship does not hold in any culture would invalidate the universal. Given the fallibility of empirical observations, observer biases, and so on, such a stringent criterion cannot be accepted. After all, the fact that an observer has not perceived a phenomenon does not mean that the phenomenon does not exist.

Nor does failure to replicate in another culture a study that was apparently well done in one culture automatically mean that cultural differences interact with the phenomenon. If this happens, the first thing to ask is whether the study does replicate in the original culture, particularly when variations in sampling of subjects, stimuli and response continua are introduced. Furthermore, one needs to examine rival hypotheses for non-replication, such as unusual subject selection or sampling, inadequate controls of relevant variables (e.g. subject motivation to please the experimenter, or disrupt the experiment), nonequivalence of the response format, differential familiarity with the experimental treatments, and differential reactions to being a subject in an experiment. As long as such factors operate *within* a culture, it is not necessary to infer cultural differences as explanations for nonreplication. In short, cultural differences can be inferred only when (a) they are embedded in a nomological network which shows substantial cultural similarities, thus eliminating most of the above rival hypotheses as plausible alternative explanations for nonreplications, and (b) when there is substantial evidence supporting the construct validity of the measurements of the key variables of the network. Thus very strong multimethod and multiobserver evidence that the phenomenon of the relationship does not occur is required to accept the view that a psychological process is not a universal. (Triandis 1978, 1–2)

The passage begins reasonably enough by stating that unduly severe criteria for universals would be unrealistic, owing to the numerous sources of error in both intra- and cross-cultural studies. Some of the major ones are then spelt out, moving gradually to the position that exceptionally strong evidence is required to prove that a phenomenon or relationship is *not* universal. Thus Triandis, using much the same kind of arguments about problems of comparisons which I pointed out, ends up with the opposite conclusion. Quite apart from the fact that the transition from the start to the end of the argument is sudden and unexplained, such a stance on psychological universals is in my view highly questionable. It asserts in effect that any observed phenomenon or postulated relationship can be taken as universal, the onus being on those who deny this status to provide proof. Any observation or experimental finding would automatically qualify as a universal, and since a negative proof would require considerable expenditure of time and resources, it is unlikely to be forthcoming in the majority of cases. In other words, there would be such a plethora of so-called 'universals' that the term would cease to have much meaning.

My own preference is therefore to maintain the burden of proof on those who claim to have discovered a universal. It is they who will have to show that underlying the rich variety of behaviours across human cultures particular elements, usually not readily discernible by the naked eye, remain constant. For psychology surely shares with other disciplines the aim, succinctly expressed long ago by Poincaré, of finding 'similarities hidden under apparent discrepancies'.

## References

Deregowski, J. B. (1968) 'Difficulties in pictorial depth perception in Africa', *British Journal of Psychology* 59, 195–204
——, Muldrow, E. S. & Muldrow, W. F. (1972) 'Pictorial recognition in a remote Ethiopian population', *Perception* 1, 417–25
Ekman, P. (1973) 'Cross-cultural studies of facial expression', in Eckman, P. (ed.) *Darwin and facial expression.* New York: Academic Press
Forge, A. (1970) 'Learning to see in New Guinea', in Mayer, P. (ed.) *Socialization.* London: Tavistock
Hochberg, J. & Brooks, V. (1962) 'Pictorial recognition as an unlearned ability: a study of one child's performance', *American Journal of Psychology* 75, 624–8
Holmes, A. C. (1963) *A study of understanding of visual symbols in Kenya.* London: Oversea Visual Aids Centre
Hudson, W. (1960) 'Pictorial depth perception in sub-cultural groups in Africa', *Journal of Social Psychology* 52, 183–208
—— (1967) 'The study of the problem of pictorial perception among unacculturated groups', *International Journal of Psychology* 2, 89–107
Jahoda, G. & McGurk, H. (1974a) 'Development of pictorial depth perception: cross-cultural replications', *Child Development* 45, 1042–7
—— & McGurk, H. (1974b) 'Pictorial depth perception in Scottish and Ghanaian children', *International Journal of Psychology* 9, 255–67

—— & McGurk, H. (1974c) 'Pictorial depth perception: a developmental study', *British Journal of Psychology* 65, 141–9

——, Cheyne, W. M., Deregowski, J. B., Sinha, D. & Collingbourne, R. (1976) 'Utilization of pictorial information in classroom learning: a cross-cultural study', *Audio-Visual Communications Review* 24, 295–315

——, Deregowski, J. B., Ampene, E. & Williams, N. (1977) 'Pictorial recognition as an unlearned ability', in Butterworth, G. (ed.) *The child's representation of the world*. New York: Plenum Press

Kilbride, P. L., Robbins, M. C. & Freeman, R. B. (Jr). (1968) 'Pictorial depth perception and education among Baganda school children', *Perceptual and Motor Skills* 26, 1116–8

Leach, M. L. (1977) 'Pictorial depth interpretation: a prerequisite to pictorial space comprehension', *International Journal of Psychology* 12, 253–60

McGurk, H. & Jahoda, G. (1975) 'Pictorial depth perception by children in Scotland and Ghana', *Journal of Cross-Cultural Psychology* 6, 279–96

Miller, R. J. (1973) 'Cross-cultural research in the perception of pictorial materials', *Psychological Bulletin* 80, 135–50

Mundy-Castle, A. C. (1966) 'Pictorial depth perception in Ghanaian children', *International Journal of Psychology* 1, 289–300

Nicholson, J. R. & Seddon, M. (1977) 'The understanding of pictorial spatial relationships by Nigerian secondary school students', *Journal of Cross-Cultural Psychology* 8, 381–400

Ofori, R. E. (1970) 'Pictorial depth perception in some Ghanaian school children', Legon: Unpublished honours dissertation

Olson, R. K. (1975) 'Children's sensitivity to pictorial depth information', *Perception and Psychophysics* 17, 59–74

Omari, I. M. & Cook, H. (1972) 'Differential cognitive cues in pictorial depth perception', *Journal of Cross-Cultural Psychology* 3, 321–5

—— & MacGintie, W. H. (1974) 'Some pictorial artefacts in studies of African children's pictorial depth perception', *Child Development* 45, 535–9

Opolot, J. A. (1976) 'Differential cognitive cues in pictorial depth perception among Ugandan children', *International Journal of Psychology* 11, 81–8

Rosch, E. (1977) 'Human categorization', in Warren, N. (ed.) *Studies in cross-cultural psychology*. London: Academic Press

Segall, M. H., Campbell, D. T. & Herskovits, M. J. (1966) *The influence of culture on visual perception*. Indianapolis: Bobbs-Merrill

Triandis, H. (1978) 'Some universals of social behavior', *Personality and Social Psychology Bulletin* 4, 1–16

Wohlwill, J. F. (1973) *The study of behavioral development*. New York: Academic Press

# 3    Tallensi children's drawings[1]

*Meyer Fortes*

The material I am here presenting was collected by my late wife Sonia
L. Fortes and myself during our first spell of field work among the
Tallensi of Northern Ghana in 1934–7. At that time, as I have
described elsewhere (1945, 1949) the Tallensi had been brought
under administrative control only twenty-five years before our
coming. There were no missions or schools among them, the nearest
missionary being ten miles away in the neighbouring tribal area of
the Gorisi (or Nankanse as they were known to the Administration)
and no police or dispensary or colonial civil servant nearer than seven
miles away in the Gorisi tribal area. The first batch of Tallensi boys
to be sent to school, numbering at most a dozen, had been recruited
by the well-known process of a District Commissioner's arriving in
a settlement and demanding from the chief or senior-lineage head a
boy to be sent away to school. One of the oldest of these boys, on
leaving school, worked for me as a clerk and, at first, as interpreter.
He was barely literate and his command of English was limited. The
most significant areas of acculturative experience for the Tallensi was
through labour migration and dry-season small-scale trading journeys
to the southern regions. But the main product of these economic
activities was a very limited inflow of European trade goods and some
money, and the acquisition by some of the men of a smattering of
pidgin English. In short, in 1934–7, Tallensi tribal culture had been
only marginally influenced from outside. Typically, children were
normally nude until the beginning of puberty. Maidens remained
nude, except for a cloth or leather 'back flap' some eight inches long
and two or three inches wide hung on a waist cord over the division

[1] I published a short note on the drawings here discussed in 1940 (Fortes 1940). Recently
a selection of the drawings has been examined in a paper by Dr J. B. Deregowski (1978).
He cites these drawings as evidence that it 'would be erroneous to suggest that a universal
grammar of drawing can be derived by examination of drawings from Western
populations only'.
    I am indebted to the Leverhulme Foundation for a grant towards secretarial assistance
in the preparation of this paper.

between the buttocks, until their first pregnancy. They were then ritually fitted out with a perineal band hitched on to the waist cord in front and tucked under the groin onto the waist cord behind.

Our subjects were mainly children though we also obtained drawings from a few youths in their late teens and early twenties. The children (cf. Fortes 1938) were adept at plaiting reed bangles, waist bands and necklets of quite complex design. Reporting on this at the time I wrote 'This demands skill of eye and hand as well as ingenuity.' I noted that there was a considerable element of play in this activity, and some effort to compete, and added that it was worth observing that plaiting is a repetitive procedure.

I also referred to the children's favourite pastime of modelling miniature clay figures three to six inches high, and proportioned accordingly, of people, horses, cattle and other animals. Little girls made clay cooking pots and played at housekeeping with the figures of people, and small boys played similarly with the figures of men, horses and cattle. The figures varied much in quality but the best were quite realistically representational. Humans had eyes, nose and mouth shown by putting small holes in the face. Figures of women always showed breasts and occasionally the enlarged belly of pregnancy as well as a slit between the legs to stand for the vulva, usually also decorated with a tuft of hair snipped from the artist's head. The figures of men were not given genitals but I collected one such figure in which the man was shown to have the enlarged scrotum due to elephantiasis that was not uncommon among elderly men. Figures of chiefs, mounted on horses, were always dressed up in bits of cloth and equipped with a hat modelled in clay. It was noticeable that human ears were never modelled. Figures of cattle had horns, and bulls and stallions were equipped with scrota.

It seemed to me that what was aimed at in these figures was a three-dimensional spatial diagram, with discriminatory anatomical features shown, rather than a portrait, hence representing rather the child's concept of a man or woman or animal or object than a visual image of it. All the same these figures do suggest that these children had a clear grasp of three-dimensional objects in space. Tallensi culture, I should add, was at that time markedly lacking in any form of art or developed decorative products. The women sometimes decorated the walls of a room with lozenge-like blobs and irregular lines of chevrons, but the nearest thing to a work of art would have been the spread-eagle flat bas-relief of a crocodile of chameleon very crudely modelled in mud on the surface of some ancestor shrines.

Let me now turn to the drawings. In addition to the 'tribal' children who had never been away from home or ever before seen, let alone used, pencil or crayon and paper, we also elicited drawings from some school-children of the same cultural background. I will come to them presently.

There is one point I do want to emphasize, though it will seem superfluous in the light of more recent cross-cultural research in cognitive and perceptual abilities. In the 1930s controversy about the alleged 'pre-logical' mentality of 'primitive peoples' was still rampant. When, therefore, I first discussed these drawings at a meeting of the British Psychological Society in 1940 I made a special point of asserting that the evidence of my 'natural history' observation over two years of close contact with the Tallensi, added to the evidence of responses obtained to the non-verbal tests I had tried out, left me in no doubt as to their cognitive abilities. I stated that there was not the slightest doubt that Tallensi children and adults perceived, remembered and thought about the world around them in accordance with the same laws of cognitive behaviour as govern our perceptual and cognitive activities. Apparent differences, I said, were of cultural not psychological origin. Thus any peculiarities that might seem to appear in the drawings could not, a priori, be attributed to peculiarities of mental constitution in a genetical sense.

In view of some of the questions and comments that came up when I presented this material at the Cambridge conference, I think it will be useful to record the description I wrote on the spot of my first 'drawing session' with some Tallensi children. This was on 18 March 1934, three months after our arrival in Taleland. A group of about a dozen boys of ages from about 6 to 16 had gathered in our compound. With a box of colour pencils and a package of quarto paper I sat down in the middle of the group. I took a pencil and a sheet of paper and drew, very roughly (for I am no draughtsman) a 'picture' of an animal. I then handed a pencil to one of the bigger boys and simply said 'you write' (golh – literally, to make lines). After some hesitation he took the pencil (in his right hand – on this and other occasions we noted some children who used the left hand) bent over the sheet of paper and laboriously covered it with haphazard squiggles like those shown in Fig. 3.1.[2] Meanwhile I distributed pencils and papers amongst the others and noticed that all began by

---

[2] Colour pencils were used in all the drawings but it has been found to be impracticable to reproduce the specimens illustrating this paper in colour. I have, where relevant for particular specimens, indicated what colours are used. The arrow marks the edge of the paper which the subject faced.

Fig. 3.1 Area ABC, all green, elsewhere mainly blue and a few brown squiggles.
Subject: boy ± 12 years

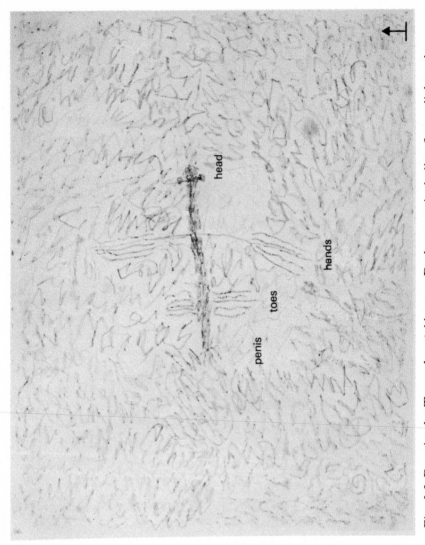

Fig. 3.2 Drawing by Tenga, boy ±11 years. Darker area, including figure, light red; lighter area, orange

covering the surface of the paper with similar meaningless scribble. They worked away diligently, each bent over his own paper, paying no attention to one another. After a while I suggested that they should draw a cow or a donkey but no-one responded. They continued scribbling often rotating the sheet of paper. Then one boy produced a drawing which he said was 'a man'. I suggested that the others should also 'do a man', whereupon Tenga, whom I guessed to be about 11 years showed me his drawing (Fig. 3.2).

Crude and diagrammatic, it could have passed for the work of a 3- to 4-year-old English child. Describing to me what he had drawn, the boy pointed to the 'head' and 'ears' at the 'top' of the $3\frac{1}{2}$-inch by a quarter-inch stripe that represented the 'body'. Lower down he pointed to the 'arms', shown by thin lines sticking out on each side, and the five disproportionately long lines representing the 'fingers' at the end of each 'arm'. Further down five similar lines on each side were the 'toes' and the last half inch of the 'body' was described as the 'penis'. With variations this was the formula followed by all the subjects.

After the introductory scribble stage came, generally, such a diagrammatic or conceptual representational stage and that was as far as any of the subjects got. One feature of the stage exemplified by Fig. 3.2 however deserves comment. It will be noticed that the drawing of the 'man' is roughly in the centre of the page with the scribble now appearing as a framing background but characteristically covering the whole of the space offered by the sheet of paper. A similar pattern appeared in the work of several other boys once they had passed the scribble stage. It might be suggested therefore that a 'figure' and 'ground' *Gestalt* did emerge (cf. remarks below, p. 58) in the drawings after the subjects had familiarized themselves with the use of pencil and paper, but with the peculiar feature that the 'ground' was perceived as empty space that had to be filled in. It is of added interest that some of the boys drew the man in a perpendicular position relative to their own posture whereas others drew the figure horizontally to themselves or at an angle and in a corner rather than centrally. None showed their work to any of the others, or drew my attention to their efforts, and none of them tried to imitate my drawing or that of any other boy.

Having seen Tenga's 'man' I suggested that he might draw a woman, which he promptly did following the same formula but putting in, as the distinguishing feature, 'breasts', not the genital. This was the way a woman was typically represented by all the subjects, in keeping, of course, with the way women were visually distinctive in contrast to males.

Next morning the same group, considerably augmented, arrived early – uninvited – and asked for pencils and paper. They set to work eagerly and I particularly noticed how each worked for himself at first. There was much chatter but it seemed to have no reference to what they were actually drawing. After a while, one or two turned to look at what their neighbours were doing. Most begun with the scribble and then went on to draw a person, animal or object, often rotating the paper or reverting to scribble after a drawing, quite clearly aiming to fill up the blank space. Asked to explain the scribble, they would shrug a shoulder and say 'don't know'. Two of the oldest boys (14 to 16 years, as near as I could ascertain) continued for two hours filling up every corner on both sides of the sheet. Several used pencils of different colours. Watching them, I intervened once or twice with a suggestion of a subject to draw but none of the boys followed these suggestions. Each went on doing what he wanted to do, enjoying the activity as a game.

The pattern of activity shown at the beginning changed very little after the second or third attempt. I regret to say that I did not keep a record of the number of successive drawing sessions that any of the boys, and later also some girls, attended. But a good example of the typical pattern of change can be seen in the specimens of Gbong's (age 14) work. His first attempt was mainly scribble. Even a tree-like blob in the top left hand corner was not given a name by him (Fig. 3.3). His second effort had a more definite structure, with identifiable figures of a 'donkey', a 'man' (note 'penis') and a 'woman' horizontally presented in a demarcated space but all superimposed on the usual scribble (Fig. 3.4). This pattern was repeated two days later, the figures being more distinct, however, and the scribble appearing more recognizably as the ground against which the figures stood out. Equally typical is the change from scribble to recognizable match-stick figures and ground, as in the drawings of Oanyelib (age about 13) (Fig. 3.5).

Age differences clearly influenced performance, the older boys (15 to 18 years plus) showing greater maturity and confidence in their drawings and attempts at realism not found with younger boys, though always within the limits of the diagrammatic formula. Yinera, a rather aggressive lad of about 15 years, was drawing figures of humans and animals (horizontally and upside-down however) very firmly on top of his scribble by the end of his first session (Fig. 3.6).

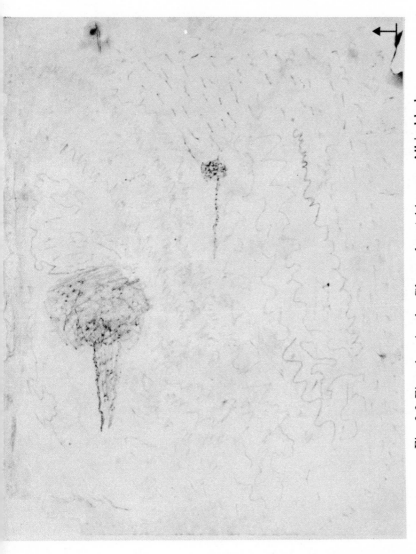

Fig. 3.3 First drawing by Gbong, boy ±14 years. All in black

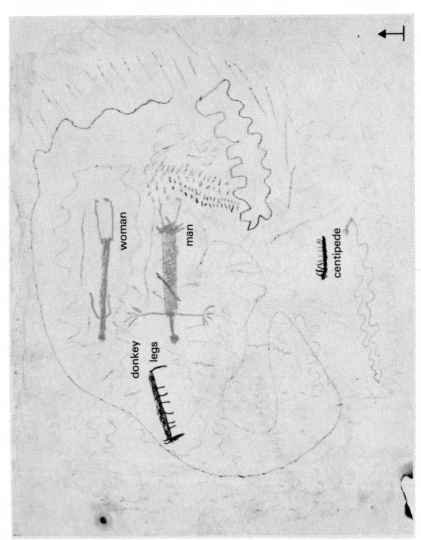

Fig. 3.4 Second drawing by Gbong. Figures of 'man' yellow; the rest of area all black

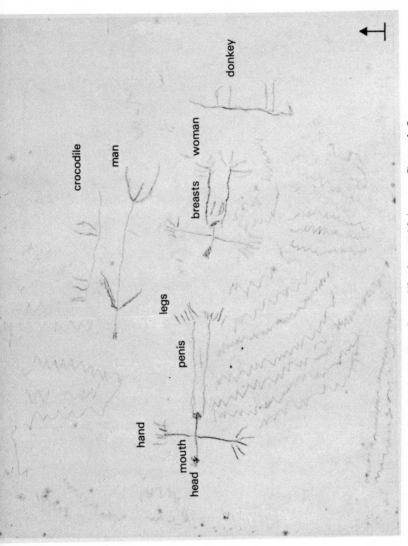

Fig. 3.5 Drawing by Oanyelib, boy ±13 years. Central figures black, other areas lighter colours

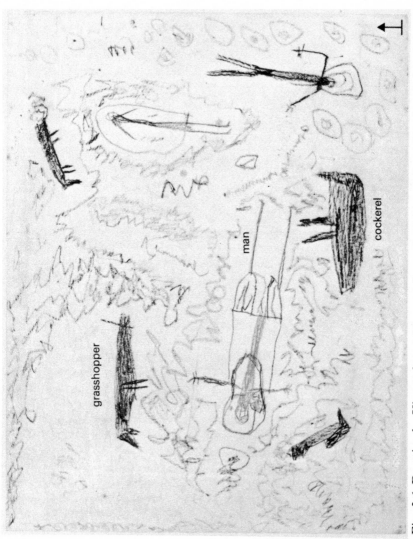

grasshopper

man

cockerel

Fig. 3.6 Drawing by Yinera, boy ±15 years. Several colours used – cockerel, red; larger man, orange and yellow, other figures black and orange. Background black, brown, green, blue, orange.

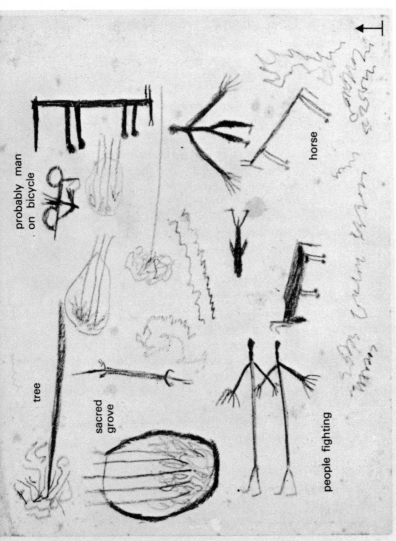

Fig. 3.7 Drawing by Piisim, boy ±15 years. Cow (right-hand corner) red, other figures all blue

More impressive is the work of Piisim, a lad of about 17 years (Fig. 3.7). I was struck by his quick grasp of the situation when he joined the group, by the eagerness with which he settled down to the task and by the way he worked steadily at it for two hours. Though still within the limits of the diagrammatic formula, his (like Yinera's) drawings suggest an attempt at a realistic rather than a simply conceptual representation of what he was depicting. Notice, in particular, the red cow and the grove of trees in his drawing. Considering that this was his first acquaintance with pencil and paper, the firmness of his lines and rings is noticeable, especially in contrast to the drawings of such much younger boys as Tenga (Fig. 3.2 above), though, like them, he placed the human figures on the paper horizontally to himself. That age and maturity might well have been the significant factors is confirmed by the drawings of Sinkawol, a young man of about 22 years (Fig. 3.8). His representation of a man, though still in accordance with the children's formula and even, like some of their drawings horizontally placed, shows a similar attempt at realism and the same firmness of line as Piisim's.

It is of interest to add – as indeed the drawings already considered suggest – that individual differences among the boys were easily detectable. Compare, for instance, Oanyelib's drawing (Fig. 3.5 above) with that of Kyekambe who was the same age, about 12 to 13, as Oanyelib but more intelligent and more curious to understand what we were trying to find out (Fig. 3.10).

As the specimens already considered show, a striking feature of all the drawings, especially in the initial scribble stage, but at later stages too, was the way that the boys set about filling up, almost obsessionally, the whole of the spatial field presented by the blank sheet of paper. To begin with it seemed to be just a way of acquiring familiarity with the unfamiliar blank visual surface of the paper and of learning how to use the pencil. But even after enough practice to become familiar with the paper and the use of the pencil, the propensity to fill up the space persisted, as if the paper were perceived as only a blank surface not as a bounded frame. It is noticeable how common it is for the drawings to have been, apparently, slapped on without cognizance of the objective shape, orientation and boundaries of the sheet of paper. As I put it to myself in the idiom of the thirties, it seemed as if the boys, with a few exceptions, had no perception of a *Gestalt*-type 'figure and ground' setting which the objectively framed visual surface could provide for their drawings. Interesting confirmation came from a remark of a boy who, having filled up one side of his

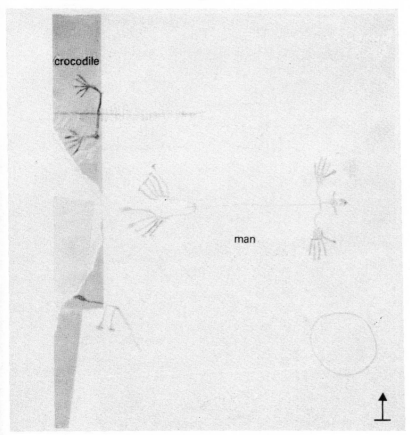

Fig. 3.8 Drawing by Sinkawol, youth ± 22 years

paper was busy with the other side. As he came to the edge he said, stopping abruptly, 'there's no more space left' (*fal* = vacant space as, for example, on a seat or in a room). On another occasion I saw a boy of about 8 years intently bending over his paper and going over the edge on to the floor to finish his drawing. Further confirmation is apparent in the unusual drawing by Zong, aged about 14 years (Fig. 3.9). As can be seen, he actually drew a frame for his scribbles roughly following the edges of the paper as if he had not realized that these constitute a definitive frame.

As regards the drawings of humans, animals and objects, it is evident that they have a constant form right through all ages to adulthood. The commonest formula is the match-stick, spindly,

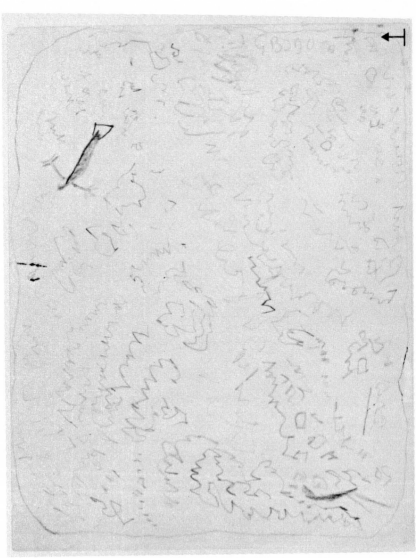

Fig. 3.9 Drawing by Zong, boy ± 14 years. Figure of 'man' top right-hand corner purple, frame purple; elsewhere green

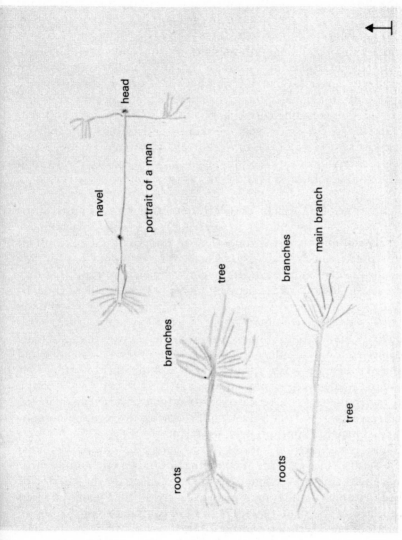

Fig. 3.10 Drawing by Kyekambe, boy ±12 years. All figures in brown

figure but there are also some figures filled out to show bulk or volume. Fundamentally, the figures are functional diagrams projecting in an abstract formula the relative positions and spatial relationships of the different diacritically significant parts of the human or animal body, or the object. The position of each part in relation to the whole and the significant indicative features such as the male genital, female breasts, animal legs, fingers or toes, etc. are the elements emphasized. Relative proportions, for example of head and thorax, are not objectively correct. What the notation primarily represents is the visual and functional prominence and significance of the part depicted – for example, drawings of a man with fingers and toes looking longer and larger than the skimpy neck of the whole foot (cf. Figs. 3.3, 3.5 and 3.8). There are relatively few attempts at presenting volume – i.e. objects in three dimensions, and these take the form of thickening the lines, so to speak, as if volume is perceived as 'thickness' (cf. Fig. 3.6).

What conclusions can be drawn from these data? As I noted at the onset, these Tallensi children were perfectly able to perceive humans, animals and objects in the round and to translate these perceptions into representations, scale models as it were, in the toy figures they modelled in clay. But faced with paper and pencil, it seems that they fell back on the most rudimentary concepts (? internalized models) of the items in the outer world they were trying to depict, resembling in this way children under about 5 years in our culture. Such match-stick models of humans, animals, etc. convey the minimally indispensable visual information needed in order to recognize and respond with appropriate action to the data of the world outside. This principle is effectively exploited in advertising. When I was writing this paper there was a repeated fire-warning advertisement in the press consisting of a large human figure depicted by large photographs of actual matches appropriately arranged.

There is no question here of innate perceptual incapacity. That these performance patterns of children and adults in the 'untouched' tribal environment were functions of learning and of what used to be called cultural conditioning is made clear by the next lot of drawings I collected at the same time. These were collected from a group of school-boys and girls aged about 10 to 17 years who were boarders at the central middle school in Gambaga. These children all came from the cluster of linguistically and culturally very closely-related tribes which include the Tallensi and their neighbours. How closely related these tribes are is indicated by the fact that I conversed easily

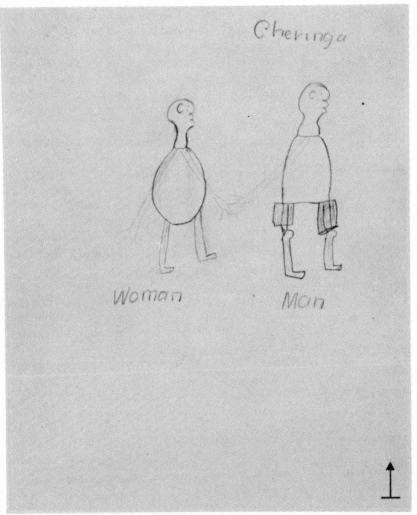

Fig. 3.11 Drawing by schoolboy Cheringa, 12 years, 1934. Note the 'diacritical' representation of the short trousers to distinguish the man, whereas the woman is left without specific distinguishing features

with these children in the Tallensi dialect. Though some of these boys and girls had been at school for five or six years, their standard of literacy in English was very low, and as I found later when I met some in their home communities during school holidays, when at home they 'reverted' completely to traditional habits.

The school-children were asked first to draw a man and a woman and then to draw anything they fancied. The latter turned out to be conventional classroom drawings, mostly in colour, of the kind that were common in primary schools fifty years ago – an orange on a plate, or a tree or a motor car, as these might be drawn by a 7 or 8-year-old English child. The samples of drawings of a man and a woman are similarly in the convention of the English schoolbooks the children used (Figs. 3.11 and 3.12).

The significant point about this, in contrast to the children in the tribal environment is the way the visual space is used. There is no attempt to fill up the space. Instead an attempt is made to depict the object as visually isolated, as a figure against the ground represented by the sheet of paper and roughly centrally to the framed space. In contrast to the spontaneous manner of the 'bush' children, these school-boys and girls set about the task with a degree of strenuous application, that showed they had not fully mastered the skill required for the task. Drawing faces in profile was clearly difficult and most of the drawings look as if they are a compromise between childish representation in European style and graphic symbolization in the 'bush' manner. At all events, there can be no doubt that the way these children perceived the sheet of paper as a bounded space and the way they attempted to represent persons and objects were the results of school experience. They had learned to relate their percepts and concepts to a flat bounded surface in accordance with European models presented to them in their schoolbooks. Yet there could be no doubt, as I easily ascertained from conversations with them, that they saw and thought about the world outside in no way differently from their 'bush' brothers and cousins. Indeed the childish ($\pm 6$-year-old) quality of their drawings by European standards showed how deeply these 10 to 17-year-old children were still fixed in their traditional culture – as is ingenuously shown in Fig. 3.11.

The implication is clear that the way Tallensi children – or for that matter, adults – represented their percepts and concepts of things in the world outside them was fundamentally determined by cultural conditioning and training, not by genetic ('innate') factors. This is very nicely confirmed by the third group of drawings of which some specimens are here shown (Figs. 3.13 and 3.14). These were collected in 1970 in the same Tallensi settlement where my first specimens were collected in 1934, but this time in the local primary school which was now attended by at least 70 per cent of the children between the ages of 5 and 13. These subjects were children and grandchildren of the

Fig. 3.12 Drawing by schoolboy Labugli, 16 years, 1934. Note that his images of a man and a woman are based on the way they looked in the tribal area, not the school area

Fig. 3.13 Drawing by Tindan Nyoka, Tallensi schoolboy, 12 years, at Tongo Primary School, 1970. Head in black pencil, shirt yellow, belt in pencil, trousers green

Baan Kawbena P6 27/1/70

Fig. 3.14 Drawing by Baan Kawbena, Tallensi schoolboy, 13 years, at Tongo Primary School, 1970. Head and body in black pencil, cap green, pipe and leg red, gun held by concealed hand red, object behind gun and shod feet green

population which provided the sample of drawings in 1934–7. As will be seen, they drew a man in a clearly European style, mostly in profile – interestingly enough, with few exceptions, facing left, as is said to be the case with European children – and mostly with the parts of the body shown 'in the round' and in reasonable proportions. Like the earlier batch of school-children they saw the paper as a framed ground for the figure, not as an empty space to be filled up. And it is worth noting how much more skilful their drawings are than are those of the first generation of school-boys and girls. It is interesting to add that when I tried to get some boys of school-going age, but who were not attending school, to draw a man – or anything they liked – I met with a firm refusal. The boys said that 'writing' (*golhug*) was 'a thing for schoolboys not for us'.

And a final observation. I took out to the field, in 1934, a set of Dr Margaret Lowenfeld's test material consisting of fifty-four flat wooden geometrical pieces, squares, triangles and lozenges, with sides of about an inch and a quarter, each shape including three pieces in each of six colours. The task was simply to put the pieces together on a sheet of quarto paper into any sort of arrangement that the subject might fancy. This, of course, is a rigid material which cannot be used to depict the world outside. For Tallensi it was also totally unfamiliar material and the task would very likely have seemed quite prepostrous, a white man's game, even odder than the drawing exercise, from the point of view of normal Tallensi activities and interests.

With this material, too, the tribal subjects all tried to fill the whole space. Younger children made no attempt to arrange the pieces coherently by shape or colour; they slapped down the pieces at random. The older children, from about 11 to 12 years upwards, and the adults usually tried to achieve some sort of arrangement of the pieces, for example a line of squares followed by a line of triangles and then a group of lozenges, sometimes with obviously intended alternation of two colours, but without any patterned connection between the lines. In contrast, normal English children tested by Dr Lowenfeld commonly made a perfectly distinguishable pattern in the centre of the frame or working outwards from the centre.

When I showed the Tallensi efforts to Dr Lowenfeld she said they were exactly like the work of mental defectives! Needless to say none of the Tallensi subjects, least of all adults like Sinkawol, could by any criterion be regarded as mentally defective. The explanation of their performance must be in the absence of culturally given familiarity with the material and with models of what to do with it. If mental deficiency in our society is a sign of the absence of some internal organizing capacity, then the absence of culturally-given organizing directives among these Tallensi children might quite possibly result in performance similar in appearance to that of an English mental defective. Without a clear apprehension of the nature and uses of the material in terms of their normal perceptual and cognitive experience, and no other clues as to how to deal with it, the arrangements they could achieve were bound to have a minimum of structure – the minimum that is given by mere repetitive juxtaposition.

A minor feature of the drawings here discussed deserves comment. We deliberately gave our subjects colour pencils in the hope of eliciting responses to colour differences. The pencils were presented haphazardly mixed in a box and the children were left free to pick and choose among them. In the event it was obvious from the outset that they made no effort to choose but simply picked the first that came to hand, often changing pencils at random as the task proceeded. Asked to explain their use of colours, the majority of the unschooled subjects said something like 'I don't know' though some of the older ones said something like 'It looks nice like this' without further elaboration. It seemed clear that colour preferences played no part in the performance of these subjects. Colour preferences seemed to be more apparent in the drawings of the school children. In some cases this was in obvious imitation of pictures seen in books. But these children also were content to say that the colours they used were chosen because they looked 'nice'. Among the 1934 group no attempt was made to use colour differences or similarities in patterned ways, but their 1970 successors did make use of colour to add pattern to their drawings. It seems that schooling has a training effect in this respect as well as on drawing skill. I need hardly add that the unschooled subjects had no difficulty in discriminating between colours, both perceptually and verbally.

### References

Deregowski, J. B. (1978) 'On re-examining Fortes' data: some implications of drawings made by children who have never drawn before', *Perception* 7, 479–84

Fortes, M. (1938) 'Social and psychological aspects of education in Taleland', *Africa*, Mem. xvii (reprinted in Fortes 1970, ch. 8)

—— (1940) 'Children's drawings among the Tallensi', *Africa* 13, 239–95

—— (1945) *The dynamics of clanship among the Tallensi.* Oxford University Press

—— (1949) *The web of kinship among the Tallensi.* Oxford University Press

—— (1970) *Time and social structure and other essays.* London: Athlone Press (LSE monographs on social anthropology 40)

# 4    Space and community behaviour: a discussion of the form and function of spatial order in settlements

*Roland Fletcher*

## Concepts and procedure: introduction

This study is based upon the assumption that information about external circumstances is received through sense impressions and then made into ordered patterns by the human brain. The brain is regarded as a finite analytic and data storage system (Baddeley 1972) which operates as if classifications of reality enable the brain of each individual to cope with information by arranging it in manageable, discrete, yet interrelated categories. The categories used may be tacit or, like verbal languages, consciously recognized by their users. These classifications also aid communication between individuals by means of consistent though potentially modifiable categories.

In this paper I shall concentrate on the nature of a non-verbal, tacit and material operation whereby human beings attempt to order their spatial context. I shall be concerned with the way in which inanimate objects, such as the buildings in a settlement, express an ordered spatial message.[1] My concern is *not* the supposed 'ideals' behind the pattern but rather is the nature of the material signals as a message system about how space is organized in the settlement. The particular spatial message apparently used by any one community consists of a pattern of structures which repetitiously express a parsimonious basic dimensional order. It is the repetitious and parsimonious nature of the message which aids the ease with which human beings can move around and interact within their settlement.

[1] The 'concepts' and 'ideals' approach used in Fletcher 1977 is unnecessary and is replaced by a 'messages' model. The shift is crucial since it obviates the issues about 'ideals' and 'actuality' that a concepts approach raises (Fletcher 1978).

*Purpose of the paper*

My topic is the nature and role of the ordered, material spatial messages that human communities seem to use in small-scale settlements. The paper is a brief summary of work on a contemporary Ghanaian settlement and a workman's settlement of the second millennium BC in Egypt.

Communities in small-scale settlements behave *as if* they use a model of the horizontal plane of space to locate people and structures in their settlements Though anthropologists have discussed the verbal classification of space (Cunningham 1964; Alkire 1970, 17–23) they have rarely considered the arrangement of walls, posts and other structural features as a classification *in itself* of the horizontal plane of space. The structural form of a settlement divides that plane into discrete though interrelated parts and provides the frame with which the community interacts and within which it orders its life.

That human beings use unstated classifications of space is apparent from their proxemic behaviour. Different human groups have their own preferred spacings for various kinds of social interaction (Hall 1966; Watson 1972; Bauer 1973). These preferences are usually only recognized when they are infringed; otherwise they are taken completely for granted. One fascination of books such as *Body language* (Fast 1970) is that the use of this kind of message system has to be pointed out to the users. Clearly, the analysis of proxemic behaviour shows that people are capable of consistent selection and recognition of distances without the use of any measuring device other than estimation by the eye. In doing so they may be quite unaware of the spatial order which they create, a conclusion as applicable to structures as to persons.

*Research procedure*

Small-scale settlements occupied by user/builders were studied because they are most likely to illustrate spatial patterning. In a small settlement most members of the community can be assumed to be familiar with the spatial pattern created around them. User/builder examples ensure that *as near as is possible* the structures used by a community are spatial forms that each builder intended to create or is at least willing to tolerate. The structures will in some way express and constitute a spatial model for the community.

*Selection of spacings.* The critical problem in a study of dimensional order is the selection of the features to be measured. There is an infinity of possible measurements; therefore some selection is necessary. But the selection must try to be consistent, otherwise any desired result could be obtained by judicious choice of convenient examples. There is, however, a permanent ambiguity that even with clear specifications, no observer could ever presume to have recognized every specified spacing.

*Similar linked entities.* I have followed the specifications applied in proxemic studies because these provide simple criteria and help to maintain a connection between studies of personal and structural location. Distances between *similar linked* entities are used (Fig. 4.1). Lengths of walls, i.e. the distance between the ends of the wall, are included but diagonals of rooms are not. For circular structures the radius is taken. This procedure followed a crude condition defined by interpersonal spacing, i.e. as human beings approach one another, each person is at some point located at the edge of the other's personal space (Hall 1968). Accepting the simplistic idea of a circular personal space, the distance between the two similar linked entities, whether persons or elements of structures, is then equivalent to the radius of a circle.

*Spacing categories.* Identifying the spatial categories to be studied was the next task. This must unavoidably proceed through the bias of the researcher's own categories (Gerber, Greenfield & Wright 1974). My own bias is to perceive settlement structure in terms of categories such as doorways and courtyards. This bias might be at variance with the *tacit* classes of entities, or the verbal labels actually used by the community.

For instance, the class of doorwidths includes widths from all entry spaces regardless of the specific use of that entry. Widths from human used doorways and the entries to animal pens are plotted to provide a distribution of widths which can be characterized by a measure of central tendency (e.g. a mean or median) and a measure of variation from the mean (e.g. standard deviation or interquartile range). Two alternative patterns of distribution can then be distinguished, either unimodal or polymodal, i.e. those for which there is a clear tendency for values to cluster at one point and those where there is more than one central tendency for the values. These distributions must be considered to reflect different types of classification of spacings. For

Personal space in plan view:
proxemic distance X

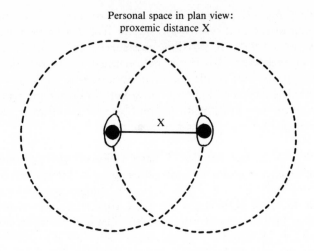

Structural equivalents in plan view

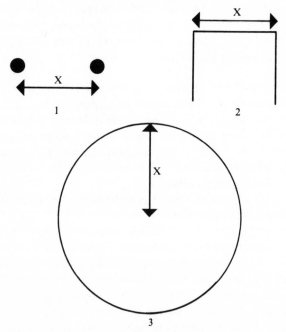

Fig. 4.1

example, a situation where the widths of small doorways, for animals other than man, form the lower tail of a smooth distribution of all doorwidths should be distinguished from the case where animal doorways produce a distribution peak of widths distinguishable from, even if partly overlapping, a distribution for human used doorways. The latter case, unlike the former, must be accepted as an indication that the community behaves as if it distinguishes the two categories of doorways, whether or not people in the community can state such a view.

Wherever possible, a consistent and appropriate class interval for grouping the dimensions should be applied to the distributions of familiar categories in order to present the regularities revealed in the distributions. One reason for the studies presented here is to illustrate that simple procedures can indicate the order in spatial arrangements without requiring elaborate statistical presentation and analysis. The studies do not, however, claim to present *the* form of a community's spatial reflection of the order which is actually present and which might be understood in a variety of different ways. The quality of a proposed pattern depends on its consistency with, and its capacity to predict, other features of the community's behaviour.

### *Expected spatial patterns : (Fig. 4.2)*

*Central tendencies.* If the central tendency of each of the available distributions of linear dimensions is unrelated to any other central tendency, then a plot of the differences between adjacent central tendencies (which I now refer to as separations) against the dimensions of the lower central tendency should produce a scatter of separations containing no order. This is the dimensional equivalent of randomly hitting some of the keys on a piano, starting at the lower end of the keyboard and proceeding to the other end. Each note produced is like a central tendency: the pitch differences between successive notes are like the separations between the dimensional central tendencies. If the notes are taken at random along the keyboard there will be an uneven progression in the successive pitch changes. The pitch of the notes would always be increasing but an occasional large difference could be followed by a small pitch difference, and so on with no ordered relationship between the successive notes. An initial ordering of the pitch differences would be to hit three or four keys in immediate succession; then jump several keys and hit all of the next three or four keys and so on. A

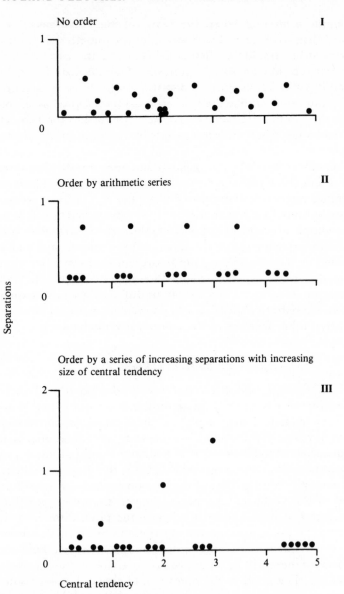

Fig. 4.2 Expected spatial patterns

distinction would be made between bunches of small pitch differences separated by large jumps in pitch. Likewise a concentration of dimensional central tendencies around particular values should produce a distinction between large and small dimensional separations.[2] If the concentrations of central tendencies possess a simple mathematical relationship, this should be apparent in the arrangement of the separations. For instance, an Arithmetic series of central tendencies would result in a series of uniform separations, while a Geometric or Fibonacci[3] series would produce a trend to increasing separations with the increase in the size of the central tendencies. The equivalent on a keyboard would be; for an Arithmetic series – strike for example every fourth key; for a Geometric series – strike the 2nd, 4th, 8th, 16th key and so on; for a Fibonacci series strike the 1st, 2nd, 3rd, 5th, 8th, 13th key and so on.

The indication of such serial trends in the spatial data does not mean that the community is specifically using such a series; only that the series description acts as a convenient mnemonic for a spatial pattern. It must once again be emphasized that a community need not be aware of the regularities in arranging space that are involved in its location of people and structures. No claim need be made that the occupants of a settlement consciously recognize or recognized the mathematical relationship identified by the researcher. What is of consequence, however, is that such relationships appear to describe the kinds of spatial messages which operate in the behaviour of a community.

*Variation.* There has been a tendency in formal studies to ignore the need for a description of variation. This limitation has been critically noted by Harris (1968, 582–91). In an analysis of the dimensional order of space some statement of the variation involved is required. Consistency in variation is needed in a community because a person's behaviour must be guided by some notion of the indeterminacy surrounding any given entity and its location. Without such a regularity for example, climbing stairs would be a difficult task.

Tolerable variation can be associated with a community's attitude to the relationship between similarity and difference. When we say

---

[2] Such clusters of small separations can also be recognized from histograms of the frequency of occurrence of central tendencies within a given class interval. A 5 cm interval presentation was used for the Deir el Medina study.

[3] Gardner (1968). In a Fibonacci series, any value is the sum of the preceding two values. See also Badawy (1965), for an attempt to apply a stringent Fibonacci rule, particularly to Egyptian temples.

that two entities are similar we are stating that they are more like each other, i.e. are nearer some standard, than they are like other entities which we recognize as different. In the similarity case the values for the two entities differ by an amount less than the acceptable variation in the size of either. Conversely, two entities we consider to be different have characteristics which differ by an amount exceeding the range of variation for any given standard, for example, the case of a bimodal distribution for doorways used by humans and those used only by other animals. The variation tolerable to a community should therefore mark the distinction between similarity and difference.

*Statistical procedure.* The distributions have been initially analysed using a Mean/Standard deviation description, based on unclassed data, to ascertain whether or not order is present in the data. These statistical measures are used because they are familiar, can be obtained by a consistent procedure from distributions in different settlements, and consequently assist comparison. However, the distributions are not 'Normal' and the Mean/Standard deviation description can thus only be used to suggest order. The actual shape of the distributions tends to show a marked positive skew.

An alternative is to use a Median/percentile range description. Apart from any other useful quality, such descriptions can be readily and easily derived, even in the field where a handy calculator may be lacking! The procedure is illustrated below for the Konkomba settlement in Northern Ghana. A Median/percentile range description reduces the skew effect of the distributions and may be obtained from smaller populations of examples. Distributions that contain ten or fewer examples are not uncommon in the small-scale settlements which I have been studying. Such populations are below the usual limit for the applicability of standard deviation descriptions. A Median/percentile range therefore helps to provide a more inclusive description. I have included the percentile ranges for distributions with only five examples and medians from distributions with as few as two examples in order to include the dimensions from as many structures as possible. This considerably increases the number of descriptions and increases the number of central tendencies for which a variation description can be provided. Since much of man's social behaviour has been acted out in small-scale settlements with restricted populations for any given spatial category, use of descriptions which can be based on only a few measurements is essential. Without such a procedure much of the potentially available information would be unusable. The statistical validity of this procedure depends upon consistent application, for example the use of one percentile range description applied to all settlements so that the resulting values will represent the similarity or difference between the variation used by different communities.

## An ethnographic example: a Konkomba settlement in Ghana

### Introduction

The Konkomba settlement discussed in this paper lies to the south of Kpandai near the Oti River in Northern Ghana (cf. Figs. 4.3, 4.4; and Fletcher 1977).[4] Thirty to thirty-five adults live in the settlement, which consists of nine occupied residence units. The community grows yams, millet and maize as their staple crops. Groundnuts are also grown but are usually marketed, as are some of the yams and part of the maize crop. Each residence unit is formed from a number of round and rectangular buildings linked by low walls to form an enclosed courtyard. Access from the courtyard to the open areas around the residence units either passes through a single door in one of the link walls or through a room. There is only one entry point for each residence unit. Walls are constructed from compacted mud. Most roofing is thatch but zinc sheet is also used for roofs of rectangular structures. Konkomba traditional buildings were circular in ground plan but rectangular buildings are now being introduced into the pattern. In the settlement studied, the first building to be erected was the large rectangular residence unit at the north end of the cleared area. The man who built it was the first Headman of the community. When he died he was succeeded by his brother who built and lives in the large, immediately adjacent residence unit. The two subsidiary courtyards of this residence unit belong to the present Headman's married sons.

### Research procedure

Table 4.1 lists the spacings measured in order to study the regularities present in the organization of structures in the settlement.

A 20 cm class interval is adequate to arrange the primary dimensions from 0 to 4 and 5 m into distinguishable unimodal distributions that

---

[4] Tait 1961; Gil, Aryee & Ghansah 1964, xxiv, 4, table 1. The Konkomba live in North-east Ghana around the Oti River and on the plains north and west of the Basare and Kotokoli Hills. In 1960 the population was counted at 110,000 people; see Prussin (1969, 38–50) for comparison to another Konkomba settlement.

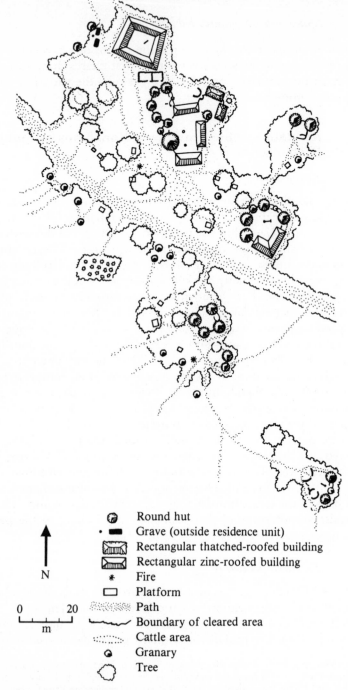

N

0        20
|_____|
    m

🕸 Round hut
· ▬ Grave (outside residence unit)
▨ Rectangular thatched-roofed building
▨ Rectangular zinc-roofed building
* Fire
▭ Platform
⠿ Path
⌣ Boundary of cleared area
⦙ Cattle area
◉ Granary
◇ Tree

Fig. 4.3 Konkomba settlement: plan 1971

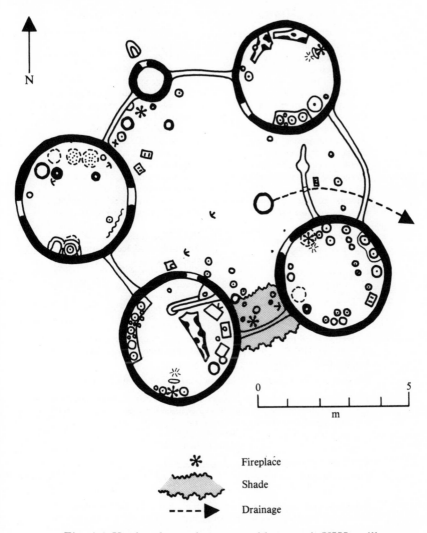

0 |———|———|———|———|———| 5
m

*      Fireplace

〰〰〰      Shade

- - - ▶      Drainage

Fig. 4.4 Konkomba settlement: residence unit VIII to illustrate
positioning of objects in huts and courtyard

TABLE 4.1. *Measured spacings : Konkomba settlement*

| | |
|---|---|
| Bath end width | Pillar dimensions |
| Bench length (incl. Arc benches) | Pillar radius |
| Bench radius | Pillar centre spacing |
| Bench width | Pillar edge spacing |
| Circle post-spacing | Rectangular building exterior length |
| Courtyard I-dimensions | Rectangular building exterior width |
| Door-width | Rectangular room length |
| Fence link post-spacing | Rectangular room width |
| Fence main post-spacing | Residence unit length ⎱ Radials |
| Firescreen wall length | Residence unit width ⎰ (not for I) |
| Granary centre separation | Residence unit centre separations |
| Granary edge separation | Residence unit II, III, IV centre separations |
| Granary platform post-spacing | Residence unit edge separations |
| Granary platform total dimensions | Round hut exterior radius |
| Link wall length | Round hut interior radius |
| Mat post-spacing | Round hut, adjacent centre separations |
| Oven exterior radius | Screen wall length |
| Oven interior radius | Stand long side |
| | Stand short side |
| | Zone II post-spacing |

Notes: This list has been revised and enlarged since the initial analysis reported in Fletcher (1977). The variation and central tendency diagrams therefore contain new and re-assessed values.

No wall widths measured. Below measurement limit for structural features.

Four categories of spacings produce polymodal distributions, covering a wide scatter of values, which provide no clear basis for sub-division by reference to any distinguishable feature of the entities:

    End walls of baths    Firescreen walls
    Link walls    Lengths of benches

Fletcher (1977, 104) includes a discussion of these spacings. They appear as dimensional adjusters, particularly to area, and suggest that a more elaborate analysis could use an area description.

Four other categories of spacing which could not be measured are:

    Chicken coops in Headman's entry hut
    Temporary fencing in baths
    Interior of rectangular ruin
    Graves

can be associated with specific categories of spacings. The larger class intervals required to present the distributions of dimensions greater than 4 and 5 m are required by the inherent errors of measurement.[5]

[5] Two measurement procedures were used: direct measurement, and triangulation survey. The scattered nature of most of the larger dimensions is not a consequence of the

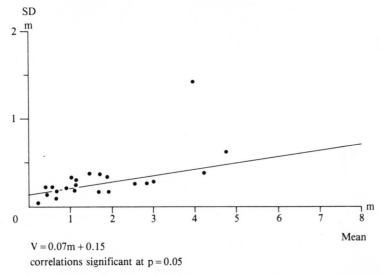

$V = 0.07m + 0.15$
correlations significant at $p = 0.05$

Fig. 4.5 Konkomba settlement: trend of variation (M/SD)

For categories of spacings with dimensions up to 15 m a class interval of 50 cm or 1 m is needed. A minimum interval of 1 m applies up to 30 m, and a 2 m interval applies for dimensions greater than 30 m. A constant class interval was applied to the dimensions of any one spacing category.

*Analysis and results*

*Order in the data.* A mean and standard deviation description indicates a consistent trend to increasing variation as the values of the central tendencies increase (Fig. 4.5). When this relationship was checked for seven other settlements in Ghana the trend appears as a general characteristic of the visual organization of horizontal space (Fletcher 1977). The increase in variation is to be expected since human estimation of distance declines in accuracy with the increase in the length being estimated (Gregory 1966, 53; Vernon 1968, 128).

measurement procedure. Surveyed dimensions of Exterior Widths of Rectangular Buildings and Centre Separations of Round Huts display a continuous distribution at a 20 cm interval.

The larger class intervals are *also* useful as a device to present the more scattered larger dimensions, whose dispersal is partly a result of the decrease in accuracy of distance estimation by the builders.

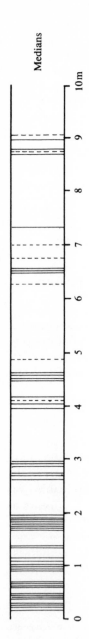

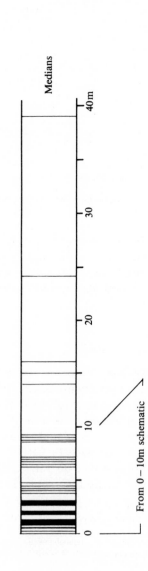

Fig. 4.6 Konkomba settlement: medians. Note: for some of the distributions around 4–10 m there are two possible medians depending on the 'lumping' (Set 1) or a 'splitting' (Set 2) treatment of the distributions.

The trend is not determined either by materials or by the position of structures in the settlement. Values from entities made of differing materials, located at different positions in the settlement, are scattered throughout the trend. This indication of order suggests that the enquiry could be usefully extended to the arrangement of central tendencies in relation to each other.

*Central tendencies.* The median descriptions of the distributions can be arranged from smallest to largest (Fig. 4.6) and the separations between them can be plotted against the medians to which they refer. When this is done, large and small separations can be distinguished. These two differing degrees of separation lie roughly on either side of the trend of variation, as if they represent the community's tacit ordering of similarity within clusters of central tendencies (the small separations) and difference between the clusters (the large separations). A severe anomaly occurs around 6–8 m where there is a break in the trend of large separations (Fig. 4.7). Discussion of the pattern must therefore be divided into two sections referring to the medians in the 0–8 m zone and to the 8–40 m values.[6]

0–8 m zone: To define the clusters we can use the trend of the standard deviations combined with the ceiling of the small separations from 1·50 m onwards. The clusters of medians can in turn be described by the median values (Fig. 4.8). The cluster medians in this zone are as follows: 0·25; 0·45; 0·65; 1·05; 1·75; 2·80; 4·45; 6·50; 8·75 m (Fig. 4.8a).

8–40 m zone: The medians for clusters in the upper zone are 8·75; 15·00; 24·00; 39·00 (Fig. 4.8b).

Comment: The cluster medians appear as a sequence in which each value is approximately the sum of the preceding two values. The sequence resembles the famous Fibonacci series which can be used as a convenient mnemonic description. Critical in this description is the series anomaly that appears around 6–8 m. The series cumulates up to 6·50 m and from there onward, but the 8·75 m value is odd. According to the series there should be an 11 m value. No *distribution* medians are present in the settlement for this dimension.[7] The nature and role of this break must now be considered.

[6] The divide is not an artifact of data collection. It occurs *within* the surveyed dimensions and is expressed in differing spacings presented *within* constant class interval.

[7] Two isolated lengths at 10 and 12 m are present. A Set 2 description adds a further isolated, 11 m dimension.

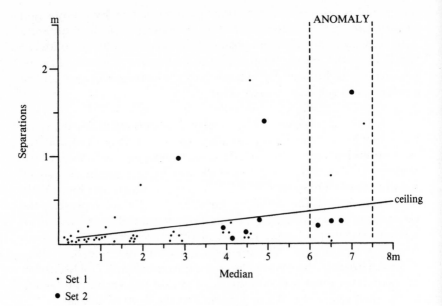

Fig. 4.7a  Konkomba settlement: median separations 0–8 m

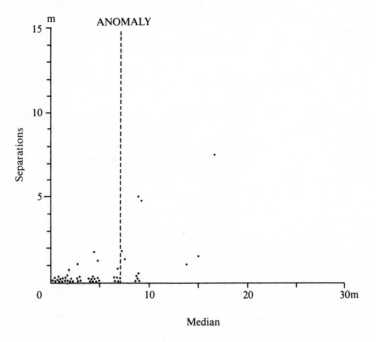

Sets 1 and 2 not distinguished

Fig. 4.7b  Konkomba settlement: median separations 0–4 m

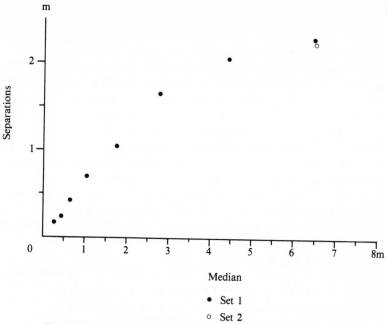

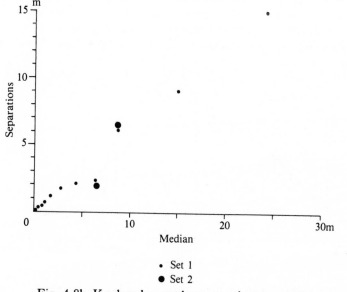

Fig. 4.8a Konkomba settlement: cluster median separations
0–8 m

Fig. 4.8b Konkomba settlement: cluster median separations
0–40 m

*Variation and the sequence anomaly.* A measure of variation based upon the range within which 40 per cent of the values occur in a distribution was found to be useful for extending the available data concerning spatial variation.[8] There are of course many different ways of describing the variation tolerable to a community. There is no assumption that this particular procedure or specific value will necessarily be the most appropriate for describing variation in different settlements. Further study will be needed to assess this issue.

The new measure of variation is used to obtain a quantified statement of the difference in the form of the distributions on either side of the 6–8 m sequence anomaly. For the classes of spacings studied, the variation for distributions with medians around 4–8 m increases abruptly (Fig. 4.9). This high level of variation is maintained for all the distribution, except one, with medians from 6–40 m.[9]

We can recognize a connection between the increase in variation and the break in the sequence of large separations. The separation between the 6·50 m cluster and the 8·75 m cluster declines into the increased variation. The distinction between clusters has apparently been lost for that separation. The 40 per cent range values can be divided either into an upper or lower trend of variation. Only those separations between cluster medians from 6·50 m and 8·75 m onwards mark differences between clusters of values, when the upper trend of variation is used. On the other hand, the separations between clusters whose medians are less than 6·50 m can only be regarded as representing differences when viewed against the lower level of variation.

8

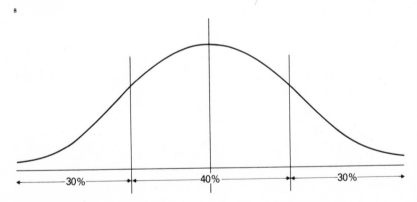

← 30% → ← 40% → ← 30% →

---

[9] The exception is a Set 2 statement for the Exterior Lengths of Rectangular Buildings, which produces a 40 per cent range that is an extension of the trend of low variation.

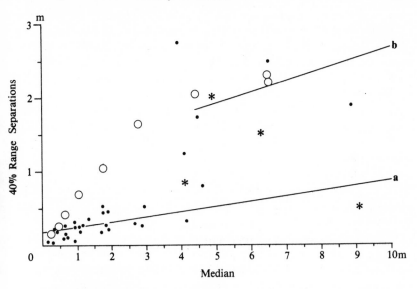

○ Separations between cluster medians
• Set 1. 40% values
✳ Set 2. 40% values
a V = 0.07m + 0.18
b V = 0.15m + 1.18
Correlations significant at p = 0.05
Note: 40% value of 7m for 39m median (Set 1)
40% value of 0.5m for 9.10m median (Set 2)
The variation regressions use these two values

Fig. 4.9 Konkomba settlement: cluster median separations and
trend of variation (median/40 % range)

An alternative is to treat all the variation values as one trend, in
which case the complementary relevant separations cover the entire
sequence from 25 cm to 40 m with the 6·50 and 8·75 m separation
subsumed in a generalized series description (Fig. 4.10).

### Nature and role of the spatial divide

The community behaves as if it uses a two-part model of space to
organize the location of entities in the settlement. If this is the case
then the dimensional break should be apparent in other aspects and
descriptions of the settlement and the behaviour of the community.

Most notably the total area of the settlement is divided into two

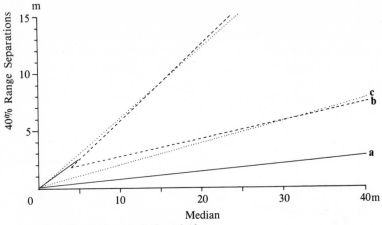

a   $S = 0.47 + 0.12$    $V = 0.07m + 0.18$
b   $S = 0.67 - 0.96$    $V = 0.15m + 1.18$
c   $S = 0.62 - 0.18$    $V = 0.18m + 0.17$

Correlations significant at $p = 0.05$

Fig. 4.10  Konkomba settlement: spatial model

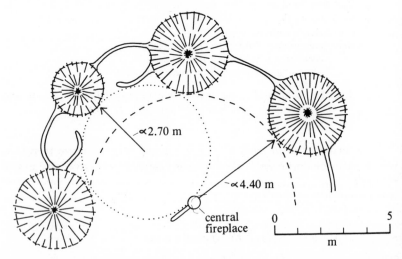

Fig. 4.11  Visual ranges in Konkomba settlement residence units

main spatial categories: the enclosed space of the courtyards and the rough, open, cleared ground around the residence units. Within a residence unit the maximum distance that can separate a person from the major structural frame of huts, rooms and link walls is about 4–5 m (Fig. 4.11). Inside this visual range the courtyards of the smaller residence units provide a maximum visual distance of about 2·60–3·10 m. That the overall space of residence units is treated as a coherent frame by the occupants is indicated by the location of fixed mortars, ovens and fire-screens in the courtyards of the larger residence units. The effect of these features is to produce the same 2·60–3·10 m visual distances as apply to the entire courtyard area of the small residence units.

Only in the open areas around the residence units are visual distances from the observer to reference points in excess of 6·50 m. The two-part model appears to complement the overall sub-division of space in the settlement. It seems that the two trends of variation are associated with the two parts of the visual-spatial pattern in the settlement. Dimensions which correspond to visual ranges with residence units need to be associated with a greater perceptual precision than is necessary outside the residence unit. Courtyards are cluttered with stools and mats, with pots or with food laid out to dry in the sun. Greater precision in observation and movement is necessary within a courtyard than in the open spaces where the only features a person is likely to meet are wood piles, timber-built platforms, graves and granaries. The formal order which is derived from measurements taken from *structures* in the settlement, appears congruent with the pragmatic functional requirements of community behaviour throughout the entire space of the settlement.

The two-part model should not be treated simply as a functional derivative of the difference between the courtyard and open space, but should be regarded as a complement to that situation. Priority cannot be allocated to the actual entities rather than to the perception that creates that space and makes its use possible. Neither the levels of variation nor the median separations are directly defined by position in the settlement or by the form of the residence units. Many of the dimensions around 1·00 m, 1·70 m and 2·08 m, with corresponding low variations occur in entities such as timber platforms *outside* the residence units. Some of the 8·70 m medians that cause the sequence break, derive from features like the lengths of rectangular buildings that are *part* of the residence units.

Therefore the location of the measured entities in the settlement

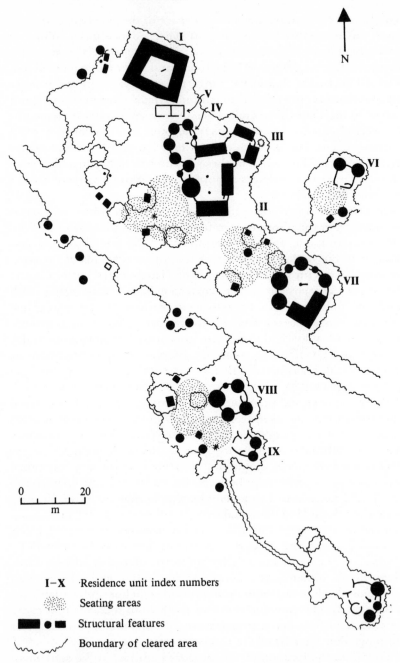

Fig. 4.12 Konkomba settlement: seating areas

is not the main factor influencing their dimensions or their variation. It is the dimensions themselves that are the complement to the variation. The specific structures occurring in the settlement are one concrete expression of the community's size estimation behaviour and its tolerance of variation. The arrangement of the residence units and open areas as zones providing particular visual distances is another expression of that response. The former states the relationship between similar linked entities; but the sequence of dimensions which appears to describe that relationship can then also be seen as a general statement of the kinds of distances into which the community tends to divide space.

The sequence of dimensions states the zones *within* which inter-action between people and structures will tend to occur, not the precise distances between such non-equivalent entities. This is well illustrated by the seating places outside residence units. In all observed cases, and particularly in the area immediately outside the Headman's residence unit, people locate themselves in places where they cannot be more than 4 to 5 m away from a reference point (Fig. 4.12). These points include trees, one small fireplace, granaries, platforms for timber and seating platforms. In limited areas outside the residence units the community has produced local visual environments equiv-alent to the frame for social activity provided by the large courtyard spaces within residence units.

When a person looks out from the single access door of a residence unit, the structures which provide reference points are either at or beyond the 6·50–8·75 m anomaly zone (Fig. 4.13). For residence units II and VI this positioning of structures defines the seating area in front of the access door. Outside the other residence units the seating area depends on the relationship between the granaries and platforms located in the zone beyond the anomaly divide. For residence unit I the area where the cattle are tethered at night also conforms to this boundary, as if the spatial divide has a direct expression in the sub-division of exterior space relative to the access door of a residence unit.

## Conclusion

The description of space in the Konkomba settlement suggests that communities behave as if they use models of space to organize the location of entities whether animate or inanimate, in the settlement area. Specific features of the spatial model correspond to prag-matic functional requirements of community life. In the Konkomba

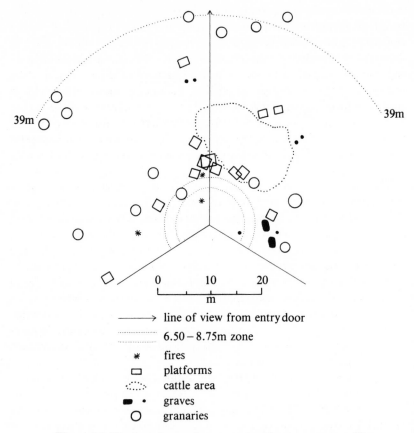

Fig. 4.13 Konkomba settlement: visual ranges out to 40 m

settlement a two-part model corresponds to the distinction between interior residence space and exterior settlement space. The maximum visual distance possible within the residence units is about 4–5 m which corresponds to the largest dimension in the 0.25 to 6.50 m sequence that has both a larger and a smaller reference value in that sequence. The variation within this visual range is relatively low, corresponding to the need for more visual precision in the crowded courtyard space. The variation for dimensions beyond this range is relatively high, corresponding to the less restrictive requirements of activity in the open spaces of the settlement. Settlement space appears as a coherent visual context in which members of the community can operate on tacit assumptions about necessary accuracies, combined with predictions about the probable dimensions that will be encountered. At the same time the structures in the settlement are constantly expressing a set of spatial signals which constitute a message about how space is to be ordered in that community (Fletcher 1976).

## An archaeological example: the settlements of Deir el Medina

### Introduction

The settlements of Deir el Medina lie on the western side of the Nile near Luxor in Upper Egypt. From about 1500–1100 BC they were occupied by a community of workmen maintained by the Royal administration concerned largely with the preparation of the tombs for the Pharaohs in the Valley of Kings (Bruyère 1939; Černý 1973).

There are two residence areas: a Main settlement at the foot of the western cliffs (Fig. 4.14) and a rest station or transit base which I shall call the Top site, on the col leading to the Valley of Kings (Fig. 4.15). At the Top site the workmen may have stayed overnight during their shift in the valley. This site contains only small rooms for sleeping and temporary storage. The workmen and their families lived in the Main settlement, around which they build their family tombs. Though the basic layout of both settlements was probably specified by the administration, the workmen appear to have built and altered their own residence units within this frame.

### Relevance of the settlements

The well-preserved residential pattern provides a convenient test case to find out whether the method applied in studying contemporary settlements can also be applied to settlements that are no longer inhabited. This should be possible because no verbal information is required from the occupants. If the data can therefore be obtained over a long time range we should ultimately be able to study the role of unstated classifications in change and adaptation, without recourse to reconstruction by analogy with present-day settlements. The value of the Deir el Medina examples is that each residence area offers an independent expression of the spatial model which the community may have used. This is of particular interest because the Top site appears superficially to possess little resemblance to its partner, and is a classic case of the settlement form often described as haphazard and unorganized.

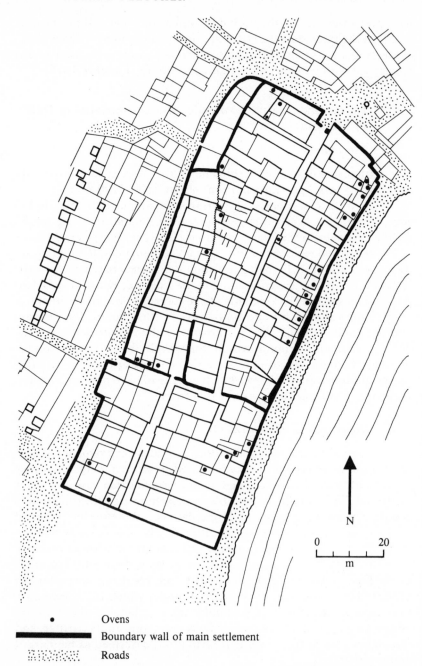

•           Ovens

━━━━━━━    Boundary wall of main settlement

∷∷∷∷∷∷    Roads

Fig. 4.14a   Deir el Medina: Main settlement (after Bruyère 1939)

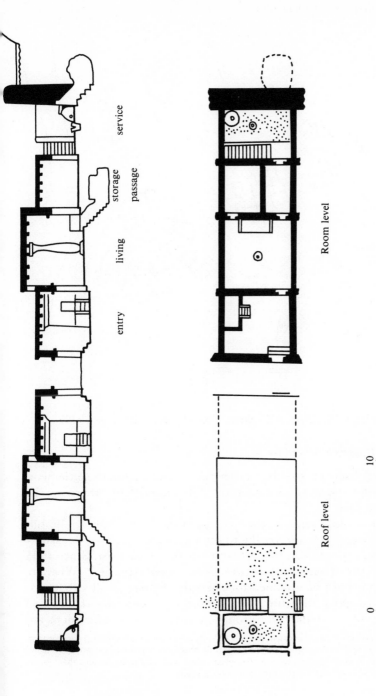

service

storage

passage

living

entry

Room level

Roof level

10

m

0

Fig. 4.14b  Deir el Medina: Main settlement. Schematic illustration of residence units (after Badawy 1965)

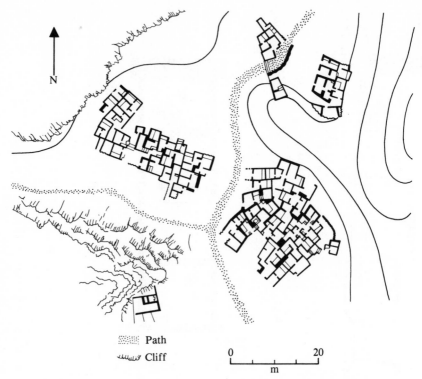

N

░░░ Path
〜〜〜 Cliff

0          20
|___|___|___|
m

Fig. 4.15   Deir el Medina: Top site (after Bruyère 1939)

### Research procedure

Table 4.2 lists the spacings measured in the Egyptian settlement. They differ, because of structural differences, from those in the Ghanaian case.

The procedure remains the same as in the Konkomba study, but there are requirements specific to the Egyptian examples. Measurements were taken from the structures as they now exist. Since 1935 some of the divans and shrines have been damaged. Where a dimension could be obtained for one side of these small structures, I have assumed that the value would also describe the ruined opposite side.[10] Medians for groups of three or more dimensions are

[10] The procedure is used because it allows inclusion of more structural dimensions in association with the eventual use of a percentile range description of variation. In using this policy it is recognized that the variation values will tend to be smaller than values from the original intact structures would have been.

TABLE 4.2. *Measured spacings: Deir el Medina, Main settlement and Top site*

| Main settlement | Top site |
| --- | --- |
| Bin interior length | Bench length |
| Bin interior width | Bench width |
| Bin/grinder exterior length | Divan length |
| Bin/grinder exterior width | Divan width |
| Bin/grinder interior dimensions | Door-width |
| Cellar entry | Niche depth |
| Column radius | Niche width |
| Column base radius | Seat length |
| Divan length | Seat width |
| Divan width | Step depth |
| Divan, edge ridge length | Step width |
| Divan, edge ridge width | |
| Divan and screen length | |
| Divan and screen thickness | |
| Door-width | |
| Niche depth | |
| Niche width | |
| Oven exterior radius | |
| Oven interior radius | |
| Shrine exterior length | |
| Shrine exterior width | |
| Shrine interior length | |
| Shrine interior width | |
| Shrine step depth | |
| Shrine step width | |
| Shrine steps length | |
| Shrine steps balustrade length | |
| Shrine steps balustrade thickness | |
| Stair step depth | |
| Stair step width | |
| Step depth | |
| Step width | |

Notes: Small structural features are common in Deir el Medina requiring the inclusion of the thickness of subsidiary walling within the measurement limit.

Major structural dimensions also included, i.e. various room dimensions. Isolated features, e.g. lone pillar pair spacings, single courtyards, a square oven and a square structure are excluded.

My labels for the parts of the Main settlement are:

| | |
| --- | --- |
| East I | – NO I–XIX, C I–III |
| East II | – NE I–XIX |
| West I | – NO XX–XXVII |
| West II | – C IV–VIII |
| South I | – 'C IV', SO I–VI |
| South II | – SE I–IX |
| (Fletcher) | – (Bruyère) |

used to describe the central tendencies. Regularities only appear at this level of detail.

Each structural group in the Top site on its own supplies insufficient medians for order to be apparent. All the median values for the Top site were therefore amalgamated in one sequence to describe the spatial pattern. In the Main settlement, descriptions of spatial order can be obtained from the dimensions up to 6 and 7 m in five of the 'sides'. West I has, however, suffered severe damage (Bruyère 1939, 297) and only displays order up to 1·50 m. There are too few medians beyond that value for order to be recognizable, except by reference to West II.

A Mean/Standard deviation statement has been used in the Top site and in the Main settlement, to indicate the presence and basic nature of the pattern of variation. A 20 cm class interval was applied, with the exception of a 25 cm interval for exterior widths of residence units.[11]

### Results

The dense packing of the structures in the Top site and Main settlement would lead us to expect a rather tighter spatial model than the Konkomba example. When the separations for the Top site are plotted, this indeed appears to be the case. An upper sequence of large separations and a lower trend of small separations are present but the large separations slump near 4 m. The cluster medians indicate a series extending to 3 m, with an anomaly at 4 m, making a break from 3 m onward (Fig. 4.16). The rounded median values for the clusters are: 0·30; 0·45; 0.70; 1·10; 1·95; 3·05; *4·10* m. The cluster medians in the Main settlement also display the 4 m slump but in addition there is a break in the sequence near 1 m (Fig. 4.17). From the clusters occurring in each 'side' rounded median values are obtained at: 0·15; 0·30; 0·45; 0·75; *0·95*; 1·10; 1·95; 3·00; 4·05; 4·90 m. With the exclusion of the italicized values the sum of adjacent cluster medians approximately equals the median for the succeeding cluster, and once again can conveniently be referred to as a Fibonacci series.

The notable feature in the Main settlement is the way the series *jumps across* the break values at 0·95 and 4·05 m, unlike the Konkomba sequence. Isolated median values, in addition to the dominant 1·10 m

[11] Exterior Widths of Residence Units were measured off the Bruyère plan. They were included because these dimensions are exceeded by some interior spacings.

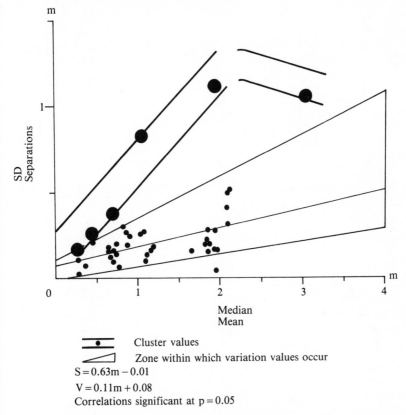

Fig. 4.16   Deir el Medina: Top site. Cluster median separations
and trend of variation (M/SD)

cluster, are scattered as far as 1·45–1·50 m,[12] while beyond the 4·00 m
value is the 4·90 m cluster which approximately equals the sum of
the 1·95 and 3·00 m values. The 4 and 5 m clusters appear in the same
relationship as the medians between 0·90 and 1·50 m.

   The standard deviations for the available distributions, as an index
of variation, conform to the already identified arrangement. In the
Main settlement the break in the medians around 1 m slumps into the
trend of variation. For both residential areas the 4 m slump is moving

---

[12] These are recognized by the histogram procedure (see note 1). As well as the repeatedly
occurring 1·10 m cluster, isolated distribution medians are also present. These are
included in Fig. 17a (1·16 m; South II; 1·44 m: West II: 1·24 in East II). In the Top
site seven medians are present between 1·00 and 1·20 m in contrast to only three between
0·90 and 1·00 m.

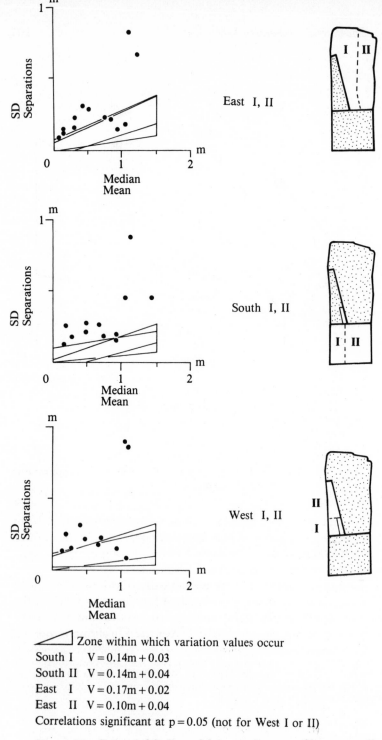

Zone within which variation values occur

South I    $V = 0.14m + 0.03$
South II   $V = 0.14m + 0.04$
East   I    $V = 0.17m + 0.02$
East   II   $V = 0.10m + 0.04$

Correlations significant at $p = 0.05$ (not for West I or II)

Fig. 4.17a Deir el Medina: Main settlement. Cluster median
            separations and trend of variation (M/SD) 0–2 m

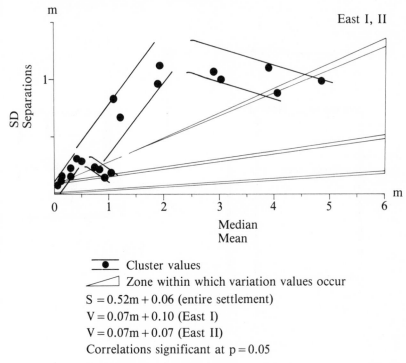

Fig. 4.17b Deir el Medina: Main settlement. Cluster median
separations and trend of variation (M/SD). East I and
II used as an illustration. 0–6 m

in to the variation trend. Unlike the Konkomba settlement there is
no apparent marked jump in the range of variation values.

### Function of the sequence and breaks

As in the Konkomba settlement the breaks connect to visual distance
limits in the utilized space. Within rectangular rooms, visual distances
to nearest reference points are specified by room width. In the Main
settlement the largest rooms are about 4 m wide and the narrow
passages are near 0·90–1·00 m wide (Fig. 4.18). These restrict the
dominant maximal (2 m) and minimal (45–50 cm) visual ranges
within the residence units. The former overlap with the last referable
cluster *before* the 4 m break and the latter with the last referable value
before the 90 cm break.

Main settlement

Top site

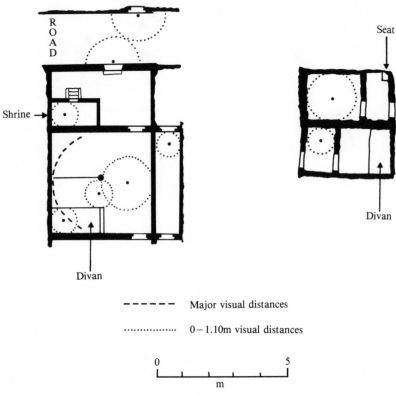

Fig. 4.18 Visual ranges in the Deir el Medina settlements

The two-part model also relates to the alternative views of space in the large rooms. As well as the primary visual referents provided by the walls, there are also subsidiary reference points such as shrines, divans and pillars. The pillars, as referents, reduce the visual distances to around 1 m. Within the shrine and divan space the visual ranges are about 45 cm. The sequence up to and including the overlap value of 1·10, covers the visual distances of sub-divided residential space.

In the Top site there is no equivalent visual distance distinction. All rooms are small with maximal visual ranges around 0·90 and 1·00 m, and minimal ones at 45–50 cm. Both ranges lie within the

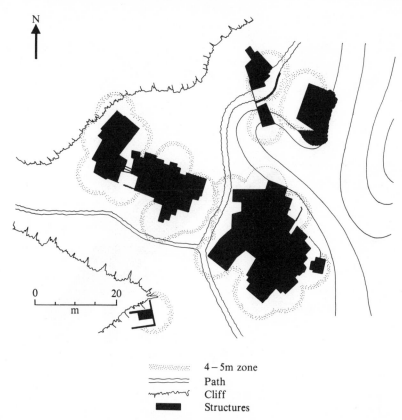

4 ‧‧‧‧‧‧‧ 4 – 5m zone
═══ Path
‿‿‿‿‿ Cliff
▬ Structures

Fig. 4.19a  Deir el Medina: Top site. Visual range around doors

smaller part of the model. There is no contrasting category of larger
visual distances within the rooms. Nor is the room space sub-divided
in the same way as in the Main settlement. The Top site divans extend
from wall to wall in a room.[13] Only a few seats and benches in the
East structural group are equivalent to the divans and shrines as
minor spatial divisions. Their 25 cm widths give minimal visual
ranges for Top site sub-divided space at about 12–13 cm, less than
the smallest identified sequence value. Interior room space in the Top
site was apparently treated as the visual equivalent of sub-divided
space in the Main settlement. This would fit the probable use of the
Top site and the divans and small rooms of the Main settlement as
rest or sleeping places.

[13] Bruyère 1939, plate xxxv, xxxvii. There is one exception in the East structural group.

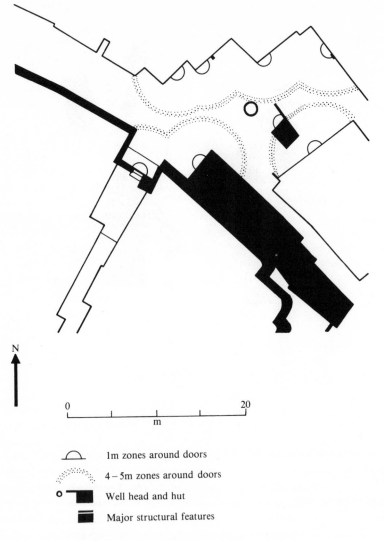

N

0                                20
                m

⌒  1m zones around doors

⋯  4 – 5m zones around doors

○◗  Well head and hut

◼  Major structural features

Note: through routes beyond the visual range out
      from each door

Fig. 4.19b  Deir el Medina: Main settlement. Visual range outside
            North gate

The Egyptian examples are also useful for checking whether a spatial model derived from only part of the location data can provide some understanding of a community's overall ordering of space. On the roadways in Main settlement, many of the residence unit entries have a clear visual zone approximately 1 m across[14] (Fig. 4.18). The limit defined by the larger part of the model should be the edge of a zone 4–5 m across. This zone and boundary are present in the Top site (Fig. 4.19a) and in the Main settlement (Fig. 4.19b).

## Conclusion

The structural form of the Deir el Medina settlements suggests that communities in the past also behaved as if they used internally coherent models of space for positioning entities within a settlement area. A Fibonacci series again serves as a *convenient* description. However, the pattern is unlike the Konkomba model because of the overlap value of the sequence at each break. It is not correct to assume that any *specific series* will always be present. We should not, I think, even presume that a Fibonacci series will always be found. Nor is the pattern of variation the same in all settlements – except for the trend to increasing variation with the increase of the dimensions.

From the Egyptian examples we may conclude that descriptions of spatial order can be obtained from uninhabited settlements. Though the ethnographic example suggests the analysis procedure, the archaeological study produces a different pattern. Here, therefore, we are not dependent upon reconstruction by direct analogy, because the research procedure can recognize different patterns. Data from these two possible sources of information, namely, occupied or abandoned settlements, are therefore complementary and should be used accordingly. Data from the present allow us to relate spatial order to social behaviour. Data from the past enable us to analyze change over time spans inaccessible in a contemporary observer's lifetime. Potentially the supply of archaeological data will allow us to ascertain whether or not human perceptual mechanisms have ever changed. We may therefore be able to assess whether spatial ordering is and *has been* a universal of human community behaviour.

[14] Bruyère 1939, plate xxix. Severe overlap cases are: NO XV and NE XI, C VII and NO XXV, C IV and SO I, SE I and Se II.

## Role and function of coherent spatial contexts: conclusions

A coherent visual context provides a consistent frame for the activities of a community. In effect, the community lives surrounded by a spatial message system. If each individual's behaviour can anticipate order and consistency in the spaces that need to be observed, then the task of assessing that physical context will not require knowing every piece of locational information (Gregory 1970). The brain can assume that certain dimensions will occur more frequently than others, and that each dominant dimension will be associated with a consistent degree of variation. The variation statement would define the uncertainty to be taken into account in response to a given dimension.

The sequence of clusters of dimensions can be regarded as a message possessing the characteristic redundancy of an information system (Clarke 1968, 88–101; Eco 1973, 57–9). A cluster provides repetition of the same signal: 'this dimension with this degree of variation'. When the eye/brain is scanning its visual context the entire continuum of possible dimensions does not need to be searched because the sequence of clusters specifies that some values occur more frequently than others. All that is required is a decision about the cluster to which the relevant dimension probably belongs. From the variation statement the eye/brain 'knows' how much avoidance will ensure that the person keeps clear of the limits of the object and can choose the appropriate route. Alternatively, if approach is required a person must behave in such a way as to pass within the expected range of variation for the object being approached.

In effect, the presence of a spatial order saves analytic effort by allowing adequate generalized response until further precision of observation is functionally necessary. The proposed spatial patterns may be regarded as reflections of the parsimonious analytic behaviour of the eye/brain. Given the opportunity and means to create a visual environment we find, rather unsurprisingly, that the human eye/brain appears to produce an *ordered* visual environment facilitating prediction and the use of consistently repeated decisions. Within the behavioural terms of the community, choice is made relatively easy.

In a sense, a settlement is rather like a beacon transmitting a message to the eyes of any observer. Though the message may become blurred by persistent and errorful replication over time, once the settlement is abandoned the structures continue to deliver the message they provided in the last moments of the community's existence. We must expect these signals to be weakened by progressive destruction. But in many settlements the structures will still provide their dimensional message long after the lives and memories of their creators have ceased.

## Acknowledgements

I have received help and encouragement from many people, too numerous to mention with sufficient generosity.

Particular assistance was given by Merrick Posnansky, Professor of Archaeology at the University of Ghana, and by his technical staff. I owe a debt that cannot be repaid to Munyimba, the Headman of the Konkomba community, and to his people. Without their social goodwill and willingness to allow me into their homes my research would not have been possible.

Without the assistance of an S.S.R.C. grant administered through the African Studies Centre of the University of Cambridge, I would not have been able to write up the Ghanaian material, nor would I have been able to work in Egypt. I am grateful to Dr S. F. Robertson and the staff of the Centre for their help and encouragement.

The staff of the French Institute of Oriental Archaeology in Cairo gave me much valuable advice. My thanks to the Egyptian Antiquities Service for permission to work in the Luxor area and to the guards at the site for their courtesy, help and good company.

Discussion with Dr David Clarke and Dr Barry Kemp has been of great value to me. My thanks to Mrs P. M. E. Altham for advice on the problems of statistical procedure. My thanks also to John Gay for the furious vigour which was applied to creating this contracted version of my conference paper. Interpretation of their advice, with any consequent error, is of course my responsibility.

## References

Alkire, W. H. (1970) 'Systems of measurement on Woleai Atoll, Caroline Islands', *Anthropos* 65, 1/2, 1–73

Badawy, A. (1965) *Ancient Egyptian architectural design: a study of the harmonic system.* Berkeley: University of California Press. Near Eastern Studies 4

Baddeley, A. D. (1972) 'Human memory', in Dodwell, P. C. (ed.) *New horizons in psychology* 2, Harmondsworth: Penguin Books, 36–61

Bauer, L. A. (1973) 'Personal space: a study of blacks and whites', *Sociometry* 36, no. 3, 402–8

Bruyère, B. (1939) *Rapport sur les fouilles de Deir el Médineh (1934–35)*. Part III, vol. XVI, Cairo: L'Institut Français d'Archéologie Orientale

Černý, J. (1973) *A community of workmen at Thebes in the Ramesside period*. Cairo: L'Institut Français d'Archéologie Orientale

Clarke, D. L. (1968) *Analytical archaeology*. London: Methuen

Cunningham, C. E. (1964) 'Order in the Atoni House', *Bijdragen tot de Taal-land-en Volkenkunde* 120, 34–68

Eco, U. (1973) 'Social life as a sign system', in Robey, D. (ed.) *Structuralism*. Oxford: Clarendon Press, 57–72

Fast, J. (1971) *Body language*. London: Pan Books

Fletcher, R. J. (1976) 'Space in settlements', unpublished PhD thesis, University of Cambridge

—— (1977) 'Space in settlements: a mechanism of adaptation', in Clarke, D. L. (ed.) *Spatial archaeology*. London: Academic Press, 47–162

—— (1978) 'Issues in the analysis of settlement space', in Green, D. & Haselgrove, C. (eds.) *Social organisation and settlement*. Oxford: British Anthropological Reports, 225–40

Gardner, M. (1968) 'Mathematical games', *Scientific American*, March, 116–20

Gerber, S. N., Greenfield, S. M. & Wright, W. E. (1974) 'Fieldwork, categorial bias, and understanding socio-cultural reality: some philosophical considerations', *Atti del XL Congresso Internationale Degli Americanisti* II, 77–83

Gil, B., Aryee, A. F. & Ghansah, D. K. (1964) *1960 Population Census of Ghana. Special Report E: Tribes of Ghana*. Accra: Census Office

Gregory, R. L. (1966) *Eye and brain*. London: Weidenfeld & Nicholson

—— (1970) 'On how little information controls so much behaviour', in Welford, A. T. & Houssiades, L. (eds.) *Contemporary problems in perception*. London: Taylor & Francis, 25–35

Hall, E. T. (1966) *The hidden dimension*. New York: Doubleday

—— (1968) 'Proxemics', *Current Anthropology* 9, 83–108

Harris, M. (1968) *The rise of anthropological theory*. London: Routledge & Kegan Paul

Prussin, L. (1969) *Architecture in Northern Ghana*. Berkeley: University of California Press

Tait, D. (1961) *The Konkomba of Northern Ghana*. Oxford University Press

Vernon, M. D. (1968) *The psychology of perception*. Harmondsworth: Penguin Books

Watson, O. M. (1972) *Symbolic and expressive use of space: an introduction to proxemic behaviour*. Reading, Massachusetts: Addison-Wesley. Current topics in anthropology 4, module 20

# 5 Taxonomic and multi-dimensional representations of reality

*John Gay*

When I began field studies in rural Liberia in 1974 on the place of agriculture in the traditional life of the Kpelle, I needed a map of the area where I was working. The Liberian government, through the kind help of the Minister of Lands and Mines, Dr Nyema Jones, provided me a 1:40,000 map showing rivers, trails, towns and hills, using the familiar two-dimensional Cartesian coordinate system of representation.

I set out to identify on that map the details of farms and sub-trails which were quite understandably left out by the geologists who had made the map. I started from the town, with map, compass and pedometer, and promptly got lost. I sketched trails where they did not belong, I had only the most infrequent glimpse of nearby hills through the rain forest, my compass was deflected by the high iron content of the hills I could not see, and my pedometer refused to adjust itself automatically to my varying pace lengths as I negotiated the swamps and hills that characterize so much of rural Liberia.

The Kpelle farmers who were guiding me through the area were curious as to what I was doing. I became curious myself, as it became clear that they knew quite well what they were doing, unlike myself. I eventually made some sense out of the map and managed to locate farms and trails, but it was only after I learned their way of mapping the region, and integrated it with my own.

Their mental map comprised a hierarchy of trails, branching from the central town to the surrounding farms. Mine was a three-dimensional Cartesian coordinate system, in which I could eventually specify the latitude, longitude and approximate altitude of a farm. My typically western map seemed at the time much less useful than stating a farm's location operationally, beginning from the town and branching out.

I tested this intuition when I subsequently collected a set of interviews with local farmers, who told me how to reach their farms

111

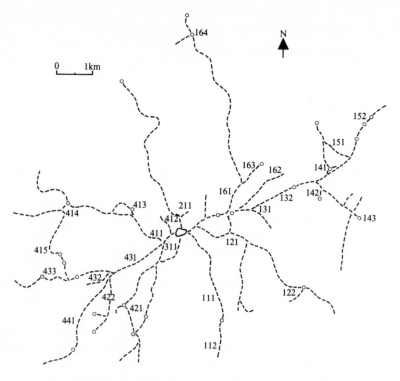

Fig. 5.1 Network of trails around the central village

from the centre of town. The formal structure was strikingly similar in all of these interviews, and strikingly efficient. The instructions would begin with a description of which trail to take from town – behind what house, near what tree, over what river. Whenever a trail divided, the farmer would name both paths, describing first the wrong and then the correct alternative. At each intersection, moreover, redundant information was given to make clear which branch to take. The process was repeated, with more redundant information as the farm came closer, until the farmer had reached the shelter at the centre of his farm. I found it finally most convenient to number the trails by reference to branch, sub-branch and sub-sub-branch as shown in the (Cartesian!) map in Fig. 5.1, where the trails and villages are shown, and where the numbers refer to specific farm areas.

The two alternatives can be described mathematically. My western alternative depends on specifying the coordinates of a point in three-dimensional space. Go to the south-west corner of 7th Avenue and 43rd Street and climb to the tenth floor.

The Kpelle farmer, on the other hand, names the nodes and branches of a tree diagram. This can be described as a network where between any two points there is only one path, unambiguously defined by the nodes and branches.

Just as my Cartesian model is an abstraction from reality, so is the Kpelle model, since there are often around a Kpelle village alternative routes between points, even though they are infrequently used.

These two models of reality have played important roles in man's attempts to understand his world. I have mentioned Descartes as the philosopher-mathematician who formalized the multi-dimensional representation. His counterpart is Aristotle, who much earlier formalized the tree diagram in the form of genera and species, down to the smallest group containing the real object in question.

Multi-dimensional representations present a variety of data in the social sciences. In geography they provide the basis for essentially all map-making. Psychology has used factor analysis, as in the case of Osgood's semantic differential technique (Romney & d'Andrade 1964). Componential analysis in anthropology in such areas as kinship was developed in the 1960s by such men as Lounsbury (Tyler 1969), Goodenough (Tyler 1969) and Romney (Romney & d'Andrade 1964). In linguistics an example is the analysis by distinctive features of the structure of phonemes by Jakobson & Halle (1956) and Chomsky & Halle (1968). At the end of the 1960s, multi-dimensional scaling was being used in such diverse disciplines as market research, the analysis of elections, comparative political systems, the sociology of employment patterns, and the analysis of disease categories, as reported in the recent survey by Shepard, Romney & Nerlove (1972).

Taxonomic representations have an equal place in current social science research. In linguistics, Chomsky (1957) and others represent the relation between deep structure and surface representation by the use of tree diagrams. The semantic classes implied by folk taxonomies have been modelled in tree diagrams as in the work of Conklin (Hymes 1964) and Frake (Hymes 1964).

Anthropologists including Crump (1973) and Boissevain & Mitchell (1973) have used taxonomies to represent a variety of social data. Networks, both minimally and completely connected, have been analysed by the geographers Haggett & Chorley (1969). Psychologists such as Cole (Cole *et al.* 1971) have used cluster analysis to represent experimental data.

The principal methods used to construct multi-dimensional models for social science data have been developed by mathematicians as well as social scientists. The basic work in factor analysis goes back to the early part of this century. The principal theorems and computer programmes in the extension of factor analysis into non-metric scaling were devised by Kruskal (1964). Biologists such as Sneath & Sokal (1973) have joined mathematicians like Jardine & Sibson (1971) to set out the principal methods in taxonomic representation.

The two models are rarely used together. Sneath & Sokal in their survey of the field of numerical taxonomy briefly discuss multi-dimensional scaling, but place little stress on it. On the other hand, the contributors to the survey of multi-dimensional scaling edited by Shepard, Romney & Nerlove use but do not depend heavily upon taxonomic methods.

In one case, d'Andrade, Quinn, Nerlove & Romney (Shephard, Romney & Nerlove 1972, vol. 2) apply both methods to disease categories. Here the possibility of meaningful interpretation seems to arise because the diseases in question can be put into a natural hierarchy and also can be described by familiar dimensions which apply to each main branch of the hierarchy. Where one of these criteria is not met, then the corresponding model cannot be used. The authors reach the following conclusion:

It appears that extensive paradigms are most likely to occur when relations are involved, as in kinship. . . perhaps because such relations make possible a great number of combinations from a small number of defining properties. Deep taxonomies, on the other hand, seem to occur when there is utility in sometimes considering a large number of elements abstractly, i.e., with reference to only a few properties, and at other times more concretely, i.e., with reference to many properties. (*ibid.*, 52)

In the same work, Rapoport & Fillenbaum (*ibid.*, vol. 2), following Miller (1969), suggest that the intuition of the researcher is the key to selecting the appropriate model. They suggest using a multi-dimensional model if the underlying organization seems of that type, or a hierarchic scheme if that seems intuitively more plausible. They give colour names as a natural example of a multi-dimensional system, and body parts as an example of a taxonomy. They conclude by suggesting that the available techniques 'be used concurrently so that one may compare the adequacy of a dimensional representation with that of a hierarchic representation in order to determine which one appears to be more appropriate' (*ibid.*, vol. 2, 130).

The possibility that the multi-dimensional representation or the taxonomic hierarchy may tell more about the researcher than about what he is studying, is very real. He who discovers a taxonomy may be so thoroughly brain-washed by Aristotle that he cannot see the forest for the tree diagrams. An equal fascination with Descartes may bring the researcher to impose a coordinate system on data which are in fact inherently organized along very different lines. Burling has asked in a well-known paper (Tyler 1969) whether componential analysis is 'God's truth or hocus-pocus'. Jack Goody (1977) has suggested that any tabular representation of oral data may be simply an imposition from the outside, overlaying rather than underlying the reality of the data.

Frake's response to Burling is appropriate. His position is that one ethnographic description is better than another if it accounts for a wider range of behaviour. He says that 'the important thing is to write ethnographic statements whose implications for behaviour are explicit and which can therefore be tested against competing statements' (Tyler 1969, 432).

I propose in this paper to attempt a set of explicit verifiable statements concerning the taxonomic model, with reference where possible to the multi-dimensional model. I conjecture that both the hierarchical model and the multi-dimensional model can be used to represent a wide variety of data, in a way that is natural and familiar, and which can be observed in real-life behaviour.

There are a variety of ways to picture a hierarchy. The most abstract has already been mentioned, namely, a minimally connected network of points. Others include a tree diagram, a star connecting peripheral points to a centre, non-overlapping sequences of nested sets contained in a universal set, a hierarchy of abstraction from greater to less specificity, a biological taxonomy of genera and species, a clustering of points in space such that the clusters themselves are further clustered and clusters never overlap, and a flow diagram without feedback. Each of these models has been used in the literature, and I will refer to some of them. They all have the same mathematical structure and can be treated according to the same rules.

I refer in this paper primarily to the tree diagram, and its equivalent forms. My claim is that the tree diagram is not only useful for representing oral and other non-written data, but is also commonly used for this purpose by people from both literate and non-literate cultures.

Table 5.1. *Taxonomy of Kpelle world organization*

|  |  |  | TOWN THINGS |  |  |  |
|---|---|---|---|---|---|---|
| PLAYING THINGS | PEOPLE | TOWN WORKS | TOWN ANIMALS | WORKING THINGS | THE EARTH* | TOWN SPIRIT |
| Dancing things | Children | Houses | Walking animals | Vehicles | Dirt |  |
| Dancers | Adults | Sheds | Birds | Medicines | Stone |  |
| Drums | Good people | Fences |  | Herbs | Sand |  |
| Horns | Evil people | Benches |  | Charms | Mud |  |
| Games | Workmen | Looms |  | Societies |  |  |
| Toys | People by status |  |  | Divining |  |  |
| Kwii music | People by appearance |  |  | Evil |  |  |
|  |  |  |  | Western |  |  |
|  |  |  |  | Household things |  |  |
|  |  |  |  | Sleeping things |  |  |
|  |  |  |  | Beds |  |  |
|  |  |  |  | Cloths |  |  |
|  |  |  |  | Mats |  |  |
|  |  |  |  | Iron things |  |  |
|  |  |  |  | Iron tools |  |  |
|  |  |  |  | Money |  |  |
|  |  |  |  | Clothing |  |  |
|  |  |  |  | Cloth washing things |  |  |
|  |  |  |  | Cooking things |  |  |
|  |  |  |  | Utensils |  |  |
|  |  |  |  | Food |  |  |
|  |  |  |  | Prepared Forest‡ |  |  |
|  |  |  |  | Traps‡ |  |  |
|  |  |  |  | Weaving things |  |  |
|  |  |  |  | Books |  |  |

## FOREST THINGS

| THE EARTH* | (ANIMALS) | ROOT CROPS | VINES | TREES | SHRUBS | WATER FOODS | MUSHROOMS)† | EVIL THINGS | TRAPS‡ |
|---|---|---|---|---|---|---|---|---|---|
| Dirt | Two-part hoof | Wild | Wild | Wild | Wild | Water | | Poro head | |
| Stone | Four-part hoof | Planted | Planted | Planted | Planted | Oil | | Sande head | |
| Sand | Claw | | | | | Honey | | Fearful things | |
| Mud | Dragging | | | | | | | Witches | |
| | Snakes | | | | | | | Genii | |
| | Snails | | | | | | | Dwarfs | |
| | Fish | | | | | | | Spirits | |
| | Worms | | | | | | | | |
| | Crawling | | | | | | | | |
| | Edible | | | | | | | | |
| | Non-edible | | | | | | | | |
| | Water | | | | | | | | |
| | Burrowing | | | | | | | | |
| | Tree | | | | | | | | |
| | Leaping | | | | | | | | |
| | Edible | | | | | | | | |
| | Non-edible | | | | | | | | |
| | Flying | | | | | | | | |
| | Birds | | | | | | | | |
| | Insects | | | | | | | | |
| | Edible | | | | | | | | |
| | Non-edible | | | | | | | | |

\* The earth is a major class of both town and forest things.
† These seven classes of edible forest things are also a sub-class of town things.
‡ Traps are a major class of forest things and a sub-class of town things.

A hierarchical representation inevitably involves a simplification of the complexities of reality. Specifically, they leave out very important interactions and cross-references certain of which are supplied by the multi-dimensional model, which, however, is also reductionist in its suppression of information about preferred groupings.

The process of simplification is probably what makes a model attractive to ordinary people as well as scholars. There is a tendency for the human mind to reduce a complex structure to a simpler structure. Not only do computer analysts prefer to store data in tree diagram form because of the relative saving in retrieval time, but also persons in the relatively non-technological societies of rural Africa, Asia and Latin America find this particular model convenient. The process of simplification whether by taxonomy or by multi-dimensional analysis, is a strategy for dealing with a mass of information, and organizing it in such a way as to make it readily available for future use.

Direct evidence for the reality of taxonomic hierarchies establishes the content and structure of the hierarchies, while indirect evidence shows that the hierarchies are present in behaviour of a type which is not designed to generate hierarchies. I consider first direct evidence, and give four examples:

The first example concerns the Kpelle classification of material things, the details of which are reported by Cole et al. (1971). Following the lead of Metzger & Williams (1966), we interviewed Kpelle adults to learn how they classify and organize 'things'. The Kpelle word seng refers broadly to what we would call things in English, and also to people, social organizations and non-countable substances. In these interviews the Kpelle had no difficulty giving superordinate and subordinate categories for things familiar to them. For instance, salt is a prepared food, belonging in turn to the classes of cooking things, household things, working things, and, at the top of the hierarchy, town things. Likewise, animals can be sub-divided into many classes and sub-classes. The result is a taxonomy which mirrors the world in which the Kpelle live, and is shown in Table 5.1.

A second piece of direct evidence is that given at the beginning of this paper. The Kpelle farmer locates his farm on a branching network of trails. He knows what lies on each branch and he knows all the intersections on the system of trails surrounding the town.

A third example is the kinship network. There are, of course, several ways of classifying individuals within a kinship system, and when all of them are considered at once, it may well be more useful to describe the total structure by a multi-dimensional coordinate system. However, we found that it made sense both to us and to our informants to consider, for instance, the system of parent–child relations in terms of a tree diagram. In unstructured interviews, the informants explicitly chose the oldest ancestor they could remember and traced one branch after another of his descendants.

A fourth example is the classification of things and events according to their relation to traditional or modern life. The word *kwii* refers throughout Liberia to modern, educated, shoe-wearing, corrupt, clean-handed, car-driving, English-speaking, upwardly mobile, money-earning people. The division of *kwii* affairs from traditional affairs, and of both types into a variety of sub-classes, is familiar and obvious to our Kpelle informants. Many of the same topics arise in this classification as in Table 5.1, but the principle of classification is different.

Of course, none of these four hierarchical models is an exact representation of reality. The taxonomy of things which fall under the word *seng* is not well-formed in every detail. For one example, traps are considered to be both forest things and town things. For a second example, root crops form an independent class of forest things, are a sub-class of trees, and are also a sub-class of cooking things.

The Kpelle trail system is likewise not uniquely specified by intersections and branches. There are a few trails which connect the branches and form rings around the central town, as shown in Fig. 5.1. However, a fact which substantiates my claim is that these connecting trails are acknowledged with reluctance, are hard to find, and in fact are scarcely more than hunters' tracks.

The kinship network is not a uniquely branching system, primarily because of marriage. If human beings could sub-divide like the amoeba, they could construct perfect hierarchies of relation. The cross-linkages of marriage make a tree diagram for kinship difficult to reconcile with the totality of the facts, even though the tree diagram remains useful for certain purposes.

Finally, there is considerable overlap and ambiguity between what is *kwii* and what is not. Persons may argue whether a given individual or a given action is modern or traditional, and which sub-branch within a major category it falls into. The classification accordingly varies with the context.

The point, perhaps, is not so much that these are perfect models, but that they are both useful and commonly used. They provide convenient representations of reality, not reality itself. My claim is only that such representations are convenient and natural to the human mind everywhere, and that both my Kpelle informants and I found them equally useful in discussing their culture and life.

The next question is whether the reality of taxonomies generated by the direct evidence of interviews can be sustained by indirect evidence. The basic technique I used for answering this question is cluster analysis, as described in the book by Sneath & Sokal (1973), a paper by Johnson (1967) and the computer program Clustan B, available at the Cambridge Computer Centre.

I will not give a detailed description of cluster analysis here, since such a description is available elsewhere. A matrix is constructed, in which each of a set of categories is evaluated by a series of diverse measures. An example is the sentence completion procedure described below, with a portion of the resulting hierarchy given in Table 5.3. Two of the sentence introducers we used in the interviews were 'I believe that...' and 'In the old days...'. The first two sentence completions in Table 5.3 appeared as responses to these as well as other sentence introducers. 'We don't attend school' was the completion of these introducers respectively eight and three times, and 'We have no money' was the completion respectively eleven and one times. The statements made in response to the twenty introducers I grouped into sixty-five response classes according to apparent similarities. The numbers of times each of the sixty-five responses was given to each of the twenty statements generates a 65 × 20 matrix, of which the examples given above form four cells.

When such a matrix is constructed, correlation coefficients can be calculated between the rows of the matrix. In this example, the responses 'We don't attend school' and 'We have no money' have very similar response patterns across the twenty sentence introducers, are correlated fairly highly and are thus joined at an early state in the construction of the taxonomy. When two categories are joined in a cluster, they are thereafter treated as one. In this way a unique tree can be constructed, from the tips of the branches back to the trunk.

I claim that it supports the reality of the interview-based hierarchies if cluster analysis reproduces the hierarchies reasonably intact. Failure to reproduce a hierarchy suggests that either cross-linkages dominate the basic pattern or that the data are better represented by other structures. In the four cases mentioned above, cluster analysis reproduced the anticipated taxonomies to a high degree, although not perfectly. Each such success can be judged for itself, since the chances of a random reproduction of a predicted hierarchy of even ten categories are essentially nil. Thus failure to reproduce one hierarchy does not discredit the method, but only its applicability to that particular case. It is possible of course, to predict several alternative hierarchies for any situation. For example, the things of the Kpelle world can be divided between modern and traditional or between town and forest, or between useful and useless. What is required is only that this method generate a hierarchy that makes sense in terms of some one of the reasonable anticipated results.

The details of the replication of the classification of material things are described in Cole *et al*. (1971). There we showed that the general outlines of the elicited taxonomy are reproduced by free association with objects or names, by the judged similarity of objects, by distributional similarity of words in sentences, and by sorting objects into groups. In each case terms from the elicited hierarchy were evaluated according to a set of diverse but consistent measures, and the resultant matrices were reorganized by cluster analytic techniques to form hierarchies for the terms.

The reality of the system of trails around the town is confirmed by relating the farm areas around the town to individuals in the town according to the degree of involvement of each individual with each farm. In the case we studied, the patterns of relation of individuals to farms allow the construction of a cluster diagram of farms, which reproduces the network of trails as described to us in the interviews, as observed by us in the field, and as shown in Fig. 5.1. Table 5.2 gives the hierarchy produced by cluster analysis. The correspondence with the actual hierarchy of trails in Fig. 5.1 is striking.

The reality of the kinship system is reflected in a similar analysis. We took the same set of individuals mentioned above and scaled their reported relationships to key persons in the community. Both the individuals and the key persons who provided the basis for scaling the individuals fall by cluster analysis into groups which display the patterns of kinship we had expected on the basis of extended interviews with leading elders.

Finally, the division of things, persons and events into modern and traditional classes appears in a cluster analysis of responses to the request to complete twenty sentences of the type mentioned above, e.g. 'I believe that...' and 'In the old days...'. A total of fifty persons from ten subject populations completed these sentences. The cluster analysis was based on the distribution of responses according

TABLE 5.2. *Taxonomy of trails around the central village*

| (I) Western group | (II) Eastern group |
|---|---|
| (A) Southern sub-group | (A) Farther sub-group |
| (1) Nearer sub-sub-group | (1) Central sub-sub-group |
| (a) 421 | (a) 131 |
| (b) 422 | (b) 132 |
| (2) Farther sub-sub-group | (2) Peripheral sub-sub-group |
| (a) 431 | (a) 141 |
| (b) 432 | (b) 142 |
| (c) 441 | (c) 151 |
| (d) 433 | (d) 152 |
| (e) 415 | (e) 122 |
| | (f) 143 |
| (B) Northern sub-group | (B) Nearer sub-group |
| (1) Nearer sub-sub-group | (1) Southern sub-sub-group |
| (a) 411 | (a) 111 |
| (b) 412 | (b) 112 |
| | (c) 121 |
| | (d) 311 |
| (2) Farther sub-sub-group | (2) Northern sub-sub-group |
| (a) 413 | (a) 161 |
| (b) 414 | (b) 162 |
| | (c) 163 |
| | (d) 164 |
| | (e) 211 |

to the different sentence introducers. The resulting hierarchy confirmed the division of assertions into *kwii* and traditional affairs, and their appropriate sub-groups. Table 5.3 gives a reduced version of the hierarchy, omitting all responses given only fifteen or fewer times.

In addition to displaying the basic division into modern and traditional affairs, the tree diagram clearly shows additional features of the culture. The two basic groups, modern and traditional, can be seen to sub-divide into positive and negative sub-groups. There are a few anomalous assignments, but the general pattern is clear.

The negative sub-group of modern matters consists of the dangers and difficulties inherent in the modern world, while the positive sub-group tells of the opportunities for advancement and success. The same pattern exists for traditional matters. In each case the negative sub-group suggests some solutions to the problems which arise. For modern matters the solutions lie in institutions such as school, church and government. In traditional affairs, the solution to problems seems to lie in the hands of God, spirits and medicine, rather than worldly institutions.

TABLE 5.3. *Taxonomy of responses to sentence introducers*

(I) Modern
(A) Bad
  (1) We don't attend school
  (2) We have no money
  (3) Parents don't help children
  (4) We smoke and drink
  (5) Pleasure is dangerous
  (6) We should attend school
  (7) We should attend church
  (8) Men can't be trusted
  (9) Government helps Liberia
  (10) There are new officials

(B) Good
  (1) We will finish school
  (2) We work for government
  (3) We go to the city
  (4) Children help parents
  (5) We work for money
  (6) Government helps us
  (7) We can attend school
  (8) Parents help children
  (9) Liberia is developing
  (10) We are healthy

(II) Traditional
(A) Bad
  (1) We need more food
  (2) We grow little food
  (3) Farming is hard
  (4) Government cheats us
  (5) Jesus died to save us
  (6) People are bad

(B) Transitional
  (1) The world is changing
  (2) We like the old ways
  (3) People fight each other
  (4) Modern ways rule us

(C) Good
  (1) We make farm
  (2) We dress well
  (3) We eat meat
  (4) Spirits exist
  (5) We live well
  (6) Farming is good
  (7) God helps us
  (8) Medicine has power
  (9) We grow much food
  (10) We grow rice
  (11) We have enough food
  (12) We should work hard
  (13) We have money
  (14) We help each other

A third sub-group is linked to traditional affairs. This sub-group consists of comments, from the traditional side, on the new domination of the modern over the traditional.

A further conclusion to be drawn from this tree diagram is that farming, in particular rice farming, is a traditional matter. None of the responses in the modern group concern farming. On the other hand, modernization and its attendant promises and perils appear in the modern group and not in the traditional sector. A conclusion might be that one challenges reality in attempting to persuade the modernizing sector of society to grow more rice, a conclusion which is supported by evidence drawn from other sources.

The cluster diagram produced in Table 5.3 is so neat, that it seemed to me perhaps a piece of good luck, rather than an authentic finding. To test this hypothesis, I systematically varied the data by the introduction of random error, and found that even with a 10 per cent probability of changing any response, the basic pattern of the cluster diagram remained. The cluster analysis represented by Table 5.3 is thus stable, in addition to confirming observations and interviews within the community.

The second, third and fourth examples given above are reported in greater detail in a volume in preparation (Gay, n.d.). In addition, cluster analysis is applied to a variety of other data in that book, and in almost all the cases the results confirm that patterns observed directly are reproduced in the tree diagrams based on indirect evidence.

The patterns produced by cluster analysis are inevitably hierarchical, based on binary choices. The process would generate a tree diagram even from totally random data. The important point for consideration is that in the case of the Kpelle data cluster analysis produces not only stable tree diagrams, but also tree diagrams which confirm the predictions I can make on the basis of direct interviews. I do not claim a conscious decision by the Kpelle to organize ideas hierarchically, even though the evidence may point in that direction. What I do claim is that a tree diagram, a nested series of sets, a taxonomy of genera and species, adequately represents the end product of thought. The model, moreover, suggests details, as in the example of modern and traditional affairs, which are consistent with the overall pattern, but which would not otherwise be obvious. The model is useful not only to confirm the basic divisions, but to go beyond them in providing significant detail.

The next step in research is to attempt to understand the processes themselves. My guess is that the widespread evidence for hierarchical models points to a mental process consisting of a sequence of choices, and amendable to representation by a flow chart of decision, as in the scheme set out by Geoghegan (Kay 1971). This is clearly the case when the path to a farm is described, since there the choices are clearly stated. What is required is a technique to identify ordered decisions, wherein the consequences of each choice are specified as clearly as in the case of paths to farms. Geoghegan's definitions, axioms and theorems may well fit the process, and should be tested in this context.

I have also analyzed the data for the second, third and fourth examples given above, to ascertain the appropriateness of the multi-dimensional model to the data. The first example, that of the hierarchy of material things, was not studied in this way, and may well be inappropriate for a multi-dimensional analysis.

The basic technique for the application of the multi-dimensional model to data is multi-dimensional scaling, as given in Kruskal (1964) and Shepard, Romney & Nerlove (1972). Using the same correlation measures as for cluster analysis, in order to provide strict comparability, I constructed three- and two-dimensional models for the data which maintained as nearly as possible the ordering of the correlations. The programme used for this purpose was developed by Sibson at the Cambridge Computer Centre.

The principle underlying this approach is the reduction of a higher-dimensional model which exactly fits a set of data to a model in two or three dimensions which suppresses some of the information contained in the data in order to give a visual representation of the remainder of the information. In the example of the sentence completion task from which I derived a taxonomy of events and beliefs, I used sixty-five response categories. A perfect representation of these categories in space requires sixty-five dimensions, one for each category, and the correlations between the responses is represented by the distances between points, appropriately normalized. The technicalities for this sixty-five-dimensional model are not important here, if for no other reason than the impossibility of visualizing it.

The programme developed by Sibson on the basis of the Kruskal paper compresses these sixty-five dimensions into some pre-selected smaller number, in such a way as to preserve the ordering of the distances between points. To give an example, if response no. 1 is more highly correlated to response no. 2 than it is to response no. 3

in the exact representation, then point no. 1 should be closer to point no. 2 than it is to point no. 3 in the lower-dimensional model. The measure of the failure to achieve this goal for all comparisons of distances is called by Kruskal the 'stress' of the model, and gives approximately the percentage of distance relations which no longer preserve their original orderings. A stress of 10 per cent or lower is very good indeed, since it means that almost all the distances follow the right pattern of relations. Even a stress of 30 per cent can be interpreted, although in such a case many points will seem displaced from their 'natural' position.

My use of this technique for the location of farms near the village I studied proved surprisingly effective. I had expected, both because the trails fell so neatly into a cluster hierarchy, and because my initial attempt to map the farms in a Euclidean fashion had not been notably successful, that analysis would find the data resistant to multi-dimensional scaling methods. On the contrary, the two-dimensional solution for the twenty-eight farm locations had a stress of only 6 per cent and the three-dimensional solution a stress as low as 3 per cent. On closer examination of the three-dimensional solution, moreover, a projection of the points onto the plane formed by axes 1 and 3 (Fig. 5.2) provides an almost exact copy of the Euclidean map (shown in Fig. 5.1) I finally did prepare for the area around the village. Dimension no. 1 can be interpreted as running from north to south, and dimension no. 3 from east to west, as shown in Fig. 5.2. Those farms which were farther from the central town had larger values on the appropriate dimensions, and those which were nearer had smaller values.

The multi-dimensional representation of the kinship system, however, is much less compatible with reality. The stress was much higher than in the case of farms, even though, as indicated above, the taxonomy of relations found by cluster analysis made generally good sense. The cluster analysis had shown a basic division between the older families in the western portion of the town and the newer families, who generally lived in the eastern portion. This division appeared as one of the dimensions in the multi-dimensional analysis. But the other sub-structures did not show up clearly in the multi-dimensional model probably because the sub-classes in the cluster analysis were formed on different principles within the two major groups. In particular, there is no evidence of any kinship structures in the multi-dimensional representation.

The analysis of the sentence completions by the multi-dimensional

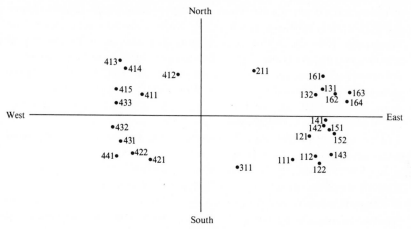

Fig. 5.2 Multi-dimensional scaling of trails around the central village

Fig. 5.3 Multi-dimensional scaling of responses to sentence introducers

scaling method reveals structure in a three-dimensional model which confirms and reinforces what we were able to learn from the taxonomy given in Table 5.3. The representation is by no means perfect, as the stress of 17 per cent makes clear. However, the main emphases of the taxonomy are repeated in the first two of the three dimensions, as shown in Fig. 5.3, where only responses made more than fifteen times are included. No obvious interpretation can be given to the third dimension.

The first dimension reflects the taxonomy's division between good and bad responses. The division in Fig. 5.3 is between the left-hand side of the model, which contains the negative responses and the right-hand side, which contains the positive responses.

The second dimension in Fig. 5.3 corresponds to the split between traditional and modern responses in the taxonomy. All the traditional responses appear in the lower half of the representation, while the modern responses are in the upper half. At the dividing line are responses which could reasonably lie in either group.

In each of the four examples, the taxonomic model has provided a useful representation of the data. The quality of the representation varies from case to case, but in none of the examples given here is the quality significantly low. The multi-dimensional analysis in some cases reproduces certain aspects of the structure presented in the taxonomy, while other aspects are ignored. In at least one case, namely the analysis of sentence completions, information can be obtained from the multi-dimensional analysis which is not present in the taxonomy, namely the strength of membership in the classes good, bad, modern and traditional.

The two models thus have a natural applicability to data drawn from the life of the rural Kpelle of Liberia. They can be applied differently in different situations, depending apparently on the efficiency with which they fit the data. We do not claim that Kpelle farmers explicitly and self-consciously apply the models, but rather that they are implicit in behaviour.

It remains to find the usefulness of these models for other peoples and cultures. Let me consider the four examples again. Further evidence about the use in ordinary life of taxonomies of familiar objects would be helpful. But it begins to appear from studies in such diverse places as the Philippines and Mexico, as well as from our Kpelle data, that probably every society organizes material objects, e.g. plants, according to some natural taxonomy, and makes active use of the system implied. In such cases, however, it is probable that the multi-dimensional approach would be less useful and less used.

Spatial representation in various communities is also well worth study. In some American cities such as mid-town Manhattan, a two- or three-dimensional model is appropriate. In Cambridge, England, with its (to an American) confusing shifts of names along the course of one street, a tree diagram, particularly in the form of a star radiating from the market, seems better. It would be useful to study the distribution of spatial models in various societies. My guess is that the taxonomic model would be universally applicable, even in New York, while the multi-dimensional approach would be less actively used, even though it might be implicit in the cognitive processing of data. The multi-dimensional model would have some specific applications, however, as in the case (provided for me in a personal communication by Paul Jorion of Clare Hall) where Breton fishermen use a non-rectangular two-dimensional system to locate good fishing grounds.

More evidence is needed concerning the patterning of kinship systems within a variety of cultures. Kinship patterns conform in some ways to taxonomies and in others to multi-dimensional models. Much effort has been devoted to the study of patterns by which people represent their systems of alliance and descent. Charts of both the taxonomic and the multi-dimensional type have been prepared for many cultures, but it is not always clear which model represents most closely the inner patterns of thought of a particular people. This is a question to which some of these techniques might be applied, and the answers might well vary greatly between different cultures.

Finally, it would be interesting to find the extent to which free and constrained expressions of belief and assertion can be modelled within a taxonomic framework or a multi-dimensional model without unduly distorting the data. Among the Kpelle both seem possible. The technique I have outlined might be useful for studying belief systems in other societies as well.

These four areas – classification of things, spatial representation, kinship, and belief systems – do not exhaust the possibilities for the taxonomic or multi-dimensional representations of reality. Many disciplines use networks and as many use coordinate systems to represent data. It is useful to ask to what areas and within what cultures each system applies.

In summary, there are two models for the representation of cognitive data that have wide application. The hierarchical model is perhaps the more widely applied and more generally applicable. The multi-dimensional model has more specialized applications. Both are available to human beings as they think about the ordinary business of daily life.

## References

Boissevain, J. & Mitchell, J. C. (1973) *Network analysis : studies in human interaction*. The Hague: Mouton

Chomsky, N. (1957) *Syntactic structures*. The Hague: Mouton

—— & Halle, M. (1968) *The sound patterns of English*. New York: Holt, Rinehart & Winston

Cole, M., Gay, J., Glick, J. & Sharp, D. (1971) *The cultural context of learning and thinking*. New York: Basic Books

Crump, T. (1973) 'Trees and stars: graph theory in Southern Mexico', Oxford: Decennial Conference, Association of Social Anthropologists of Great Britain and the Commonwealth

Gay, J. (in preparation) 'Intelligence in action: a study of agriculture among the Kpelle of Liberia'

Goody, J. (1977) 'Literacy and classification: on turning the tables', in *The domestication of the savage mind*. Cambridge University Press

Haggett, P. & Chorley, R. (1969) *Network analysis in geography*. London: Arnold

Hymes, D. (1964) *Language in culture and society*. New York: Harper & Row

Jakobson, R. & Halle, M. (1956) *Fundamentals of language*. The Hague: Mouton

Jardine, N. & Sibson, R. (1971) *Mathematical taxonomy*. London: Wiley

Johnson, S. C. (1967) 'Hierarchical clustering schemes', *Psychometrika* 32, 241–54

Kay, P. (1971) *Explorations in mathematical anthropology*. Stanford Center for Advanced Study in the Behavioral Sciences

Kruskal, J. B. (1964) 'Nonmetric multidimensional scaling: a numerical method', *Psychometrika* 29, 115–29

Metzger, D. & Williams, G. (1966) 'Procedures and results in the study of native categories: Tzeltal firewood', *American Anthropologist* 68, 389–407

Miller, G. (1969) 'A psychological method to investigate verbal concepts', *Journal of Mathematical Psychology* 6, 169–91

Romney, A. K. & d'Andrade, R. G. (eds.) (1964) 'Transcultural studies in cognition', *American Anthropologist* 66, no. 3, part 2 (special publication)

Shephard, R. N., Romney, A. K. & Nerlove, S. B. (1972) *Multidimensional scaling.* New York: Seminar Press (2 vols.)
Sneath, P. & Sokal, R. (1973) *Numerical taxonomy.* San Francisco: W. H. Freeman
Tyler, S. A. (ed.) (1969) *Cognitive anthropology.* New York: Holt, Rinehart & Winston

**Part 2**

---

**Cognitive development**

# Editorial introduction to part 2

The three papers in this section were written by psychologists who accept the scientific view of the world Gellner describes. Working within the paradigm of modern science all three subscribe to the view that human beings share a common evolutionary history and they expect to find certain common elements in the long period of individual development from birth to adulthood. Although sensori-motor development is similar in all human societies, the perplexing problems centre on the nature of the evidence with which to address the question of human universals and the forms in which such universals may be expected to occur.

Dasen introduces a distinction between performance and underlying competence in his discussion of 'strong' and 'weak' universals. He implies that we must not construe particular failures of conservation or certain gaps in spatial abilities which we measure in specific tasks as representing a lack of underlying competence. These performance failures, he suggests, signal a weak universal and indicate the effects of specific educational or ecological variables on that test performance which we consider indicative of concrete operatory thinking. Dasen is cautioning us to beware of placing too great emphasis on products and to be attentive to underlying common or universal processes. This point appears again in Bruner's Review and Prospectus when he urges that we attend to the ways in which different cultures make use of underlying universal competences.

Evidence of a strong universal is provided by the research of Dasen and the Genevan group on infants in the Ivory Coast. The data from both cross-sectional and longitudinal testing of babies is viewed as support for the structural invariances described by Piaget in his model of sensori-motor development. Evidence of sensori-motor development patterned in a similar fashion in cats and squirrel monkeys suggests that we are dealing with an aspect of development characterized by Gellner's Type I model. In the realm of sensori-motor development maturation of similar physiological mechanisms used in a shared physical environment may partially account for perceived similarities across cultures and species.

Increasing cognitive differentiation in the first two years of life supports Okonji's arguments too. He notes that development is universally marked by progressive differentiation and growing complexity in thought and that these trends override cultural diversity. Unless we specify the nature of thought such a description could again characterize non-human as well as human development.

Cultural variability provides the challenge whether we see development as increasing differentiation in the cognitive style tradition described by Okonji, as developing operativity of thought in the mode of Piaget summarized by Dasen, or in terms of the psychometric approach employed by Lloyd. Dasen shows that the ecological and the social system including formal education, relate directly to performance on various tasks assessing concrete operatory thinking. Bruner cautions us to be alert, however, to within-culture variability even where ecological demands appear uniform and compelling. Okonji grapples with aspects of socialization, social organization and authority which encourage or inhibit differentiation, particularly in aspects of visual figure-ground distinctions. Again Bruner's caution must be noted. Lloyd argues that societies selectively reward certain types of performance and the failure to achieve these particular skills, despite any underlying competencies, may perpetuate disadvantage and inequality.

In the discussion which followed the presentation of these papers at the Cambridge conference a number of participants questioned the effects of formal education on cognitive development. In drawing the strands of the discussion together Bruner suggested that even if we can agree that there are universal capacities or primitive competences we must still ponder their differing integration into higher-order skills. Different cultures with their varying educational methods and social objectives may develop them differently. These differences are a challenge to our theories. They also pose problems for societies with egalitarian ideals.

# 6 'Strong' and 'weak' universals: sensori-motor intelligence and concrete operations[1]

*Pierre R. Dasen*

For the past few years, I have been looking at Piaget's developmental psychology in a cross-cultural context, attempting to establish which aspects of cognitive development are independent of culture and which are influenced by socio-cultural variables. Piaget's theory is very complex, and it is difficult to summarize it in a few sentences without using some technical terms. Hopefully the meanings of these words will become clearer as the argument develops.

Piaget has conceptualized the child's growing understanding of the world in a series of sequentially ordered stages: sensori-motor, pre-operational, concrete and formal operational. Within each of these major stages, and during the transition from one to the next, different sub-stages, which follow rules of sequential and hierarchical ordering, can be distinguished.

Is this sequential order universal? Do individuals in various cultures acquire the same concepts, and, if so, do they follow the same developmental sequence? To this first qualitative question, which is basic to Piaget's theory, one may add a second question about the quantitative aspects of cognitive development: at what rate do individuals in a particular society move from one stage to the next?

Although each stage is characterized by a qualitatively different structure, the development from one stage to the next always follows the same functional rules of adaptation (a notion which Piaget draws directly from his background in biology) and the later stage includes the features of the earlier one in a re-ordered form. At the sensori-motor stage, the baby's actions enable him to discover the properties of objects: at the same time his actions are modified in the act of discovery. These two aspects of adaptation Piaget calls 'assimilation'

[1] The preparation of this paper was assisted by grants from the Fonds National Suisse de la Recherche Scientifique (grants nos. 1.7640.72 and 1.5550.74 to Professor B. Inhelder). Author's address: Faculté de Psychologie et des Sciences de l'Education, University of Geneva, CH-1211 Geneva 4, Switzerland.

137

and 'accommodation', and they are held in balance by internal laws of equilibration.

The sensori-motor action schemes are the basis for the later use of symbols (particularly language), which greatly increase the child's power to restructure his world on the representational level. The internalization of action schemes leads to what Piaget calls 'operations', and these will be applied not only to the physical world, but also to social interactions. Interpersonal cooperation is seen as one of the basic aspects of the reversibility of operations, and a necessary condition for the universality of operational structures.

These functional aspects of Piaget's theory have, however, received little attention in the cross-cultural literature. Most studies have been concerned with structure, or simply with performance on tasks derived from Piaget's theory (cf. Barbara Lloyd's paper in this volume). Various reviews of cross-cultural Piagetian psychology have been published recently (Dasen 1972, 1973a, 1977a; Lloyd 1972; Piaget 1974; Carlson 1975; Greenfield 1975), and I will not attempt to cover the whole of this subject in this paper. I will mainly summarize two of my own studies which seem to be of particular relevance to the topic – universals of human thought. The first is research with African babies on sensori-motor intelligence, and the second is a cross-cultural study of the passage from pre-operational to concrete operational thinking in Australian Aborigines, Canadian Eskimos and Ebrié Africans.

While searching for the characteristics of universals in this particular area of cognitive development, I found useful a distinction between 'strong' and 'weak' sequential invariance put forward by Flavell & Wohlwill (1969, 84fn), which I propose to extend, by analogy, to 'strong' and 'weak' universals. Their definition reads as follows:

A sequence is strongly invariant if it is both universally present and universally fixed in the childhoods of undamaged human beings. For instance, we imagine that all intact human infants achieve primary and tertiary circular reactions, and achieve them in that order only. A sequence is weakly invariant if, when present, it is universally fixed. One may be able to find children who do not attain A, or B, or both; but for all children who do attain both, the order of attainment is the same.

The first study I report provides an example of a strong sequential invariance or strong universal, whereas the second study gives an example of a weak sequential invariance or weak universal. In other words, all human infants seem to go through the same stages of sensori-motor development and they all reach its final level, including its extension to the symbolic function. All individuals who display concrete operational reasoning seem to have acquired it through the same sequence of stages. There are, however, some individuals who do not display the final level of concrete operations, at least in so far as it is measured by certain tasks. This performance difference should not be interpreted to imply that they would not have the capacity (or competence) to do so. Thus, the questions will be raised whether competence for concrete operations would not be a 'strong' universal (i.e. all human beings develop the underlying competence for concrete operations through the same developmental order), whereas performance would be a 'weak' universal (i.e. some human beings do not display their competence for concrete operational thinking when placed in a particular experimental situation or in their daily lives, for reasons which remain to be investigated).

## The strong sequential invariance of sensori-motor development: a study of African babies[2]

Ordinal scales have been constructed for assessing infant development in Piaget's first major stage of intellectual growth (Corman & Escalona 1969; Kopp & Sigman 1972; Uzgiris & Hunt 1975), i.e. the six sub-stages of sensori-motor intelligence (Piaget 1936, 1937). In studies of Baoulé infants aged 6 to 24 months living in villages approximately 200 kilometres north-west of Abidjan, the capital of Ivory Coast, we have used a scale for sensori-motor intelligence devised by the French psychologists Casati & Lézine (1968). In a cross-sectional pilot-study in 1971, I assessed thirty-nine infants (Dasen 1973b), and thirty-four were tested by Bovet and Othenin-Girard a year later (Bovet, Dasen & Inhelder 1974). Subsequently (1973–5), a larger longitudinal study on sixty-three babies was undertaken by Dasen *et al.* (1978).

An account of the daily life of the Baoulé is provided by Guerry (1970). Although there have been changes in agriculture and social life, child rearing in the villages follows traditional patterns. The new-born Baoulé infant is secluded with his mother for the first two weeks of life, but once the mother leaves the house, and resumes a normal routine, he is carried everywhere tied to her back. Until weaning, at about 18 months, the infant is breast-fed on demand and

---

[2] The results reported here and further details on the methods, subjects and experimental situation have been published in French by Dasen *et al.* (1978).

infants were observed to search actively for the breast, wriggling from the mother's back to her side when their cries were not heeded promptly.

In keeping with the close Baoulé mother–child relationship, testing was carried out while infants sat on their mothers' laps – in the pilot studies in their own courtyards, but in an observation-hut in the longitudinal research.

The Casati–Lézine scale, which was based upon Piaget's observations of his own children's development during infancy, allows systematic assignment of infants to the four sub-stages III, IV, V and VI. Each of these is sub-divided into A and B marking the beginning and the full accomplishment of each sub-stage. The instrument is composed of seven tasks: (1) Object permanency; (2) Distant object with string; (3) Distant object on cloth; (4) Use of an instrument; (5) Exploration of objects; (6) Combination of objects – tube and rake; and (7) Combination of objects – tube and chain.

Examples for Task (1), object permanency, give an indication of sub-stage assignment. To be classed IIIB the infant must find an object partially hidden under a cloth but still partly visible. If the infant finds a completely hidden object after having begun a grasping movement he is identified IVA. At IVB the child searches for objects under a screen even when they are hidden before the grasping movement was initiated; but if the object is moved to a second screen the infant continues to search under the first. At VA 'visible' displacement to a second screen is achieved, while ability to follow an object through an 'invisible' displacement[3] to a new location is evidence for sub-stage VB. At VIA the infant can follow an object through an invisible displacement to a second location while at VIB he can follow an object through a series of three invisible displacements.

The behaviour of the Baoulé infants was identical with that observed by Casati & Lézine in French babies; the same sub-stages were apparent, following the same hierarchical ordering. Cumulative frequencies of the attainment of sub-stages IIIB to VIB, on each of the seven tasks, were computed and compared to the French norms (Lézine, Stambak & Casati 1969), using a statistic 'V' described by Kamara & Easley (1977) which is distributed like chi-square. A summary of the results appears in Table 6.1.

Three tasks (4, 6 and 7) show a consistent and statistically highly

---

[3] The object is hidden in a box (or in the hand), the box is placed under the screen, where the object is released, and then shown empty to the subject.

TABLE 6.1. *Comparison of Baoulé results with French norms on the Casati–Lézine scale of sensori-motor intelligence (statistic 'V' of Kamara & Easley 1977)*

|  | | | | Tasks | | | |
|  | 1 Object permanence | 2 String | 3 Cloth | 4 Instrument | 5 Exploration | 6 Tube/rake | 7 Tube/chain |
| Sub-stages | | | | | | | |
|---|---|---|---|---|---|---|---|
| IIIB | 1·56 | | | | | | |
| IVA | 49·76** | 74·78** | 45·22** | | 38·73* | | |
| IVA/B | | | 25·44 | | | | |
| IVB | 51·40** | 92·84*** | 34·60 | 152·44** | 24·42 | | |
| VA | 39·23 | 65·10** | 18·35 | 130·18*** | 18·35 | | |
| VA/B | | | | 84·96** | | | |
| VB | 35·94 | −51·14** | 4·21 | 88·92*** | 8·13 | 52·41** | 43·01** |
| VIA | 26·42 | | 11·05 | 74·91*** | 10·19 | 50·63*** | 51·56*** |
| VIA/B | | | | | | 58·27** | 40·48*** |
| VIB | 29·93 | | −4·71 | 70·36** | 32·28** | 46·12** | 13·48 |

\* $P < 0.05$; \*\* $P < 0.01$. A positive 'V' value indicates an advance of the Baoulé sample, a negative 'V' value an advance of the French

significant advance of the Baoulé infants over the French norms, throughout all relevant sub-stages and the whole age-range. On the other tasks, there is usually some advance over French norms, but it is not statistically significant at all sub-stages. No advance, or even a small delay, is found in the last sub-stages on task (3), which involves the manipulation of some bizarre apparatus. The difficulty did not arise simply from lack of experience with the type of objects presented, as few Baoulé infants had had experience with the plastic tube and rake (tasks 4, 6 and 7); the difficulty appeared to be specific to the type of manipulation required, i.e. rotating around an axle. There are no everyday objects in the environment of Baoulé infants which require such an action.

It may come as a surprise that the greatest precocity occurs on tasks which involve the handling or combination of objects. The African infant has usually been described as passive, in an environment which is poor in objects (e.g. Knappen 1962; Erny 1972), and African culture is held to value social interactions rather than object manipulation (Zempleni-Rabain 1970; Mundy-Castle & Okonji 1976). Valantin (1972) has argued that African culture values axial motor development, leading to precocity in sitting, standing and walking, but does not value distal motor development, leading to a lag in the development of prehension and fine motor coordination. Similarly, Super (1976) showed that there was no overall African infant precocity in psycho-motor development, but rather an advance of those skills which are specifically taught by caretakers (mainly sitting, standing and walking).

The environment of the Baoulé infants is certainly poor in toys and other structured, technological objects, but it is quite rich in unstructured objects (sticks, stones, cooking implements, tin cans, etc.), and the child is absolutely free to explore all objects, including dangerous ones. Through naturalistic behaviour observations, we found that the Baoulé babies manipulated these objects frequently, exploring them, combining them, then using them in meaningful sequences, either conventionally (i.e. each object in its usual function) or symbolically (i.e. using an object to represent something else). Unstructured objects are particularly favourable for symbolic use.

Our observations do not support the passivity said to characterize African children, at least not in the first two years. In a structured situation where infants were presented with a fixed array of mainly familiar objects, we observed a more quiet 'style' in the handling of objects than is usual in Western children, and in some cases a more restricted use of space, but the structure and sequencing of the activities observed was identical in Baoulé and Western children.

Thus, an important conclusion may be overlooked if we attach too much attention to cultural variations and differences in the rate of development of the various sub-stages on the seven different tasks. In spite of vast differences in the cultural environment of French and Baoulé infants, the qualitative characteristics of sensori-motor development are quite similar or even identical. Not only are the structural properties of the stages, and therefore their order of appearance, identical in both groups, but the actions, schemes, and the way these are slowly built up into more complex action-patterns which eventually enable the infant to solve the more complex problems seem to be identical.

For example, Task (7) – tube and chain – appears at first sight exceedingly difficult. Why should any infant wish to combine these objects? Yet, after stage VA, almost every infant begins to search for a way of making the chain pass through the tube. When the Baoulé infant is presented with the tube and paperclip chain, not only does he try to combine them but he follows the same steps, with the same errors and finds the same successively more adapted solutions as do his French peers though, on average, at a slightly earlier age.

Dare we call these striking similarities universals on the basis of such a limited comparison? That they are not completely determined by biological factors is attested by the lack of overall precocity or delay which suggests rather the importance of particular stimulations and incitements from specific experiences. Although cultural experiences modify the rate of development in the sensori-motor stage, the overall impression is of remarkable similarity despite widely different environments.

As we move, in the next section, to a discussion of concrete operational thinking, we will come to much the same conclusion. The qualitative aspects of development, the structure of the stages, their ordering and the type of answers the children give to Piagetian tasks, seem to be quasi-universal, whereas the rates of development seem to vary under the influence of socio-cultural factors. However we will also find that the rates of development are not uniform across conceptual domains within a cultural group, but are dependent to some degree on the cultural value placed on some concepts over others.

## The weak sequential invariance of concrete operations: the example of conservation of quantity

One of the most familiar Piagetian tasks is the conservation of quantity (liquids), which is considered to be a marker of the beginning of the concrete operational stage. In this task, the child pours the same amount of water into two identical glasses; once the initial equality is well established, he is asked to pour the water from one of the containers into a glass of a different shape, say long and narrow (or wide), so that the level of the liquid changes. Then the child is asked: 'Is there still the same amount of water in the two glasses?' The child at the pre-operational stage will answer 'No, there is more (or less) because the water comes up high (or low)'. In other words, he is attending to only one of the dimensions and is not able to carry the invariance of quantity across the transformations of the display. At a second stage, the child exhibits hesitations, changing his mind either in the same situation or between situations. At the concrete operational stage (conventionally called 'stage 3'), the child is convinced that the amount of water does not change, and he is able to justify his answer in various ways.

Fig. 6.1 represents the percentages of children of different ages giving a concrete operational answer ('stage 3') on the task of conservation of quantity, using liquids. The results of three samples are shown: (1) Children from a Western, technological culture (Canberra, Australia), whose results are exactly comparable to those reported by Piaget & Inhelder (1963) for children in Geneva, Switzerland; (2) Schooled children from the same West African, Baoulé, village in which the study of sensori-motor intelligence was carried out (Kpouébo); (3) Schooled Eskimo children (Cape Dorset) from a study which will be described below. In each sample, I tested ten children at each age.

The developmental curves in Fig. 6.1 may serve as an illustration of 'strong' and 'weak' universals; more examples of such curves have been provided in other publications (Dasen 1973a, 1977a; Kamara & Easley 1977). The Kpouébo curve shows a small 'time-lag', i.e. the concept of conservation of quantity seems to be acquired about two years later than in the Canberra group; the exact status of such 'time-lags' is still under discussion (e.g. Kamara & Easley 1977; Dasen, Lavallée & Retschitzki 1979; Dasen, Ngini & Lavallée 1979), but the important aspect of the curve for the present argument is that all children eventually seem to reach the concrete operational stage

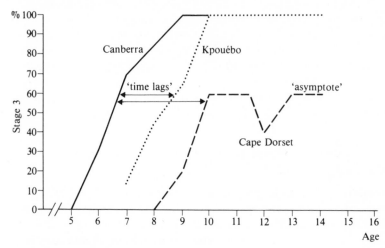

Fig. 6.1 Conservation of quantity

on this task. Such a curve therefore represents an example of a 'strong' universal.

On the other hand, the developmental curve of the Cape Dorset sample presents an 'asymptote' below 100 per cent: a plateau occurs after a certain age, beyond which no further development seems to occur. Such a developmental curve is an example of a 'weak' universal.

The interpretation of these 'asymptotes' has also given rise to some discussion, notably in terms of the performance/competence distinction (Dasen 1977b; Dasen, Ngini & Lavallée 1979). In any case, it would not be justified to interpret these curves as a reflection of the 'developmental level' or 'status' of a population as a whole. A statement such as 'Tribe X does not mature beyond the European 11-year level' (Cole & Scribner 1974, 156) is absurd, as the authors point out. What these curves mean is that some individuals give conservation answers, whereas others do not, and that the proportion of those who do, does not increase after a certain age. However, those who display concrete operational reasoning give the same answers and justifications familiar in Western children, and they also seem to have gone through the same sub-stages before reaching the concrete operational level, although this is usually an inference from cross-sectional studies, where longitudinal ones would be more to the point. Thus, in the case of conservation of liquids – and the same would be true of most other concrete operational tasks – we have examples of both 'strong' and 'weak' types: drawn together, these examples point to the fact that conservation of quantity is a 'weak' universal.

What are the cultural factors which influence the rate of development of concrete operations so markedly? This question obviously has no single answer. The study which I report below attempts to demonstrate that some of these factors may be the eco-cultural demands placed upon people living at a subsistence economy level.

## A cross-cultural study of concrete operational development[4]

According to a model proposed by Berry (1966), people tend to develop those skills which are required for a successful adaptation to their environment. More specifically, nomadic hunting people tend to develop high levels of spatial and perceptual skills and tend to be more differentiated (e.g. in terms of Witkin's field independence), whereas sedentary, agricultural populations do not need to develop spatial and perceptual skills to the same extent and tend to be less differentiated (mainly because of harsher socialization practices which are common in high population density, highly structured and hierarchical societies). Subsequently, Berry (1976) expanded his model to include several other variables, and has developed eco-cultural, socialization and acculturation indices in order to rank cultural groups more precisely. He has tested this scheme with seventeen different samples.

Applying Berry's eco-cultural model to Piagetian psychology, it is possible to predict that a sample of Eskimo children (Cape Dorset), and to a somewhat lesser degree a sample of Australian Aboriginal children (Hermannsburg) would develop concepts of topological, projective and Euclidean space more rapidly than a sample of Ebrié Africans (Adiopodoumé, Ivory Coast).

According to Piaget & Inhelder (1948), the child's initial concepts of space are topological: they are based on such characteristics as order, continuity, proximity, separation and surrounding, all other features being neglected. Gradually the child takes into account projective and Euclidean features. The understanding of projective space begins when an object can be considered in relation to a 'point of view' and the child can take into account such features as angles

[4] This study has been reported previously in Dasen (1975).

and perspective. Euclidean concepts include distance, parallelism, and vertical and horizontal coordinates.

Three tasks were selected in this study to assess spatial development:

(1) Linear, reverse and circular order. The subject has to copy a linear display of nine objects, reverse this order, and finally change a circular display into a straight line. The task assesses topological spatial relationships of neighbourhood and order, and one-to-one correspondence.

(2) Rotation of landscape models (localization of topographical positions). The subject has to locate on one landscape model rotated by 180° seven successive positions and orientations of a corresponding object placed on an unrotated landscape model. The models and objects used were adapted for each cultural group, but retain the same spatial features as originally used by Piaget & Inhelder (1948). The task assesses topological, projective, and Euclidean (metric) spatial relationships, the construction of a coordinate system, and the flexibility of spatial operations.

(3) Horizontality. This task assesses the coordination of two spatial (Euclidean) reference systems. The subject is required to draw, on corresponding outline figures, the level of water in a half-filled bottle tilted in various positions, when the water level is hidden.

Six to 14-year-old rural school children drawn from three cultural groups were tested. The groups were:

(1) Central Eskimo. The settlement of Cape Dorset is situated on the south-west tip of Baffin Island in the Northwest Territories of Canada. Its population is about 600. Cape Dorset Eskimos are well known for their artistic achievements; stone carvings and prints provide a large part of the income, together with local service jobs and welfare. But part of the food is still provided by hunting and fishing. Every family owns a house in the village, but during hunting expeditions they may still live in igloos in winter and in tents in summer. Some families live part of the year in isolated hunting camps. An excellent study of the village of Sugluk, very similar to Cape Dorset, has been provided by Graburn (1969).

(2) Australian Aborigines. The settlement of Hermannsburg Mission is situated seventy miles west of Alice Springs in the centre of Australia (Northern Territory). Its population was 554 in 1969. The cultural background of Aranda (Arunta) Aborigines has been described by Spencer & Gillen (1927), Strehlow (1947, 1965) and many others. Present-day Aborigines at Hermannsburg rely only occasionally on

hunting and gathering for their livelihood; most of their income comes from local service jobs, welfare, and cattle raising. Although the population has become mainly sedentary, many Aborigines travel frequently to other settlements and maintain their knowledge of a large area around them and keep their skill in finding their way in the seemingly monotonous desert or semi-desert.

(3) Ebrié Africans. The village of Adiopodoumé is situated seventeen kilometres west of Abidjan, the capital city of Ivory Coast. Its population is about 7,000. Most of its inhabitants are Ebrié, although some other ethnic groups are also present. The main activity is the raising of staple food (yams, plantain, and various vegetables), as well as cash crops (coffee, cocoa, and bananas). There is also some fishing in the lagoon, and some paid jobs are available in the city or at a nearby research station.

It should be noted that the cultural characteristics of the three samples come close to the requirements of Berry's model, but are not absolutely ideal. The Eskimos and Aborigines no longer rely exclusively on hunting and gathering and have become partly sedentary, whereas the African sample is somewhat heterogeneous as to ethnic background and parents' occupation.

The three samples will be labelled by the names of the locations in which they were obtained, to indicate that they are not necessarily representative of the whole ethnic groups. In particular, results may be influenced by acculturation (Dasen 1973a, 1977a); the three samples were chosen to represent approximately equal levels of acculturation, as far as this could be done across different historical and cultural backgrounds. However, no measure of acculturation, other than the author's casual observations, can be offered.

In each sample, ten subjects (as nearly as possible five of each sex) were sampled randomly within each given age group. All subjects attended the local primary school, where teaching took place in a second language, and their ages were known from reliable school records.

The results for the three spatial tasks are presented in Figs. 6.2, 6.3 and 6.4. Each point represents the percentage of subjects (out of ten at each age, and in each sample) giving a concrete operational answer (stage 3, or, in the case of Horizontality, stage 3 combined with the immediately preceding intermediate stage).

These results clearly support the eco-cultural hypothesis. On all three tasks, the rate of development is faster in the Cape Dorset (Eskimo) than in the Hermannsburg (Australian Aboriginal) sample,

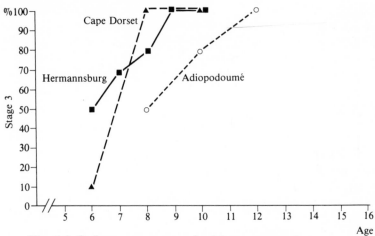

Fig. 6.2 Orders: percentage of subjects at stage 3

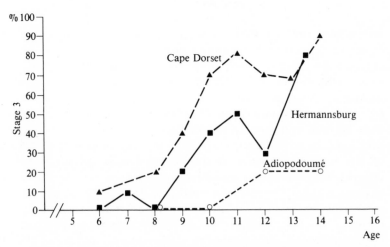

Fig. 6.3 Rotation: percentage of subjects at stage 3

and it is faster in both of these than in the Adiopodoumé (Ebrié African) sample. The statistical significance of these differences was tested according to a scheme proposed by Kamara & Easley (1977): they are all significantly different beyond the level $p = 0.05$, except for the Hermannsburg and Cape Dorset samples on task (1) (Orders).

It would be wrong to conclude from these data that the rate of cognitive development as a whole (if such a thing exists at all) is faster

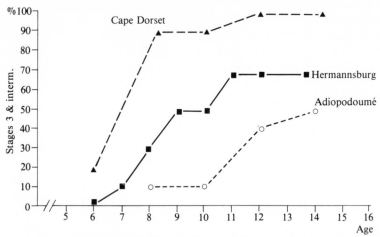

Fig. 6.4 Horizontality, part 1: percentage of subjects at stage 3
and intermediate

in Eskimos and Australian Aborigines than in Ebrié Africans. The
reverse may be true in a cognitive domain more valued by sedentary,
agricultural groups. From an analysis of ethnographic material, I
predicted, for example, that concepts of conservation of quantity,
weight and volume seem to be a necessity in an agricultural society
where the food produced has to be stored for consumption until the
next harvest, and is widely exchanged on markets. In a traditional
hunting and gathering society, such precise comparisons would seem
of less importance since food is usually collected for immediate
consumption, and it is never exchanged in markets. There is extensive
sharing within the hunting group, but this seems to be based on
qualitative rather than quantitative considerations: each piece of the
animal is valued in a different way, and it is distributed according to
social or family relationships (and the hunter sometimes gets the
worst part!). Similarly, water, which is certainly a highly valued
commodity in the Australian desert, is *not* – as far as I can tell –
measured in exact amounts. The Aborigine knows how to find
enough water to survive, and usually plans his wandering from one
waterhole to the next; he certainly needs a precise cognitive map of
his area and tremendous orientation skill to find the waterhole, but
once he gets there, he has no need for a precise measurement in
containers. Similarly, related concepts such as number are much
more developed in African than in Eskimo and Aboriginal cultures.

In order to test this second prediction from the eco-cultural model, the tasks of conservation of quantity (liquids), weight and volume were administered to the same groups of children. The task of conservation of quantity (liquids) has been described earlier in this paper. The task of conservation of weight follows the same scheme, but the materials are two identical plasticine balls, one of which is rolled out (or flattened) by the child during the experiment. The question asked is whether the ball and the rolled out (or flattened) piece are still of the same weight. A balance is used to visualize the concept. For the task of conservation of volume the same plasticine balls and their transformations are used. In addition, two identical glasses are filled with water to the same level; when the plasticine is dipped into the water, the level rises, and this is used to exemplify the idea of volume. The order of the conservation tasks was counter-balanced within each age group, to control for any order effects.

The ability to conserve concepts of quantity, weight and volume is considered an important indicator of the attainment of concrete operational thinking. However, the child does not achieve invariance of all these concepts at the same time; he usually acquires the conservation of quantity first, while continuing to give pre-operational answers for weight and volume. He then acquires the conservation of weight, and subsequently the conservation of volume. The fact that these specific concrete operational structures appear at different points in development has been described as a 'horizontal décalage'.

The results of the three conservation tasks are presented graphically in Figs. 6.5, 6.6 and 6.7.

If the age-range 12 to 14 years is considered alone, the order of the developmental curves is as expected from the hypothesis: the rate of development in the Adiopodoumé sample is significantly ($p < 0.05$) faster than in the two other samples on all three tasks. Below age 12 several discontinuities occur which are not in accordance with the hypothesis. However, the Baoulé (Kpouébo sample; cf. Fig. 6.1) correspond even more than the Ebrié to Berry's definition of a sedentary, agricultural population. The developmental curve in this Baoulé sample rises steeply from age 7 to reach 100 per cent conservation at age 10, and there is no overlap at all with the other curves.

Generally speaking, then, the eco-cultural hypothesis is also supported by this second set of data. This type of quasi-experimental design does not enable us, however, to establish causal links; further work will be needed to describe the precise mechanisms which allow

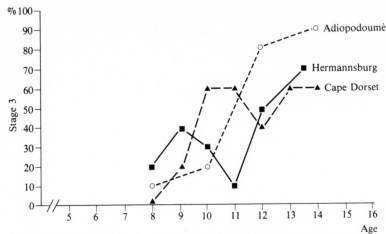

Fig. 6.5  Conservation of quantity: percentage of subjects at
stage 3

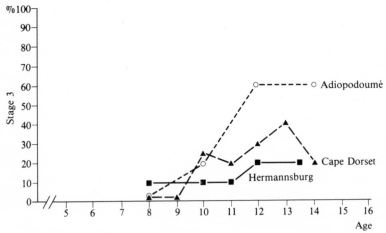

Fig. 6.6  Conservation of weight: percentage of subjects at
stage 3

some concepts to develop more rapidly. Unfortunately, little is known about these mechanisms in our own culture.

An additional point which may be of relevance is the distinction recently introduced in cross-cultural Piagetian psychology between competence and spontaneous performance (Flavell & Wohlwill 1969;

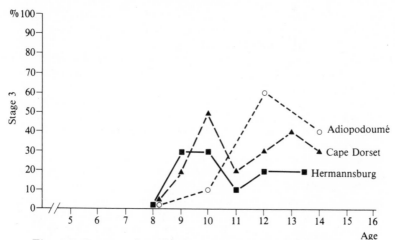

Fig. 6.7  Conservation of volume: percentage of subjects at stage 3

Heron & Dowel 1973, 1974; Dasen 1977b). From this perspective, the results presented here represent the spontaneous use of the concepts, but not necessarily the underlying 'competence'. The fact that an individual does not display a concept on first testing does not mean that he does not have the competence to use this concept if he is placed in a favourable situation (e.g. through training procedures; cf. Dasen, Lavallée & Retschitzki 1979; Dasen, Ngini & Lavallée 1979).

Thus, despite the striking cultural differences which have been demonstrated in the rate of development of concrete operations, the underlying operational structures may well be universal, as are the processes which lead to their construction, namely the basic mechanisms of adaptation (assimilation and accommodation) and of equilibration. The impact of cultural variables seems to appear in the 'functional cognitive systems' (Cole & Scribner 1974) which make it possible to use these operations in a given situation.

### References

Berry, J. W. (1966) 'Temne and Eskimo perceptual skills', *International Journal of Psychology* 1, no. 3, 207–29
—— (1976) *Human ecology and cognitive style: comparative studies in cultural and psychological adaptation.* New York: Wiley

Bovet, M. C., Dasen, P. R. & Inhelder, B. (1974) 'Etapes de l'intelligence sensori-motrice chez l'enfant Baoulé: Etude préliminaire', *Archives de Psychologie* 41 (vol. 1972), 164, 363–86

Carlson, J. (1975) 'Cross-cultural Piagetian research: what can it tell us?', in Riegel, K. & Meacham, J. (eds.) *The developing individual in a changing world*. The Hague: Mouton

Casati, I. & Lézine, I. (1968) *Les étapes de l'intelligence sensori-motrice: manuel*. Paris: Centre de Psychologie Appliquée

Cole, M. & Scribner, S. (1974) *Culture and thought: a psychological introduction*. New York: Wiley

Corman, H. H. & Escalona, S. K. (1969) 'Stages in sensori-motor development: a replication study', *The Merrill-Palmer Quarterly* 15, no. 4, 351–61

Dasen, P. R. (1972) 'Cross-cultural Piagetian research: a summary', *Journal of Cross-Cultural Psychology* 3, no. 1, 23–39 (reprinted in Berry, J. W. & Dasen, P. R. (eds.) *Culture and cognition*. London: Methuen, 1974)

—— (1973a) 'Biologie ou culture? La psychologie inter-ethnique d'un point de vue Piagétien', *Psychologie Canadienne* 14, no. 2, 149–66

—— (1973b) 'Preliminary study of sensori-motor development in Baoulé children', *Early Child Development and Care* 2, 345–54

—— (1975) 'Concrete operational development in three cultures', *Journal of Cross-Cultural Psychology* 6, no. 2, 156–72

—— (1977a) 'Are cognitive processes universal? A contribution to cross-cultural Piagetian psychology', in Warren, N. (ed.) *Studies in Cross-Cultural Psychology* 1. London: Academic Press, 155–201

—— (1977b) 'Cross-cultural cognitive development: the cultural aspects of Piaget's theory', *Annals of the New York Academy of Sciences* 285, 332–7

——, Inhelder, B., Lavallée, M. & Retschitzki, J. (1978) *Naissance de l'intelligence chez l'enfant Baoulé de Côte d'Ivoire*. Berne: Hans Huber

——, Lavallée, M. & Retschitzki, J. (1979) 'Training conservation of quantity (liquids) in West African (Baoulé) children', *International Journal of Psychology* 14, 69–82

——, Ngini, L. & Lavallée, M. (1979) 'Cross-cultural training studies of concrete operations', in Eckensberger, L., Poortinga, Y. & Lonner, W. (eds.) *Applied cross-cultural research and the development of psychological science*. Amsterdam: Swets & Zeitlinger, 94–104

Erny, P. (1972) *L'enfant et son milieu en Afrique Noire: Essais sur l'éducation traditionelle*. Paris: Pavot

Flavell, J. H. & Wohlwill, J. F. (1969) 'Formal and functional aspects of cognitive development', in Elkind, D. & Flavell, J. H. (eds.) *Studies in cognitive development*. Oxford University Press, 67–120

Graburn, N. H. H. (1969) *Eskimos without igloos: social and economic development in Sugluk*. Boston: Little & Brown

Greenfield, P. (1975) 'Cross-cultural research and Piagetian theory: paradox and progress', in Riegel, K. & Meacham, J. (eds.) *The developing individual in a changing world*. The Hague: Mouton

Guerry, V. (1970) *La vie quotidienne dans un village baoulé*. Abidjan: Institut Africain pour le Développment Economique et Social

Heron, A. & Dowel, W. (1973) 'Weight conservation and matrix-solving ability in Papuan children', *Journal of Cross-Cultural Psychology* 4, no. 2, 207–19

—— & Dowel, W. (1974) 'The questionable unity of the concrete operational stage', *International Journal of Psychology* 9, no. 1, 1–9

Kamara, A. I. & Easley, J. A. Jr (1977) 'Is the rate of cognitive development uniform across cultures? A methodological critique with new evidence from Themne children', in Dasen, P. R. (ed.) *Piagetian psychology: cross-cultural contributions*. New York: Gardner (Halsted/Wiley), 26–63

Knappen, M. T. (1962) *L'enfant Mukongo*. Louvain: Naewelaerts

Kopp, C. B. & Sigman, M. (1972) UCLA revision of the administration manual: 'The stages of sensori-motor intelligence in the child from birth to two years' by Irène Casati & Irène Lézine, unpublished manuscript

Lézine, I., Stambak, M. & Casati, I. (1969) *Les étapes de l'intelligence sensori-motrice*, monograph no. 1. Paris: Centre de Psychologie Appliquée

Lloyd, B. B. (1972) *Perception and cognition from a cross-cultural perspective*. Harmondsworth: Penguin Books

Mundy-Castle, A. C. & Okonji, M. O. (1976) 'Mother–infant interaction in Nigeria', Manuscript, Department of Psychology, University of Lagos

Piaget, J. (1936) *La naissance de l'intelligence chez l'enfant*. Neuchâtel: Delachaux & Niestlé. English translation: *The origins of intelligence in the child*. London: Routledge & Kegan Paul, 1953

—— (1937) *La construction du réel chez l'enfant*. Neuchâtel: Delachaux & Niestlé. English translations: *The construction of reality in the child*. New York: Basic Books, 1954. *The Child's construction of reality*. London: Routledge & Kegan Paul, 1955

—— (1974) 'Need and significance of cross-cultural studies in genetic psychology', in Berry, J. W. & Dasen, P. R. (eds.) *Culture and cognition*. London: Methuen, 299–309

—— & Inhelder, B. (1948) *La représentation de l'espace chez l'enfant*. Paris: PUF. English translation: *The child's conception of space*. London: Routledge & Kegan Paul, 1956

—— & Inhelder, B. (1963) 'Les opérations intellectuelles et leur développement', in Fraisse, P. & Piaget, J. (eds.) *Traité de psychologie expérimentale*. Vol. 7: *L'intelligence*. Paris: PUF, 109–55

Spencer, B. & Gillen, F. J. (1927) *The Arunta*. London: MacMillan

Strehlow, T. G. H. (1947) *Aranda traditions.* Melbourne University Press
—— (1965) 'Culture, social structure and environment in Aboriginal Central Australia', in Berndt, R. M. & Berndt, C. H. (eds.) *Aboriginal man in Australia.* Sydney: Angus & Robertson, 121–45

Super, C. M. (1976) 'Environmental effects on motor development: the case of "African infant precocity"', *Developmental Medicine and Child Neurology* 18, no. 5, 561–7

Uzgiris, I. C. & Hunt, J. (1975) *Assessment in infancy: ordinal scales of psychological development.* University of Illinois Press

Valantin, S. (1972) 'Problems raised by observations of children in various cultural environments', *Early Child Development and Care* 2, no. 3, 276–89

Zempléni-Rabain, J. (1970) 'L'enfant Wolof de 2 à 5 ans (Sénégal): Echanges corporels et échanges médiatisés par les objets', *Revue de Neuropsychiatrie Infantile* 18, nos. 10–11, 785–98

# 7    Psychological differentiation

*Ogbolu Okonji*

I must confess that when I received the invitation to attend the Cambridge conference I was puzzled because I was not sure how I could talk about 'universals of human thought' from the rather scanty evidence from Africa with which I am familiar. However, despite my doubts about the meaning to attach to the notion of 'universals' in the African context I found the problem intellectually challenging. I was also encouraged by the democratic tone of the letter of invitation which virtually permitted one to define one's own area of interest and discuss it in one's own way.

It was easy for me to assume that thinking itself is a universal human characteristic and to feel that there must be aspects of thinking (especially in terms of structure and function, but not necessarily of content) which one can consider universal to all human beings at least within some historical time space. Such universals need not be constant but there may be 'basic regularities' (to use Margaret Mead's (1950) expression) in human thinking behaviour which one can legitimately expect not only because of the common biological heritage of all human beings but also because some problems of existence and living appear to be common to all human beings irrespective of cultural and ecological differences. Evidence for the physiological bases of thinking is accumulating as the volume edited by McGuigan & Schoonover (1973) amply illustrates and it stands as further support in a search for universals.

The concept of psychological differentiation comes to mind when considering universals of human thought. Development viewed in terms of the differentiation or increasing specialization both of function and structure is a powerful concept which has been used to explain the growth of the individual and the species. It is a particularly attractive idea in this context because the notion of psychological differentiation as developed by Witkin and his colleagues (1962) has been used in cross-cultural studies in almost all parts of the world.

157

In addition the theory which Witkin has presented considers biological factors as aspects of the differentiation process and holds that increasing differentiation or complexity of thinking is pan-human and overrides particular cultural experiences (cf. Werner 1948; Witkin *et al.* 1962; Piaget 1963).

Although there have been no direct studies of the universality of the concept of psychological differentiation with special reference to the cognitive style aspect there is some indirect evidence which suggests such universality and it is often assumed in cross-cultural studies. Vernon (1973) has traced the origins of the concept of cognitive styles to the Greeks and Romans whose notion of somatic typologies would appear to share common features with our contemporary notions of cognitive style. I have suggested (Okonji 1974) that there may be pan-cultural links between personality types and modes of thinking on the basis of having shown the presence of such personality typologies and associated cognitive styles in African societies.[1]

## Cognitive differentiation: factor-analytic evidence

The presence of a factor which can be described as an analytic style of thought has been suggested in the cognitive structure of Africans from a number of factor-analytic studies and this factor would appear to be similar to that reported for Euro-American peoples. Irvine (1969) has described the structure of abilities in a variety of African cultural groups from an extensive survey in Kenya, Zimbabwe–Rhodesia and Zambia involving over 5,000 people. From his analysis he was able to identify factors which he labelled 'g' (general reasoning), 'v.ed.' (verbal educational ability) and 'n.ed.' (numerical educational ability) following conventional psycho-metric practice. He found, however, that the factor k.m. (spatial and mechanical ability) – which seems to be closely related to the cognitive style dimension of field dependence and independence identified by Witkin – appeared to be present in varying degrees in the different cultural samples. Although the relationship between spatial and mechanical ability and field dependence follows theoretical expectation, Irvine & Sanders (1972) have raised some doubts about the

[1] Among my own people (an Igbo group of Southern Nigeria) a person's way of doing things may be described as 'floating on the surface' (*ona ekpo no enu*) as against the deep, wise and thoughtful person. In many ways the former type of person shares common characteristics with the global, field-dependent individual.

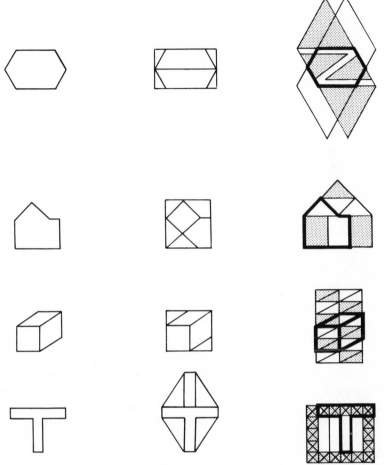

Fig. 7.1 Embedded Figures Test

practice generally adopted in cross-cultural research, of using the Embedded Figure Test (EFT) (see Fig. 7.1) to assess cognitive style since results on the EFT appear to be affected by schooling.

Claeys (1972), in a factor-analytic study of the intellectual structure of teachers in the Congo, reported the presence of a factor similar to field dependence-independence which he considered varied with 'adoption of a Western attitude'. Grant (1972) has argued, on the basis of evidence from South Africa, that intellectual differentiation is greater in urban educated Africans than in illiterate people from

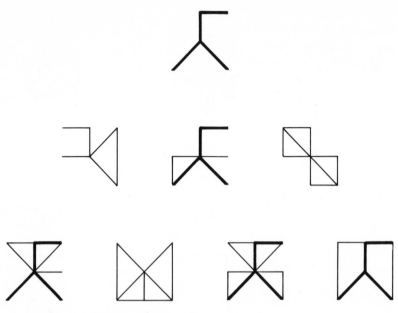

Fig. 7.2 Hidden Patterns Test

rural areas. Vernon (1969) administered a variety of psychological tests including spatial/perceptual tasks to samples of males of different socio-economic backgrounds from Britain, Jamaica, Uganda (East Africa) and Canada (Indians and Eskimos). He found that the usual ability factors were distributed differently among the various groups. In fact it seemed that Witkin's field dependence dimension emerged as a factor in the cognitive structure of the people in the diverse cultures included in the sample.

El Abd (1970) administered a battery of cognitive tests to secondary and university students in Uganda. The students came from different ethnic groups as well as different socio-economic backgrounds and the groups of tests included the Hidden Patterns Test (see Fig. 7.2). El Abd concluded from the factor analysis of his results that the structure of intellect among his sample was similar to that reported in studies with Western samples. He observed: 'Another interesting point is that Factor IV, of the computer varimax rotation, sustains Vernon's observation that there is a link between flexibility of closure and spatial orientation. This might be due to the fact that in dealing with the tasks of both factors the examinee's intellect has to retain a given figure in a distracting field' (p. 431). Finally, MacArthur, in a series of studies (cf. 1970, 1974) in which a group of Nsenga of Zambia were included, found a factor common to a number of the usual tests of cognitive style.

It seems clear from the studies reviewed above that the construct of cognitive style is as valid for describing an aspect of the cognitive structure of Africans as it has proven to be for characterizing the intellectual abilities of Europeans and Americans. The evidence suggests, however, that formal Western-type education may influence the elaboration of this apparently universal cognitive structure.

### Witkin's approach to differentiation: cognitive style

In this section an effort is made to examine the main postulates of Witkin's theory in the light of findings from cross-cultural studies in an attempt to assess the extent to which his theory can be shown to be universal. One of the main postulates of Witkin's theory is that an individual's degree of psychological differentiation is self-consistent within and across domains. This implies that an individual's performance in tasks requiring disembedding, even though they usually tap the visual perceptual domain, is consistent not only within the perceptual system as a whole but across other domains such as the articulation of body image and the sense of separate identity in the social fields. This postulate, though largely supported in studies undertaken in Euro-American societies, has been challenged by Wober (1966) on the basis of his own research results from studies with Nigerians. Citing the findings reported by Beveridge (1939) along with his own data, Wober has put forward the notion of 'sensotypes' and argued that the intake and proliferation of information from the various sense modalities differs according to culture and more particularly with ecology, so that the elaboration and relative importance or salience of these modalities will differ from one eco-cultural system to another. In his own study Wober used a modified version of the Rod and Frame Test (RFT) (see Fig. 7.3) for assessing the field dependence-independence of Southern Nigerians who are primarily agriculturalists living mainly in an area of rain forest. The RFT was administered in such a way that to determine whether the rod was perpendicular in the tilted frame it was necessary for subjects on some trials to use visual clues while on others to rely on information about the tilt of the chair they were sitting on from their own bodies, i.e. proprioceptive cues. The assumption underlying Wober's procedures was that since West African cultures included

Fig. 7.3 Rod and Frame Test (after Wober)

considerable elaboration of the proprioceptive and aurally perceived world, Nigerians would perform more adequately, i.e. identify deviations from the true horizontal or perpendicular, when the RFT trials relied upon proprioceptive feedback for a correct response than when the information was supplied visually. In this context correct identification is an indication of field independence. In comparing his findings with those of earlier American studies Wober found that Nigerians on the whole performed better than Americans when proprioceptive cues were accentuated but that this was not the case when performance depended on visual information. Furthermore, he reported in a later study (Wober 1969) that the usual strong relationship between performance on the RFT and the EFT, often considered alternative measures of field dependence-independence, was not replicated in Nigeria. Wober concluded on the basis of these results that 'it would appear that "style of cognitive functioning" is not so uniform throughout all fields on an individual's expression as had originally been supposed by Witkin' (p. 194).

The notion of 'sensotypes' is plausible but there have been a number of questions raised concerning Wober's empirical study and its theoretical implications. The assumption that the aural and proprioceptive domains are more important for West Africans in particular and all Africans generally was based on observation of the popularity of dancing and music as traditional cultural art forms. The prominence given to dancing in Nigeria and other African countries in 'festivals of art' seems to lend some support to Wober's conclusion concerning the popularity of dancing but what is apparently not given adequate consideration is that dances are also meant to be appreciated visually. The importance of visual enjoyment is demonstrated by the saying of the Igbo of Nigeria to the effect that blindness is the worst disease an individual can suffer. I have also shown (Okonji 1974) that many other African cultural groups attach a great deal of importance to visual perception; this is epitomized in a Shilluk proverb which states: 'The Shilluk only believe what they see' (Lienhardt 1954). In an attempt to explore an aspect of the self-consistency issue a battery of tests of cognitive style have been intercorrelated in some studies undertaken in Africa. These studies include those of Berry (1966), Dawson (1967a, b), Okonji (1969, 1973), MacArthur (1970, 1971, 1972, 1974) and Baran (1971). In many of these studies the RFT failed to correlate with other measures of field dependence-independence such as the EFT, Block Design (BD) and Human Figure Drawing Test (HFDT) but the latter three measures tended to correlate with each other consistently.

Elsewhere, outside Africa, a similar pattern of results has been reported. The study of Bergman & Engelbrektson (1973) in Norway may clarify the position. They correlated and factor analyzed data on the performance of ninety-three male students on the EFT, RFT and three other reference tests and on the basis of their analysis concluded that 'field dependence as assessed by RFT and EFT, is not a unitary trait but is determined by at least two factors: a factor specific for the RFT situation and a Gestalt psychological factor figural transformation...moreover, RFT and EFT had quite different factor patterns and shared only 4 to 16 % common variance' (p. 946). This same view is echoed by Pascual-Leone (1974) from his organismical studies: 'The mental processes which overcome the embedding context is similar in the RFT and EFT in the sense that both processes are operative. However, in the case of EFT[1] the mental process of RFT is different because for EFT this process is figurative' (p. 13).

## Cognitive style and personality

African studies of the personality aspects of psychological differentiation also raise doubts related to the problem of consistency across
perceptual domains. Some time ago I suggested (Okonji 1969) that
the aspect of cognitive style which had to do with personality
characteristics as distinct from perceptual and intellectual functioning
might be more susceptible to cultural moderation. This issue has not
yet been directly investigated but indirect evidence from studies in
Nigeria is quite suggestive. Lovegrove (1974), using the Eysenck
Personality Inventory (EPI) among Igbo students in an advanced
teachers training college in Nigeria, found no significant correlations
between Emotionality (E), Neuroticism (N) and the ability measures
he used. One of his explanations for these results is that 'the Igbo
are commonly regarded by those who are familiar with their life style
as being confident, outgoing, hardworking and hospitable' (Lovegrove
1974, 33). The implication is that most of the students may be
outgoing and socially independent but that most of them may also
be global and unanalytical in their cognitive functioning. In another
study involving Nigerian secondary school pupils in Lagos aged
between 17 and 22 years, Akinjagula (1974) found no significant
correlations between the EFT and scores on the Maudesley Personality
Inventory. An item analysis of responses to the personality measure
showed that over 90 per cent of the pupils of both sexes answered
extrovertedly to the items assessing sociability. The incidence of
extroversion in the sample as a whole (eighty-five pupils) was 70 per
cent. In explaining this result Akinjagula noted that Nigerians value
sociability highly, hence everyone strives to be sociable and outgoing
even if this is only a verbal or outward stance.

## Age-related changes

An important aspect of Witkin's conceptualization of psychological
differentiation is its developmental nature. In both cross-sectional
and longitudinal studies Witkin and his colleagues have shown
age-related changes in the ability to differentiate figure and ground
and reported improvement from childhood till early adulthood when
the ability to differentiate begins to stabilize. There are suggestions
that it may also show a decline in old age.

Age-related patterns of change have been reported in Africa as well
as from other areas. Jahoda (1970) found that among a sample of

Ghanaian University students those aged 25 years and below were more field independent, as reflected in their performance on the RFT and BD, than older students. Okonji & Olagbaiye (1974) found a highly significant linear age trend in performance on the Children's Embedded Figures Test (CEFT) for a sample of Nigerian primary school children in age groups 7 plus, 8 plus, 9 plus and 10 plus years. Using Coates' (1969) Preschool Embedded Figures Test (PEFT) Olowu (1974) in a study of 3, 4 and 5-year-old Nigerian boys and girls also found a clear linear age trend with differentiation increasing on the PEFT.

These African studies as well as others undertaken cross-culturally (cf. Witkin & Berry 1975) indicate a pan-cultural age-related change in the development of cognitive style showing a tendency for individuals to be more articulated in cognitive style as they grow older or until 30 to 40 years though a gradual decline may then begin. A note of caution is in order here. Most of the studies are cross-sectional, use parametric trend analysis (with the exception of the studies by Okonji & Olagbaiye 1974, and Olowu 1974) and seem to treat age as an independent variable without taking adequate account of confounding factors related to socio-cultural changes. The existing studies have contributed rather little from the point of view of helping to map out the developmental pattern of psychological differentiation universally or even within different cultural groups. One can only say that because of its organismic features the developmental pattern of psychological differentiation is most likely to have universal features.

### Sex differences

The earlier studies by Witkin and his collaborators observed sex differences in cognitive style with American males tending to be more analytic and differentiated than American females but later studies by Witkin and others have shown less pronounced sex differences. Berry's (1966) well-known study of the Eskimo which reported for the first time in any ethnic group an absence of sex differences in cognitive style has stimulated interest in this question. Since Berry published his findings and these were confirmed by MacArthur (1967) the study of sex differences in psychological differentiation has been extensively investigated cross-culturally (cf. Stewart 1974).

The cross-cultural evidence on sex differences shows some persistent though uneven, in terms of magnitude, differences in psychological differentiation usually favouring males. Men have a more articulated cognitive style than women in most cultures. In Africa, Asia and Latin America sex differences of this nature have been frequently and consistently reported in the literature (e.g. Kato 1965; Berry 1966; Canavan 1969; Okonji 1969; Mebane & Johnson 1970; Pande 1970a, b; Baran 1971; MacArthur 1972; Britain & Abad 1974; Chandra 1974; Witkin *et al.* 1974; Holtzman *et al.* 1975).

Among Jews who have retained their traditional orthodox religious ideology, on the other hand, females have been found to be more field-independent and articulated in their cognitive styles than males (e.g. Dershowitz 1971; Weller & Sharan 1971; Meizlik 1973). Currently the question is whether the instances of hunting and gathering societies and those of the orthodox Jewish sub-cultural groups are exceptions to a universal trend, a trend which some theorists have suggested has its basis in the hypothesis that females lateralize earlier and have less specialized cerebral hemispheres than men (Cohen *et al.* 1973; Sperry 1973; Pascual-Leone 1974).

## The origins of individual and group differences in cognitive style socialization

Witkin and his collaborators have argued that both environmental and biological factors are influential in the development of cognitive style. The environmental factors which have been isolated include socialization and family practices, cultural factors including socio-cultural change and ecological factors. In the area of socialization and family practices Witkin (1967) has specified the dimensions of mother–child interaction which are associated with differences in field articulation. These are techniques related to physical care and mother–child separation, socialization concerned with maternal control of the child's impulses and aggression, and mother's personal maturity. But individuals are not socialized in a vacuum; they grow up in specific cultural settings and are part of particular kinship networks which are embedded in a given ecological context. All of these factors are closely interrelated.

Many studies of socialization and family practices as they affect the development of cognitive style are of a global nature. I have attempted to relate specific family practices and socialization techniques with assessment of psychological differentiation in a study carried out in Uganda (Okonji 1973). Boys aged between 5 years 6 months and 5 years 10 months from both high and low income groups were assessed using the Portable Rod and Frame Test (PRFT), the Children's

Embedded Figures Test (CEFT) and the Coloured Raven Progressive Matrices. Mothers were required to complete a detailed questionnaire covering topics such as parents' age, education, occupation, information on family size, quality of housing, maintenance and nurturance of the child to be assessed, as well as data on his independence training. Methods of communication with the boy and maternal teaching strategies were observed directly in the laboratory. When the scores of the boys on the measures of cognitive style – PRFT and CEFT – were correlated with measures of independence training and maternal teaching strategies the correlations were low and non-significant.

Studies which have been more successful in showing a relationship between socialization and cognitive style in African societies have used ethnographic reports or retrospective accounts from adults of how they were disciplined as children. Berry (1966) required his adult subjects to make ratings of the strictness of their parents in bringing them up. His subjects were selected from among an Eskimo group and the Temne of Sierra Leone. Generally his results showed that children who rated their parents as 'more strict' performed in a relatively more field-dependent manner on the EFT and BD than those who rated their parents as less severe. In an earlier study Dawson (1967a, b) had used a similar procedure among the Mende and Temne of Sierra Leone. In the ethnographic literature describing these groups the child-rearing and family practices were seen as differing considerably and children's ratings of parental strictness and maternal dominance were in line with these accounts. In this study Dawson found a significant correlation between maternal strictness and dominance, and field dependence as measured by performance on the EFT and BD. Although the relationship between paternal strictness and field dependence was in the expected direction it was not significant though Dawson did report a significant relationship between the number of wives a man had and the cognitive style of his children. This finding is consonant with the view which has become more common in the literature that 'the extended family, the polygamous family, and the father-absent family...share the characteristics of providing a female salient surround from which strong male role models are lacking' (Witkin & Berry 1975, 57). This type of argument also suggests the possibility of some differences in the cognitive styles of children reared in matrilineal as contrasted with patrilineal kinship systems which would relate to differences in the position of women in the two types of social systems. No studies have

168    OGBOLU OKONJI

as yet been reported from matrilineal societies. MacArthur (1970, 1971, 1974) has also found child-rearing indicators to be associated with measures of cognitive style particularly with respect to independence training.

Witkin's postulated relationship between socialization practices and cognitive style is supported by African studies generally but my own study which related specific socialization practices with measures of cognitive style failed to produce a clear pattern of results.[2] This may indicate that the atomization of socialization practices is unrealistic and artificial since the practices never occur in isolation during socialization. Nevertheless, the need for clarification of the concepts used in socialization studies and cognitive style is evident.

### Other cultural factors

As I have noted earlier other cultural and social factors may also have important influences on the origins of cognitive style. These factors include authority patterns and social stratification in the larger community, the amount of emphasis placed on conformity to cultural norms, rural/urban differences, cultural contact and acculturation stress.

Hovey (1971) has chosen a global but suggestive approach in a pioneering study of the cultural factors which influence cognitive style. He compared some African societies (Masai, Ganda, Fon, Ashanti, Venda, Lamba, Ndubu, Chagga, Azande, Nuer, Tiv, Tallensi) to establish theoretically the relative position of each of these societies on the field dependence-independence dimension of cognitive style. These societies were selected from a cross-cultural summary because they could provide information on other cultural variables relevant to cognitive style theory. Finally by the use of multi-variate analysis Hovey attempted to isolate from the range of background factors those factors which predicted his hypothetically assigned position on the field dependence-independence dimension. From this analysis he produced a list of variables which made the highest contribution to the prediction of field dependence-independence. The list of variables is almost overwhelming and unilluminating in the end but the main usefulness of the study may lie in pointing out some cultural factors which may be associated with cognitive styles

[2] Holtzman et al. (1975) obtained a similar result showing a relationship between socialization and cognitive style at a global level but not with specific socialization variables.

in African societies. There is clearly a need, however, to go beyond this global and theoretical comparison to the actual administration of tests measuring cognitive style, to individuals from the societies which have been placed at different points on the global-articulated dimension of cognitive style solely on the basis of ethnographic evidence. Nonetheless, Hovey's conclusion that African societies appear to manifest different levels of articulation and would be differently placed on a global-articulated dimension lends further support to the view expressed earlier that the concept of cognitive style can be validly applied in cross-cultural research in Africa.

The role of pressure for social conformity on the development of cognitive style has been investigated in a number of cross-cultural studies. Most of this research has upheld the view that societies in which there is an insistence on almost unquestioning obedience to authority (religious, social or political) both in the larger society and in the family inhibit the development of an articulated cognitive style among its members and actually facilitate the development of global style. Studies that compare traditional and non-traditional societies, rural and urban societies and villages and towns or cities, indicate the importance of the pressure for conformity in the development of cognitive style.

Along with the studies of Berry and Dawson already discussed other research in Africa has reported differences in cognitive style among rural and urban peoples (e.g. Du Preez 1968; Baran 1971; Smith 1971 – all in South Africa; Okonji 1969 in West Africa). Traditional African societies are well known for their socialization which places emphasis on obedience, responsibility and respect for societal norms. I have reviewed the ethnographic literature from different parts of Africa and shown how pervasive these practices are (Okonji 1973). The only experimental study in Africa (of which I am aware) addressing this question was carried out by Munroe & Munroe (1972) among the agricultural Kikuyu of Kenya; they found that the pressure for obedience was high. In another study (Munroe, Munroe & Daniels 1973) the degree of socialization pressure for conformity was compared in three East African societies. In an Asch-type situation where an individual may either agree (conform) or disagree with the false reports of experimenter-provided stooges, the Kipsigis, a pastorally oriented people were more conformist than either of the two agricultural peoples, the Gusii and the Logoli. These findings are in agreement with the existing literature on cognitive style.

## Ecological factors

Closely related to the socio-cultural factors are the ecological dimensions. It is in fact very difficult to tease out these ecological variables. Ecological factors are intricately bound up with socialization practices and social organizational patterns especially with reference to the degree of 'tightness' or 'looseness' of social structures and authority patterns. Indeed, one is at a loss to understand whether or not there are really any ecological factors which do operate independently of the other socio-cultural factors. It has however been argued correctly that certain ecologies call for special spatial organizational skills for the survival of those who live in them. Ecologies like those of the Eskimo which are monotonous and relatively unvariagated make it necessary for the individuals who grow up in them to learn to structure their environment and to be able to discriminate and attend to minute details within them.

There is some evidence from Africa (Munroe & Munroe 1971; Nerlove, Munroe & Munroe 1971) showing that the range of experience with environmental exploration influences the development of some spatial ability. The spatial skills of the Eskimo and other hunting and gathering peoples may be due to their wide exploratory experience arising from this way of life or to the physical nature of terrain which we considered earlier, or to both.

The suggestion emerges quite strongly from the foregoing discussion that in the search for universals of human thought especially as it concerns strategies of thinking, the investigation of modes of socialization, itself a universal phenomenon, may be fruitful while bearing in mind some methodological problems which I have not dealt with here, it is possible to state, at least tentatively, some emerging trends from both African and other research concerned with psychological differentiation:

(i)   The existence of an analytical-global dimension in thinking strategies among individuals in different cultural groups seems fairly well established.

(ii)  Self-consistency within and across domains in cognitive style is demonstrable except in relation to social sensitivity and personality which are most susceptible to cultural modification.

(iii) The patterns of sex differences in psychological differentiation with particular reference to thinking styles are predictable on the basis of the theory of psychological differentiation, given adequate information concerning socialization practices and eco-cultural context in which they take place. Though the evidence from Africa, Asia and Latin America is more consistent with Witkin's original view that males are more field-independent than females, the evidence now available from America, and from hunting and gathering peoples, and from Orthodox Jews, is such that one can not uphold the idea of a universal pattern of sex differences.

(iv) The age-related developmental aspects of differentiation appear to be universal, i.e. differentiation increasing with age up to about 30 years, then stabilizing and finally declining in old age.

(v) The bio-social origins of differences in cognitive style seem to be the same among all human groups that have been studied across the world.

## References

Akinjagula, O. (1974) 'An experimental study of extraversion–introversion: field dependence-independence among Nigerians', Honours thesis, University of Lagos

Baran, S. (1971) 'Development and validation of a TAT-type projective test for use among Bantu-speaking people', Special report PERSO 138. Johannesburg, South Africa: National Institute of Personnel Research Council for Scientific and Industrial Research

Bergman, H. & Engelbrektson, K. (1973) 'An examination of factor structure of Rod and Frame Test and Embedded Figures Test', *Perceptual and Motor Skills* 37, 939–47

Berry, J. W. (1966) 'Temne and Eskimo perceptual skills', *International Journal of Psychology* 1, 207–29

—— (1967) 'Independence and conformity in subsistence level economy', *Journal of Personality and Social Psychology* 7, 415–18

—— (1974) 'Differentiation across cultures: cognitive style and affective style', in Dawson, J. L. M. & Lonner, W. J. (eds.) *Readings in cross-cultural psychology*. Hong Kong: University of Hong Kong Press

Beveridge, W. M. (1939) 'Some racial differences in perception', *British Journal of Psychology* 30, 57–64

Britain, S. D. & Abad, M. (1974) 'Field dependence: a function of sex and socialization in a Cuban and American group', Paper presented at the American Psychological Association, New Orleans, September

Canavan, D. (1969) 'Field dependence in children as a function of grade, sex and ethnic group membership', Paper presented at the Annual meeting of the American Psychological Association, Washington

Chandra, S. (1974) 'Cognitive development: Indians and Fijians', Paper presented at the 2nd Conference of the International Association for Cross-Cultural Psychology, Queen's University, Kingston, Ontario, August

Claeys, W. (1972) 'The factor structure of intelligence among teachers in the Congo', in Cronbach, L. J. & Drenth, P. J. D. (eds.) *Mental tests and cultural adaptation*. The Hague: Mouton

Coates, S. W. (1969) *Preschool Embedded Figures Tests* (manual), Palo Alto, Calif.: Consultive Psychologist Press

Cohen, D. B., Piscataway, N. J., Stanley, B. & Silverman, A. J. (1973) 'Field dependence and lateralization in the human brain', *Archives of General Psychiatry* 28, 165–7

Dawson, J. L. M. (1967a) 'Cultural and physiological influences upon spatial-perceptual process in West Africa', Part I, *International Journal of Psychology* 2, 115–28

—— (1967b) 'Cultural and physiological influences upon spatial-perceptual process in West Africa', Part II, *International Journal of Psychology* 2, 171–85

Dershowitz, Z. (1971) 'Jewish subcultural patterns and psychological differentiation', *International Journal of Psychology* 6, 223–31

Du Preez, P. D. (1968) 'Social change and field dependence in South Africa', *Journal of Social Psychology* 76, 265–6

El Abd, H. A. (1970) 'The intellect of East African students', *Multivariate Behavioural Research* 5, 423–33

Grant, G. V. (1972) 'The organisation of intellectual abilities of an African ethnic group in cultural transition', in Cronbach, L. J. & Drenth, P. J. D. (eds.) *Mental tests and cultural adaptation*. The Hague: Mouton

Holtzman, W. H., Diaz-Guerrero, R., Swartz, J. D. & Lara-Tapia, L. (1975) *Personality development in two cultures: a cross-cultural longitudinal study of school children in Mexico and the United States*. Austin: University of Texas Press

Hovey, R. L. (1971) 'Cognitive styles in African cultures: the global and articulated', Unpublished PhD thesis, Michigan State University

Irvine, S. H. (1969) 'Factor analysis of African abilities and attainments', *Psychological Bulletin* 71, 20–32

—— & Sanders, J. T. (1972) 'Logic, language, and method in construct identification across cultures', in Cronbach, L. J. & Drenth, P. J. D. (eds.) *Mental tests and cultural adaptation*. The Hague: Mouton

Jahoda, G. (1970) 'Supernatural beliefs and changing cognitive structure among Ghanaian University students', *Journal of Cross-Cultural Psychology* 1, 115–30

Kato, N. (1965) 'A fundamental study of rod and frame test', *Japanese Psychological Research* 7, 61–8

Lienhardt, G. (1954) 'The Shilluk of the Upper Nile', in Forde, D. (ed.) *African worlds: studies in the cosmological ideas and social values of African peoples*. Oxford University Press

Lovegrove, M. (1974) 'Extraversion, neuroticism and ability amongst Igbo students', *West African Journal of Educational and Vocational Measurement* 2, 24–34

MacArthur, R. S. (1967) 'Sex differences in field dependence for the Eskimo: a replication of Berry's findings', *International Journal of Psychology* 2, 139–40

—— (1970) 'Cognition and psychological influence for Eastern Eskimos and Nsenga Africans: some preliminaries', Paper presented at the Memorial University of Newfoundland Symposium on Cross-Cultural Research, St Johns, October

—— (1971) 'Mental abilities and psychosocial environment: Ingloolik Eskimos', Paper presented at Mid-Project Review, International Biological Programme, Ingloolik Project, Toronto, March

—— (1972) 'Some ability patterns: Central Eskimo and Nsenga Africans', Paper presented at the 20th International Congress of Psychology, Tokyo, August

—— (1974) 'Differential ability patterns: Intuit, Nsenga, and Canadian whites', Paper presented at the 2nd Conference of the International Association for Cross-Cultural Psychology, Queen's University, Kingston, Ontario, August

McGuigan, F. J. & Schoonover, R. A. (eds.) (1973) *The psychophysiology of thinking: studies of covert processes*. New York: Academic Press

Mead, M. (1950) *Male and female*. London: Golancz

Mebane, D. & Johnson, D. L. (1970) 'A comparison of the performance of Mexican boys and girls on Witkin's cognitive tasks', *American Journal of Psychology* 4, 227–39

Meizlik, F. (1973) 'Study of the effect of sex and cultural variables on field independence/dependence in a Jewish sub-culture', Unpublished Masters thesis, City University of New York

Munroe, R. L. & Munroe, R. H. (1971) 'Effect of environmental experience on spatial ability in an East African society', *Journal of Social Psychology* 83, 15–22

—— & Munroe, R. H. (1972) 'Obedience among children in an East African society', *Journal of Cross-Cultural Psychology* 3, 395–9

——, Munroe, R. H. & Daniels, R. E. (1973) 'Relation of subsistence economy to conformity in three East African societies', *Journal of Social Psychology* 84, 149–50

Nerlove, S. B., Munroe, R. H. & Munroe, R. L. (1971) 'Effect of environmental experience on spatial ability: a replication', *Journal of Social Psychology* 84, 3–10

Okonji, M. O. (1969) 'Differential effects of rural and urban upbringing on the development of cognitive styles', *International Journal of Psychology* 4, 293–305

—— (1973) 'Child-rearing and the development of cognitive style in Uganda', Pre-publication draft of a monograph to be published by the University of Lagos Press

—— (1974) 'African approaches to the study of behavior,' Paper presented at the 2nd Conference of the International Association for Cross-Cultural Psychology, Queen's University, Kingston, Ontario, August

174    OGBOLU OKONJI

—— & Olagbaiye, O. (1974) 'Egocentrism and psychological differen-
tiation: a cross-cultural perspective', Paper presented at the 2nd
Conference of the International Association for Cross-Cultural
Psychology, Queen's University, Kingston, Ontario, August

Olowu, A. A. (1974) 'Cognitive style among Nigerian preschool children
in age, sex, and socio-economic status dimensions', Honours thesis,
University of Lagos

Pande, C. G. (1970a) 'Performance of a sample of Indian students on a
test of field-dependence', *Indian Journal of Experimental Psychology*
4, 46–50

—— (1970b) 'Sex differences in field-dependence: confirmation with an
Indian sample', *Perceptual and Motor Skills* 31, 70

Pascual-Leone, J. (1974) 'A neo-Piagetian process: structural mode of
Witkin's psychological differentiation.' Extended version of a paper
presented at the 2nd Conference of the International Association for
Cross-Cultural Psychology, Queen's University, Kingston, Ontario,
August

Piaget, J. (1963) *The origins of intelligence in children.* New York:
W. W. Norton. (Originally published in 1936 as *La naissance de
l'intelligence chez l'enfant.*)

Smith, T. V. G. (1971) 'Acculturation and field-dependence among the
Xhosa', *Journal of Behavioural Sciences* 1, 121–3

Sperry, R. W. (1973) 'Lateral specialisation of cerebral function in
surgically separated hemispheres', in McGuigan, F. J. & Schoonover,
R. A. (eds.) *The psychophysiology of thinking : studies of covert processes.*
New York: Academic Press

Stewart, V. M. (1974) 'Sex and temperament revisited: a cross-cultural
look at psychological differentiation in males and females', Paper
presented at the 2nd Conference of the International Association for
Cross-Cultural Psychology, Queen's University, Kingston, Ontario,
August

Vernon, P. E. (1969) *Intelligence and cultural environment.* London:
Methuen

—— (1973) 'Multivariate approaches to the study of cognitive style', in
Royce, J. R. (ed.) *Multivariate analysis and psychology.* New York:
Academic Press

Weller, L. & Sharan, S. (1971) 'Articulation of body concept among
first-grade Israeli children', *Child Development* 42, 1553–9

Werner, H. (1948) *Comparative psychology of mental development.* New
York: Science Editions

Witkin, H. A. (1967) 'A cognitive style approach to cross-cultural research', *International Journal of Psychology* 2, 233–50

—— & Berry, J. W. (1975) 'Psychological differentiation in cross-cultural
perspective', *Journal of Cross-Cultural Psychology* 6, 1–87

——, Dyk, R., Paterson, H. E., Goodenough, D. R. & Karp, S. A. (1962)
*Psychological differentiation.* New York: Wiley

——, Price-Williams, D., Bertini, M., Christiansen, B., Oltman, P. K., Ramirez, M. & Meel, J. van (1974) 'Social conformity and psychological differentiation', *International Journal of Psychology* 9, 1, 11–29

Wober, M. (1966) 'Sensotypes', *Journal of Social Psychology* 70, 181–9

—— (1969) 'Adapting Witkin's field-dependence theory to accommodate new information from Africa', in Price-Williams, D. R. (ed.) *Cross-cultural studies*, Modern Psychology Readings. Harmondsworth: Penguin Books

# 8    Cognitive development, education and social mobility

*Barbara Lloyd*

In this paper I examine data collected from two groups of Yoruba children and ask whether it is meaningful to talk about universals of intellectual growth. I argue that answers can only be offered with reference to specific assessment procedures and that these methods and their interpretations are embedded in particular psychological theories. The problem of choosing between solutions arises since different theories lead to different conclusions about the course of cognitive development.

In the second part of the paper I suggest that rather than seeking criteria for selection among the solutions within psychological theory, attention may be directed to the social world in which these children participate. From an analysis of the educational system of Western Nigeria and in particular its selection mechanisms it appears that a model stressing differences has the best predictive validity. Since this description, of ever-increasing disparity between the two groups of children, is personally unacceptable it seems worthwhile considering what contribution psychologists may make to altering the situation.

The children whom I studied in Ibadan participated in research on physical growth at the Institute of Child Health in the University of Ibadan from 1962 until 1976. The two samples, one from Oje – a traditional quarter in the indigenous Yoruba city of Ibadan – and the other composed of children from Yoruba families in which the mother had completed secondary schooling or its equivalent, were originally selected to provide maximum contrast on a set of physical measures. The criteria of admission to the Elite sample were set in what has proved to be a reasonably successful effort to provide growth data reflecting development in near optimal conditions. From analyses of lying height, weight and head circumference Janes (1975) has shown that Elite boys surpass Oje children on all measures and that Elite boys equal or surpass British norms based upon Tanner's studies. However, consideration of small growth spurts and dips suggests that

176

TABLE 8.1. *Design of 1968 study: number of children tested*

| Age group (years) | 3½ | | 4½ | | 5½ | | 6½ | | 7½ | | |
|---|---|---|---|---|---|---|---|---|---|---|---|
| Sex | M | F | M | F | M | F | M | F | M | F | Totals |
| Oje | 4 | 4 | 4 | 4 | 4 | 4 | 4 | 4 | 4 | 4 | 40 |
| Elite | 4 | 4 | 4 | 4 | 4 | 4 | 4 | 4 | 4 | 4 | 40 |

Piagetian tasks, Oddity Learning and Binet administered to all children.

*Restudy in 1973: number of children tested*

| Age group (years) | 8½ | | 9½ | | 10½ | | 11½ | | 12½ | | |
|---|---|---|---|---|---|---|---|---|---|---|---|
| Sex | M | F | M | F | M | F | M | F | M | F | Totals |
| Oje | 3 | 3 | 3 | 3 | 4 | 4 | 4 | 4 | 4 | 4 | 36 |
| Elite | 4 | 4 | 4 | 4 | 4 | 4 | 4 | 4 | 3 | 4 | 39 |

Piagetian tasks: 8½ years only, Binet administered to all children. Percentage loss in restudy: Oje, 10, Elite, 2½.

*1973 replication: number of children tested*

| Age group (years) | 3½ | | 4½ | | 5½ | | 6½ | | 7½ | | |
|---|---|---|---|---|---|---|---|---|---|---|---|
| Sex | M | F | M | F | M | F | M | F | M | F | Totals |
| Oje | 3 | 4 | 4 | 4 | 4 | 4 | 4 | 4 | 0 | 0 | 31 |
| Elite | 4 | 4 | 4 | 4 | 4 | 4 | 4 | 4 | 0 | 0 | 32 |

completely optimal growth has not yet been achieved by the Elite sample.

## Cognitive development

My own studies have included research on social background factors and on attitudes towards rearing children (Lloyd 1966, 1967, 1969). In addition, in 1968 and again in 1973, I assessed children from the two growth study samples on various cognitive tasks. In the first study eighty children aged 3½ to almost 8 years were seen individually three times. In the 1973 restudy seventy-five children from the 1968 sample were re-examined and sixty-three new children between the ages of 3½ and almost 7 years were also tested. Table 8.1 shows the children who participated in each study divided in groups according to family background, age and sex. It can be seen from Table 8.1 that only one Elite child and four Oje children were lost in the restudy. Two of the Oje children had died (and one girl returned to the north before completing the Intelligence Test).

The first session in the 1968 assessment programme was devoted to examining children with a variety of Piagetian tasks which would require concrete operations for full understanding. The second session explored oddity learning and in the third a double-translated Yoruba version of the Stanford-Binet Intelligence Scale was administered. The oddity learning tasks were eliminated in the 1973 study due to a failure to discriminate among individuals. At the youngest age levels many children showed no improvement in either of the two sets of thirty-six learning trials while at the oldest age Elite performance was often almost without error. Differences which could be explained in terms of family background were found and an overall Elite superiority was clear from visual inspection of the results but restrictions on variance which both total failure and errorless performance imposed precluded statistical analysis (Lloyd 1971a).

My original assumption had been that performance on the learning task would be the least susceptible to cultural influences while the standard intelligence scale would yield the greatest differences between Oje and Elite children and that performance on the various Piagetian tasks would fall somewhere in between. In the terms of this discussion, I had assumed the universality of the learning process in the oddity problems, i.e. learning a concept with reinforcement for correct responses but without other informative corrections would result in similar behaviour in Elite and Oje children. Furthermore, I predicted increasingly greater differences on measures of Piagetian and psychometric intelligence. My prediction about oddity learning performance was wrong. I have not systematically explored the sources of difference in the behaviour of Elite and Oje children but observations during training suggested different scanning as well as different response strategies with Oje children failing to examine the five stimuli and choosing instead one particular position in the array.

The Piagetian tasks and the Binet were used again in 1973. While all the children recruited for the replication study were tested with both of these instruments the Piagetian tasks were used only with the youngest group in the restudy, i.e. the children who had been $3\frac{1}{2}$ to almost 4 years in 1968 and were $8\frac{1}{2}$ to 9 years old in 1973. The Piagetian tasks were not given to the older groups as near errorless performance would be expected for all $9\frac{1}{2}$ to 10-year-old Elite children and for many, though not all, Oje children of this age. The Binet was re-administered to all available children from the 1968 sample.

In the discussion of possible universals of cognitive development I shall first consider both sets of data based upon the Piagetian tasks and then examine the two sets of Binet results.

## The Piagetian model of development

Piaget's early studies of children's thinking which described age specific stages were challenged almost fifty years ago by results from non-western cultures. An accumulating body of new cross-cultural evidence has recently been accompanied by an interest in the universality of Piaget's structural analysis of cognitive development despite fluctuations in age of specific stages. I considered (Lloyd 1972) some of these questions by first comparing Piagetian and psychometric concepts of intelligence, by then examining cross-cultural studies of conservation which require concrete operatory thinking, and finally by speculating about the likelihood of finding evidence for the universality of formal operations. At about the same time Dasen reviewed the cross-cultural Piagetian literature and brought to his analysis the added sophistication of a Genevan training in psychology (Dasen 1972). When his summary was published in 1972 non-western data on sensori-motor development scarcely existed and the now compelling arguments for the universality of sensori-motor intelligence were just evolving. Thus the major portion of Dasen's review was devoted to the development of concrete operations and the horizontal décalages of specific concepts typical of this stage. Both summaries supported Peluffo's (1967) earlier hypothesis that the concrete operations would be found in members of any society with agriculture and handicrafts. The specific ages and orders in which the ability to handle such different problems as the conservation of substance, weight and volume or hierarchical classification developed were examined closely. Subsequently, emphasis has shifted to analyses of sequential delays in cognitive growth and explanations have been offered in terms of westernization, urbanization, formal schooling and language, or in idiosyncratically rich socialization such as having a father who is a professional potter (cf. Cole & Scribner 1974).

Piaget wrote in 1966 of the need for cross-cultural studies to unravel two biological and two social factors influencing cognitive development but little attention has been given to the former. Experiential variables of a particular nature, which can be grouped under the second social factor specified by Piaget, have, as I have already noted, received most consideration. My Yoruba data can contribute little towards disentangling the four factors as it is likely that both the biological variables noted by Piaget and experiential aspects of education and family sub-culture could be invoked to explicate any Oje/Elite differences in operatory development. In my design these factors are confounded in that the homes of Elite children provide not only education and intellectual stimulation but also superior nutrition, hygiene and medical care.

My original selection of tasks to measure the development of concrete operations was determined by the ages of children available for study at the Institute of Child Health and by the wish to use techniques which had been clearly described in published accounts. Thus the collection included three conservation problems – identity and equivalence of number, and continuous quantity after Almy (1966),seriation using rods of different lengths and colours as described by Inhelder & Piaget (1964) and free and structured classification tasks replicating Lovell, Mitchell & Everett (1962). One innovation was to examine each child twice on conservation of number identity and of equivalence, once using the standard test materials, i.e. inch-cube red and yellow bricks, and once with everyday Yoruba objects, i.e. blue and red cough sweets bought in Oje market. The testing was undertaken on both occasions by Yoruba, female undergraduates who had some familiarity with Piaget's theory of development and who were trained and encouraged to elicit optimal performance from all the children.

In analyzing the 1968 data I have used a numerical scoring system rather than the usual stage description. By this method each aspect of a child's response, including the production of an adequate justification for an operatory decision, is assigned a value. Tuddenham (1971) has reported a similar procedure. Both of these approaches are closer to the quantitative analysis of test performance than to the subtler inferences usually required in the diagnosis of Piagetian stage development.

Averages for the total scores on the six Piagetian tasks are presented in Table 8.2 by age, for Oje and Elite children. These scores could range from 0 to 30. The values for the $7\frac{1}{2}$-year-old group in the original study have been placed within the 1973 results to make clear the apparently steady progress towards completely operatory

TABLE 8.2. *Six Piagetian tasks : total scores*

1968 results ($N = 80$)

| Age group (years) | $3\frac{1}{2}$* | $4\frac{1}{2}$ | $5\frac{1}{2}$ | $6\frac{1}{2}$ | $7\frac{1}{2}$ |
|---|---|---|---|---|---|
| Oje | 1·5 | 7·7 | 8·8 | 15·3 | 17·4 |
| Elite | 4·4 | 9·7 | 17·2 | 20·7 | 23·6 |
| Oje/Elite difference | 2·9 | 2·0 | 8·4 | 5·4 | 6·2 |

1973 results ($N = 78$)

| Age group (years) | $3\frac{1}{2}$ | $4\frac{1}{2}$ | $5\frac{1}{2}$ | $6\frac{1}{2}$ | $7\frac{1}{2}$† | $8\frac{1}{2}$* |
|---|---|---|---|---|---|---|
| Oje | 1·6 | 4·4 | 11·0 | 16·0 | 17·4 | 21·0 |
| Elite | 5·0 | 8·9 | 15·0 | 20·0 | 23·6 | 26·6 |
| Oje/Elite difference | 3·4 | 4·5 | 4·0 | 4·0 | 6·2 | 5·6 |

* $3\frac{1}{2}$-year-olds in 1968 }
  $8\frac{1}{2}$-year-olds in 1973 } repeated measures on same children.
† $7\frac{1}{2}$-year-olds' 1968 values repeated for 1973 table.

performance. The direction of difference follows that of the physical growth data: Elite children perform at consistently higher levels than Oje children. Statistical evidence for this conclusion comes from analyses of variance undertaken on each set of data. Family background was assessed as a main effect along with age and sex and was highly significant, i.e. $P < 0.001$. The other main source of variance to reach significance was age (again at the level, $P < 0.001$). Since sex was not significant the scores for boys and girls were combined for tabular presentation. None of the interaction terms were significant.

The absolute difference between Oje and Elite performance at given ages varies in the two sets of data but the overall pattern of development appears similar and the 1968 values for $7\frac{1}{2}$-year-olds fit into the gap in the 1973 results. Although the 1973 testing was carried out by different undergraduates and under the supervision of Mr Bundy, a Lecturer in Psychology at the University of Lagos, rather than my own, the similarity is sufficient to suggest the reliability of the procedure. Both sets of results support the hypothesis that in the two samples the children are moving towards completely operatory behaviour though a delay of at least one year is evident in the performance of Oje children.

Commenting on the Piagetian battery Mr Bundy concluded that while, as a set, the tasks appeared well within the experiences of both samples children he had reservations about the anticipatory seriation exercise and free classification. He noted that some children lacked experience with paper and pencil and felt this might interfere with performance on the anticipatory drawing of the ordered rods, while the twenty-four objects of the free sort, he believed, were confusing and hindered potential classifying.

The particular difficulties noted by Mr Bundy lend additional weight to an earlier decision to examine in detail only the conservations. In a study using the 1968 data I have shown (Lloyd 1971b) that Yoruba conservation results are as good or better than those of the American children described in the monograph from which the procedures were adapted. Only on number conservation which required the ability to count to eleven did Oje children have more difficulty than their American counterparts. Comparisons with other African groups were favourable though Yoruba performance did not match the near-errorless results of $7\frac{1}{2}$- to 8-year-old Tiv children (Price-Williams 1961).

The random assignment for the first assessment on conservation of number and equivalence of either local or standard test materials to half the individuals in each of the age by sex by family background cells of the total design allowed measurement of the effects of practice as well as of difference in stimulus material. A practice effect was found in both sets of data significant at $P < 0.05$, but the use of different materials did not influence performance directly. Practice did not interact with materials though in the 1968 analysis of variance a number of interactions with materials were significant. The easiest to interpret was a materials by sex interaction with males performing a little better when bricks were used while females were better with sweets. Further clarification can be obtained by considering the means for the materials by sex by family background interaction which showed the sex typing by materials only for Elite children while Oje boys performed at higher levels than girls whichever stimulus material was used in testing.

A similar analysis of the 1973 data replicated the main effects of age, family background and practice; however, the only significant interaction was materials by sex by practice. Boys performed at higher levels when bricks were used in the second testing while girls were better if sweets were used second. There is no ready answer to why the results should be different in 1973 though there is the possibility of an examiner effect as all the examiners were female in 1968, while Mr Bundy supervised all data collection in 1973. Although the particular interactions which achieved significance were different the effect was in the same direction with boys performing better on bricks and girls on sweets.

The similarity in the quantitative analyses of results from the two assessments with the Piagetian tasks can be interpreted as evidence of the reliability of the procedures. They allow conclusions to be drawn about test materials, practice and age differences.

Familiar, linguistically easier to encode materials do not significantly affect Yoruba children's performance though other studies in the literature preclude a strong statement such as that operatory thinking is unaffected by the figurative content of the tasks, i.e. by stimulus material. In studies with American children, Uzgaris (1964) using four sets of stimuli to test conservation of substance, weight and volume, found an effect for materials. So too did Lester & Klein (1973) comparing conservation of area. In one version of the task they used a pair of green boards to represent farms on which buildings were placed in different arrangements, while in the other two sets of six cubes each were used and the arrangement of cubes varied. Not surprisingly, rural Guatamalan children found the first test of conservation easier and their mothers too judged the first stimulus material more familiar. This cross-cultural result allegedly showing a change in performance as a function of materials probably involves a change in task also, i.e. the transformations of space which are required are modified along with the change in materials. The most cautious conclusion which can be drawn is that the stimulus changes used in studying Yoruba children were not of sufficient magnitude to affect thinking.

The effects of practice are clearer. Lester & Klein reported some improvement when retesting a month later but the practice effect here was immediate and replicated in the second set of data. This improvement cannot readily be explained in terms of cognitive growth and seems more likely to reflect the effect on performance of familiarity with the task rather than a change describable in terms of cognitive structures.

Taken together these results make one chary about drawing conclusions about universals of development. Although the data can be interpreted in terms of a milieu effect (family background) there are also highly specific experiential factors, i.e. practice, contributing to the results. A direct challenge to the generally accepted view that the rate of development of the concrete operations is modified significantly by milieu comes from Kamara & Easley (1977). They have presented a methodological critique of the cross-cultural Piagetian literature to sustain their attack on the view, accepted by Piaget himself, that children who grow up in societies little influenced by western culture will fall behind by anything from two to seven years in the development of concrete operations. They see active manipulatory experience, be it with manufactured objects or sand, mud and water, as the source of a universal structured, cognitive competence as described by Piaget. However, they note major shortcomings in the cross-cultural research on conservation which make it difficult to verify or refute this hypothesis. These are analyzed under four headings: (1) inaccurate age determination, (2) linguistic and cultural communication failures between the researcher and the children studied, (3) lack of an adequate statistical model to evaluate the results which have been produced as evidence for the retardation effect, and (4) the use of rigidly administered tests which measure performance rather than techniques designed to elicit underlying cognitive competences.

A strength of the Kamara & Easley argument is their demonstration of ways in which research can be improved along each of the dimensions noted. Taking Kamara's work in Sierra Leone as an example they show (a) how to overcome the problem of determining chronological age, (b) the benefit of belonging to the non-western culture whose members are the subjects of study, (c) statistical methods for analyzing Piagetian stage results, and (d) an example of competence testing and analysis using a Temne protocol.

Since my own original analyses were based directly on performance and as the research satisfied Kamara & Easley's criticism on points (a) and (b), i.e. the dates of birth are precise and the interviewers were Yoruba, I decided to re-analyze some of the conservation data in a manner more closely resembling a search for competence and to test the results using the statistic provided by Kamara & Easley. Specifically I did this by looking at conservation of equivalence and continuous quantity, but disregarding number, since Elite children, who on average begin schooling at 4 years 2 months (Lloyd 1966) have an advantage on the number task which reflects training as well as thinking. In diagnosing competence on the equivalence conservation I used both trials: if after practice on the first equivalence task a child could then give evidence of operatory thinking in terms both of judgement and justification, he was counted as a conserver.

Classification by stage, family background and age is shown in Table 8.3. Inspection of the distribution of non-conservers, inter-

TABLE 8.3. *Conservation of equivalence (E) and continuous quantity (Q): number of children at each stage by age and family background*

1968 results (N = 80)

| Age group (years) | 3½–4 | | 4½–5 | | 5½–6 | | 6½–7 | | 7½–8 | |
|---|---|---|---|---|---|---|---|---|---|---|
| | E | Q | E | Q | E | Q | E | Q | E | Q |
| **Oje** | | | | | | | | | | |
| Non-conserver | 8 | 7 | 3 | 2 | 3 | 2 | 0 | 0 | 0 | 0 |
| Intermediate | 0 | 1 | 5 | 6 | 5 | 6 | 4 | 6 | 3 | 2 |
| Conserver | 0 | 0 | 0 | 0 | 0 | 0 | 4* | 2 | 5 | 6* |
| **Elite** | | | | | | | | | | |
| Non-conserver | 3 | 4 | 0 | 2 | 0 | 0 | 0 | 0 | 0 | 0 |
| Intermediate | 5 | 4 | 8 | 6 | 5 | 6 | 3 | 3 | 1 | 2 |
| Conserver | 0 | 0 | 0 | 0 | 3 | 2 | 5* | 5* | 7 | 6 |

1973 results (N = 78)

| Age group (years) | 3½–4 | | 4½–5 | | 5½–6 | | 6½–7 | | 8½–9 | |
|---|---|---|---|---|---|---|---|---|---|---|
| | E | Q | E | Q | E | Q | E | Q | E | Q |
| **Oje** | | | | | | | | | | |
| Non-conserver | 7 | 6 | 6 | 5 | 4 | 1 | 0 | 1 | 0 | 0 |
| Intermediate | 0 | 1 | 2 | 3 | 2 | 7 | 5 | 5 | 3 | 4 |
| Conserver | 0 | 0 | 0 | 0 | 2 | 0 | 3 | 2 | 4* | 3 |
| **Elite** | | | | | | | | | | |
| Non-conserver | 7 | 5 | 4 | 3 | 0 | 0 | 0 | 0 | 0 | 0 |
| Intermediate | 1 | 3 | 4 | 5 | 5 | 7 | 3 | 7 | 1 | 0 |
| Conserver | 0 | 0 | 0 | 0 | 3 | 1 | 5* | 1 | 7 | 8* |

\* Conservers outnumber others in all other categories.
E = conservation of equivalence; Q = conservation of continuous quantity.

mediate and conserving children indicates that differences in the 'competence' of Elite and Oje children of the same age are not great. Kamara & Easley's static for testing the proportions of conservers by age group across two samples was used to compare Oje and Elite children on equivalence and continuous quantity in 1968 and in 1973. None of the four comparisons were statistically significant though on continuous quantity, where there was only one assessment upon which to base a diagnosis of level of development, the probability of these proportions occurring by chance was $P < 0.10$. Conventionally the null hypothesis is not rejected but it should be noted that the test proposed by Kamara & Easley errs on the side of caution.[1] Closer inspection of Table 8.3 reveals certain anomalies. Unlike the 1968 results, on equivalence only Elite children showed a majority of conservers by $6\frac{1}{2}$ to 7 years. On three of the four comparisons the competence of the $8\frac{1}{2}$- to 9-year-olds failed to surpass that of the $7\frac{1}{2}$- to 8-year-olds in the 1968 study. Thus rather than the steady but slower progress towards operatory thinking shown in Table 8.2 this analysis yields a different conclusion on the delay issue.

Returning to a consideration of the universality of delays in operatory development, it now appears that different conclusions are possible depending upon the method of analysis employed. The problem of choosing an appropriate assessment of operatory thinking is a familiar one (Smedslund 1969) and not unique to cross-cultural investigations. The conflict between the two conclusions can be construed in terms of competence and performance or perhaps between the behaviourist and cognitive approaches in psychological research (cf. Goodnow 1969). Before attempting to choose one of the two I will present the results of assessment with the Stanford-Binet Intelligence Scale.

### Binet intelligence testing

In choosing the Binet Scale I was aware that it would reveal differences between Oje and Elite children but I preferred it to other individual tests of intelligence because of its variety of objects and tasks. As with any scale of this type the Binet depends heavily on language, especially at older ages. A great effort was made to develop an adequate and appropriate Yoruba translation though in so doing the standardization of items by age was lost. This problem is particularly acute for the vocabulary sub-test and is typified by the difficulty encountered in translating 'muzzle' (as in 'muzzle your dog'). There is no precise Yoruba equivalent but to achieve the same sense Abraham, in his standard Yoruba–English dictionary, lists a word composed of the Yoruba elements for 'cover the mouth'. Children speaking Yoruba would find the Yoruba term easier as they could interpret the constituent morphemes while children tested in English would be confronted with the single morpheme, muzzle, which cannot be decomposed.

In 1968 we succeeded in persuading almost all Elite children aged

---

[1] As a value of $P = 0.5$ is assigned to cells in which no children appear as conservers the test is probably biased against rejecting the null hypothesis.

$3\frac{1}{2}$ to 8 years to accept the Yoruba version of the Binet. Mr Bundy and his assistants encountered greater difficulty while testing children who ranged from $3\frac{1}{2}$ to almost 13 years. Although all assessment was designed to elicit optimum performance Mr Bundy noted that five different linguistic variants could be identified and that their effects could not be evaluated systematically. Along with pure Yoruba and English versions of the test Mr Bundy distinguished coordinate bilingual ability as well as compound bilingualism weighted to either Yoruba or English.

An additional source of difference in Oje and Elite behaviour is the well-documented association between performance on the Binet and education. Free primary schooling from the age of 6 has been provided in Western Nigeria since 1956 but the educational experiences of children in the two samples vary considerably. When I matched 12-year-old Oje and Elite girls to compare performance on a seriation matrix I found that while Oje girls of 12 years were in Primary Classes 4, 5 or 6, the Elite girls of the same age were already in Form I or II of secondary grammar schools. Elite children not only start school earlier but attend better schools with smaller classes and more highly trained teachers.

Results of assessment with the Binet are presented in Table 8.4 as average Mental Ages (MAs). I have not transformed these scores into IQs because of the problems of standardization and even these values should be interpreted with caution. There is a difference in performance levels in 1968 and 1973 with the latter consistently lower. This may reflect differences in the language used in assessment as well as the employment of stricter criteria in 1973. Overall the pattern of Oje/Elite differences is in line with expectation, though the increasing difference with age is both clearer and achieves statistical significance in the comparison at nine age levels in the later testing (cf. Lloyd & Easton 1977).

In the analysis of variance on MAs in each set of data the main effects of age and family background were highly significant ($P < 0.001$). Sex was not significant nor were any of the interactions in the original data. Similarly, in the regression of MA on Chronological Age (CA) the slopes of the regression lines for the two groups showed no statistically significant difference. Here the 1973 results differ. The interaction of family background and age was significant ($0.01 < P < 0.05$) and the corresponding regression analyses showed significant differences in the slopes of the regression lines of MA on CA for the two samples. Given the age range from $3\frac{1}{2}$ to almost 13

TABLE 8.4. *Mean mental age (MA) scores*

*1968 results (N = 80)*

| Age group (years) | 3½ | 4½ | 5½ | 6½ | 7½ |
|---|---|---|---|---|---|
| Oje | 3·2 | 5·0 | 5·7 | 6·6 | 8·2 |
| Elite | 5·0 | 6·1 | 7·7 | 9·1 | 11·1 |
| Elite/Oje difference | 1·8 | 1·1 | 2·0 | 2·5 | 2·9 |

*1973 results (N = 138)*

| Age group (years) | 3½ | 4½ | 5½ | 6½ | 8½ | 9½ | 10½ | 11½ | 12½ |
|---|---|---|---|---|---|---|---|---|---|
| Oje | 2·92 | 3·62 | 4·67 | 5·08 | 6·17 | 7·29 | 8·29 | 9·58 | 9·12 |
| Elite | 3·46 | 4·71 | 6·21 | 7·00 | 9·00 | 9·58 | 11·37 | 12·92 | 12·75 |
| Elite/Oje difference | 0·54 | 1·09 | 1·54 | 1·92 | 2·83 | 2·29 | 3·08 | 3·34 | 3·63 |

3½, 4½, 5½, 6½, 7½-year-olds in 1968 ⎫ same children.
8½, 9½, 10½, 11½, 12½-year-olds in 1973 ⎭

years, the classic effect frequently shown in social-class comparisons among American children appeared. A performance deficit in children from less privileged homes increases with age. This result can be viewed as a universal in the sense that intelligence testing reliably produces evidence of such an increasing difference when children from diverse backgrounds are compared.

With these Binet results there is yet another set of data and a further model with which to consider universals of cognitive development. The question can then be formulated – which of the three descriptions of growth should be considered the most appropriate representation of universal aspects of intellectual development: a difference which eventually disappears (first Piagetian analysis), the possibility of no or minimal difference (Piagetian stage analysis) or an ever increasing disparity in performance?

Evaluation of the three descriptions of Yoruba cognitive development may be clarified by considering a fourth, that of Kagan & Klein (1973). They argue, concerning universals of cognitive growth, that 'there are few dumb children in the world if one classifies them from the perspective of the community of adaptation, but millions of dumb children if one classifies them from the perspective of another society' (p. 961). This conclusion was reached after demonstrating that while Guatamalan village infants show a cognitive deficit along such dimensions as attention, object permanence and fear of strangers in infancy, they eventually perform as well as American children on tasks measuring recall and recognition memory, perceptual analysis and inference. Specifically the thrust of their attack is against the common assumption that early retardation is irreversible and the obvious ceiling effects on their tasks in childhood, i.e. the near-perfect performance of American children at age 6 matched only by Indian children at 10 or 11 years, is interpreted as evidence for the universality of the basic cognitive competences these tasks are held to reflect.

In my own pursuit of cognitive universals I have mused for some time about the facile nature of the Kagan & Klein argument. Perhaps the most obvious criticism, that in viewing development from an evolutionary perspective it is inconceivable that man as a species could fail to have developed a set of common cognitive competences, is already well known (cf. Piaget 1971; Cole *et al.* 1972). Another source of unease is the worry which I share with Cole & Bruner (1971) about the search for competences which are unrelated to situations and cultures. Thinking in this vein I have felt the need to reframe the question and to ask: which model of cognitive development might best predict the future achievements of Elite and Oje children in formal education and in society?

## Education and social mobility

The heritage of British rule is clearly seen in Nigerian educational institutions and values. A formal, literary schooling is widely desired. Commenting on the development of grammar school education from 1859 to 1970 Adeyinka has written: 'Nigerians tend to look on secondary grammar school education as a necessary qualification for entry into highly rewarding white collar jobs' (1973, 371). Despite the recent rapid growth in the number of grammar schools Adeyinka admits ruefully that demand has consistently outstripped available facilities. Perhaps of greater concern for the nation is his observation that those children who do obtain the coveted grammar school education no longer wish to farm nor are they willing to return to small village communities. In an equally gloomy manner he comments that the post-secondary facilities were woefully inadequate. In 1970, Adeyinka reports, the number of grammar schools in Nigeria had grown to 524. The goal of most grammar school students was the University but in that same year the five Nigerian universities offered only about 2,000 places to new entrants. A consequence of this restriction has been that teacher training and technical college places are sought, not only for the vocational preparation which they offer, but as an alternative route by which eventually to reach university.

Peter Lloyd (1974, 91) has summarized the educational journey to a high status position in the occupational system in a flow diagram describing the progress of a hypothetical 1,000 children in Western Nigeria entering the primary school system in 1957. It shows that only half the number, 500, reach Primary 6 and there sit the school leaving examination. Of the 300 who pass this examination sixty obtain grammar school places and of the forty-five who eventually sit the West African School Certificate, thirty obtain a pass. Even then the passage to university is not won, for only half the remaining thirty achieve the necessary Higher School Certificate. Five students gain the qualifications for university through teacher training colleges and private study but even so, of the initial 1,000 only twenty have achieved their desired goal and passport to a high status job. Perhaps the ultimate irony is that only 25 per cent of those who gain a coveted university place can hope to receive financial support through scholarships or other public forms of aid.

Coming from the tradition of cross-cultural psychology with its emphasis on culture-fair tests and universal cognitive competences I was dismayed to observe the severity of the selection processes which operate in the educational system and which determine later social and occupational success. Even if we were to argue that Peter Lloyd's model is time bound to the period between 1956 and 1970 or to take issue with the statistical information on which it is based, the overall impact of the analysis is difficult to escape. Surprisingly few children are chosen to remain in primary school, are then able to pass the primary school leaving examination or gain a place in a grammar school or eventually to achieve their ambition of a university degree. In the everyday life of Yoruba children one can ask pragmatically what are the relative chances of children from different family backgrounds achieving their educational and occupational objectives. The answer to this question may help us choose which of the four models of Elite and Oje intellectual development appears most adequate (realistic).

My question probably seems naive as most observers of the Nigerian educational process (and possibly that of many other nations) would accept as a social universal the proposition that the financial capacities of parents have a considerable impact on the training their children receive. Although free primary schooling in Ibadan has been provided since 1956, parents must still buy books and uniforms. Secondary education, whether in sought-after grammar schools or in secondary modern schools, until very recently entailed fees which had to be met by parents or other relatives. Similarly, university education had to be paid for largely by the student or his family. Thus throughout the system ability to provide money for fees may determine further participation. A more disturbing question is whether parental means can also ensure success in examinations, not through corruption but through legitimate channels. Shiman (1971), reporting on research carried out in Ghana, has shown that children who attend private fee-paying primary schools rather than those in the state system have a greater chance of passing the common entrance examination for secondary schooling. He noted that the private sector, which depended for prosperity on examination results, provided a virtual cram system in which subjects which were not assessed on common entrance were ignored, while attention focused on reading, writing and arithmetic. A system of private primary education exists in Ibadan and most Elite children either attend fee-paying schools or, through parental influence, are enrolled in select state schools which offer special tuition. In addition, Elite parents can assist their children with homework or employ tutors to give additional lessons outside of school hours.

Thus far we have considered the indirect advantages which can be provided by parents but additional questions can be asked about the developmental advantages, both physical and psychological, which Elite children may have in meeting the demands which the educational system presents. The common entrance examinations used by the more prestigeous secondary grammar schools for selection in Nigeria are administered by the West African Examinations Council. They consist of timed, group-administered tests which sample achievement and aptitude in English and Arithmetic. Since 1973 there have been no sample items and the tests begin after the instructions are given. I have not been able to learn whether all children who sit the common entrance are given practice on old tests at school but it is a widespread procedure in private primary schools for Elite children in Primary 5 actually to sit the examination a year early. Their success is reflected in the considerable number of 10- and 11-year-olds in the first form of grammar schools. Thus the Elite child may make rapid progress through the formal structure with years to spare should they require additional attempts to pass School Certificate or Higher School examinations. Furthermore, those Elite children who fail in their first attempt have had practice under the actual conditions and may well do better when in Primary 6 they are the appropriate age.

The common entrance examination is in part an intelligence test and thus similar to the Binet which I administered. It contains vocabulary items, and other verbal tasks similar to those used in the older ages of the Binet. If anything, the common entrance examination might be expected to exaggerate the differences which testing with the Stanford-Binet revealed in the performance of Oje and Elite children as they grew older. Unlike the Yoruba version of the Binet, the common entrance is given only in English though the achievement section is of course related to local tuition. Both tests are concerned with performance but the Binet was administered individually and informally with the interviewers encouraging children to do their best while the common entrance is given formally in official and impersonal public places. Children are aware that many more sit the examination than gain places at grammar school and, I suspect, this perception may be realistically stronger for non-Elite children. Thus of the four models considered earlier, the description of increasing Oje and Elite differences in MA appears to have ecological validity and be best able to predict the future educational achievement and occupational attainment of children from the two samples.

Although this conclusion may be warranted I am not offering it as a justification for the *status quo* nor as external evidence of the validity of the Binet based model of cognitive development. Rather I wish to draw attention to the procedures of secondary school selection which appear to depend upon or at least replicate the results of measuring performance on the Stanford-Binet. The special advantages which children from educated families enjoy and thus the bias inherent in such a model of cognitive development have been noted by a Nigerian researcher.

Obemeata (1973) has commented upon the widespread use of intelligence tests for selection, particularly in secondary schooling, and has also noted that children from privileged homes not only attend better schools but often speak English at home. He conceptualized the problem of unequal access to good test performance around the linguistic issue and suggested the use of local metaphors and examples from Nigerian culture. I would argue that these changes alone would not be enough to have a major impact. I found a statistically significant and increasing difference in the performance of Oje and Elite children on the Stanford-Binet despite the provision of a carefully adapted test and the willingness of interviewers to administer it in that variant of Yoruba-English with which the child was most comfortable. It seems reasonable to argue that any test so designed as to assess the highest thinking skills and to examine taught content are bound to show differences as long as children have grossly unequal access to informal training and teaching.

This theme has been explored by Ogunlade (1973) who examined the school performance of children in two primary schools attached to teacher training colleges in Ile-Ife, a major Yoruba town. Teaching in such schools would be above average, yet in his analysis of 120 children in Class 4 he found a highly significant difference in the performance of children from families he classified as literate and illiterate. Thus after four years of schooling the effects of different home environment are still reflected in performance. Ogunlade concluded by urging '. . . it is reasonable to suggest that if the existing gulf between children of literate and illiterate parents is not to be further widened, a sort of compensatory education should be provided for the child of illiterate parents' (1973, 432).

Both the researchers quoted above share my view that the performance model, to which participation in the educational system as it now functions approximates, is not a veridical representation of the range of intellectual competence of Nigerian children. This theme was also reflected in Shiman's (1971) worry that the common entrance examination as used in Ghana lacked validity since the subsequent performance in the School Certificate examinations of children from private primary schools was only marginally better than that of children from state schools. While it may be the case that secondary grammar schooling can provide equally good training for children from different family backgrounds, especially at boarding schools, the problem of differential access remains and should not be disguised by abstract discussions of shared cognitive competences. In most countries at the present time education appears to be the key to future occupational achievement.

What then should be the goal for cross-cultural psychology? As well as developing elegant theories, controlled data and ivory-tower discussions of universals of cognitive development, should we not be involved in studies aimed at effecting change in the educational system and career structure? At this point I am very hesitant for not only is such a task of daunting magnitude but I am prepared to take to heart the criticism of Nigerian psychologists about 'people who live in glass houses'. Even if we had been able to draw clear lessons from experience with compensatory education in the United States or in high priority areas in England we could not hope to export these to Nigeria without modification.

The search for abstract universals tied neither to situations nor cultures may indeed be theoretically and methodologically unsound but I feel we should not allow the pursuit of even elegant and well-founded universals to blind us to social reality. We may be able to show flaws in descriptions of an ever-increasing disparity in the performance of Oje and Elite children but these considerations should not be allowed to divert attention from inequalities which do affect the future of these children.

### References

Adeyinka, A. Ade (1973) 'The development of secondary grammar school education in Nigeria 1859–1970: an historical analysis', *West African Journal of Education* 17, 371–82

Almy, M., Chittenden, E. & Miller, P. (1966) *Young children's thinking.* New York: Teacher's College Press

Cole, M. & Bruner, J. S. (1971) 'Cultural differences and inferences about psychological processes', *American Psychologist* 26, 867–76

——, Gay, J., Glick, J. & Sharp, D. W. (1972) *The cultural context of learning and thinking.* London: Methuen

—— & Scribner, S. (1974) *Culture and thought : a psychological introduction.* New York: Wiley

Dasen, P. (1972) 'Cross-cultural Piagetian research: a summary', *Journal of Cross-Cultural Psychology* 3, 23–39

Goodnow, J. J. (1969) 'Research on culture and thought', in Elkind, D. & Flavell, J. H. (eds.) *Studies in cognitive development.* Oxford University Press

Inhelder, B. & Piaget, J. (1964) *The early growth of logic in the child,* translated by Lunzer, E. & Papert, D. London: Routledge & Kegan Paul

Janes, M. D. (1975) 'Physical and psychological growth and development', *Journal of Tropical Pediatrics and Environmental Child Health* 21, Special issue, 26–30

Kagan, J. & Klein, R. E. (1973) 'Cross-cultural perspectives on early development', *American Psychologist* 28, 947–61

Kamara, A. I. & Easley, J. A. (1977) 'Is the rate of cognitive development uniform across cultures? A methodological critique with new evidence from Themne children', in Dasen, P. R. (ed.) *Piagetian psychology : cross-cultural contributions.* New York: Gardner (Halsted/Wiley)

Lester, B. M. & Klein, R. E. (1973) 'The effect of stimulus familiarity on the conservation performance of rural Guatemalan children', *Journal of Social Psychology* 90, 197–205

Lloyd, B. B. (1966) 'Education and family life in the development of class identification among the Yoruba', in Lloyd, P. C. (ed.) *The new elites of tropical Africa.* Oxford University Press (for the International African Institute)

—— (1967) 'Indigenous Ibadan', in Lloyd, P. C., Mabogunje, A. L. & Awe, B. (eds.) *The City of Ibadan.* Cambridge University Press (for the Institute of African Studies, University of Ibadan)

—— (1969) 'Antecendents of personality and ability differences in Yoruba children', in Jolly, R. (ed.) *Education in Africa : research and action.* Nairobi: East African Universities Press

—— (1971a) 'The intellectual development of Yoruba children: a re-examination', *Journal of Cross-Cultural Psychology* 2, 29–38

—— (1971b) 'Studies of conservation with Yoruba children of differing ages and experience', *Child Development* 42, 415–28

—— (1972) *Perception and cognition: a cross-cultural perspective.* Harmondsworth: Penguin

—— & Easton, B. (1977) 'The intellectual development of Yoruba children: additional evidence and a serendipitous finding', *Journal of Cross-Cultural Psychology* 8, 3–16

Lloyd, P. C. (1974) *Power and independence*. London: Routledge & Kegan Paul

Lovell, K., Mitchell, B. & Everett, I. R. (1962) 'An experimental study of the growth of some logical structures', *British Journal of Psychology* 53, 175–88

Obemeata, J. (1973) 'Cultural and linguistic variables in intelligence test scores', *West African Journal of Education* 17, 423–8

Ogunlade, J. O. (1973) 'Family environment and educational attainment of some school children in Western Nigeria', *West African Journal of Education* 17, 429–32

Peluffo, N. (1967) 'Culture and cognitive problems', *International Journal of Psychology* 2, 187–98

Piaget, J. (1966) 'Nécessité et signification des recherches comparatives en psychologie génétique', *International Journal of Psychology* 1, 3–13

—— (1971) *Biology and knowledge*. University of Chicago Press

Price-Williams, D. R. (1961) 'A study concerning concepts of conservation of quantities among primitive children', *Acta Psychologica* 18, 297–305

Shiman, D. A. (1971) 'Selection for secondary school in Ghana: the problem of choosing the most capable', *West African Journal of Education* 15, 173–7

Smedslund, J. (1969) 'Psychological diagnostics', *Psychological Bulletin* 71, 237–48

Tuddenham, R. D. (1971) 'Theoretical regularities and individual idiosyncracies', in Green, D. R., Ford, M. P. & Flamer, G. B. (eds.) *Piaget and measurement*. New York: McGraw-Hill

Uzgiris, I. C. (1964) 'Situational generality of conservation', *Child Development* 35, 831–41

# Part 3

---

# Language

# Editorial introduction to part 3

The three papers in this section discuss strategies in communicating ideas at the levels of vocabulary choice, sentence construction and literary composition. In each case, language may follow the ordinary usage sufficient for ordinary circumstances, or it may rise to the challenge of circumstance by using strategies of an uncommon but quite comprehensible nature.

The papers reject the idea of a single, culture-bound universal rule peculiar to each particular language. They assert rather that language is more like a kit of tools which can be used selectively to achieve diverse results. Tanzanian students, competent in both Swahili and English, show regular preferences for one or the other, depending on the context (Lemon). Relative clauses are formed according to an elegant and parsimonious rule, but there are alternative strategies when the rule forbids the construction of such clauses under particular circumstances (Comrie). Oral composition is not rigidly restricted, as the Parry-Lord theory would suggest, but allows composition either by formulae or by individual word choice (Finnegan). The particular choice of language or grammatical strategy or literary device, is dictated by the needs of both logic and social context.

As a result, the papers give a foundation for explaining the fact which Gellner finds a problem in his General Introduction; namely, that tolerably acceptable mutual translation is always at least possible. Comrie asserts that there is a common logic for explicating the information contained in the five basic portions of a statement. Lemon shows that bilinguals can use the languages at their command in consciously selective ways. And Finnegan shows how bits of information can be fitted in diverse ways into literary expression. Thus there is convertibility of the currency used in sentence construction, organization of ideas, and literary expression. None of the cultures investigated is narrowly limited, certainly not in competence and also to some extent not in performance.

This convertibility of linguistic currency is in part what makes possible translation between visions of the world. It is true that there are always idiosyncratic pockets which are relatively resistant to interpretation. But these are the exceptions to an overall universal ability to speak to one another and have ourselves understood.

Bruner speaks in his Review and Prospectus about the diverse ways in which the universal functional requirements of societies are met. There are certain functional requirements which may be ascribed to language as well. These papers suggest that the functional requirements of language may include features remarkably similar to features of Gellner's one privileged world of enquiry. The implication may be that Gellner unnecessarily restricts these features to his newly-emergent world of modern science. Among other things, languages allow elements within statements to be modified in such a way as to admit the addition of further information (Comrie), and they allow a choice of strategies for the most effective (Lemon) and the most expressive (Finnegan) communication of information. To the extent that all languages do so, they possess at least implicitly what Bruner calls universal competences, competences that have been articulated in a public and symmetrical way in the detribalized world of the scientist.

The general discussion after the presentation of the papers at the Cambridge conference elaborated on this theme, by pointing out that the sub-routines which are conventionally used within a society can be modified and varied to take into account unusual circumstances. As Bruner put it, there are standard tasks and conventional solutions, but there are always people within every society who are breaking out of the conventions, in order to find new ways to cope. To the extent that this happens, the convention-breakers must belong at least in principle to the same public, unprivileged world of the authors of these papers. Perhaps we are not so different after all, or perhaps our difference lies in the explicitness of our commitment to breaking through the sub-routines, even of conventional scholarship.

**Language and learning: some observations on the linguistic determination of cognitive processes**

*Nigel Lemon*

In any culture language is the principal medium through which formal knowledge is communicated and acquired. If universals of human thought are to be represented in ordinary natural language, then it follows that the same thought must be capable of representation in markedly different languages. Such universals of thought would therefore have to be independent of the verbal labels used to represent them, so that a single concept could be represented by a number of linguistic forms and a single word could represent more than one concept. For example, the concept which the English speaker represents by the word 'bird' can be assumed to be equivalent to the concept which the Swahili speaker refers to as *ndege*. However, the fact that the Swahili speaker refers to both bird and aeroplane by this same word *ndege* does not necessarily imply that a Swahili speaker would expect aeroplanes to be covered in feathers or to flap their wings on take-off.

The philosophical tradition which implied a formative influence of language on the processes of thought was probably established by von Humboldt and his neo-Kantian successors. However, it is in the writings of a linguist, Edward Sapir, that the possibility of some form of linguistic determination of such processes can be most clearly discerned. Sapir's opinions were more balanced and moderate than those of his predecessors and he simply asserted that language, socially conditioned as it is, shapes the way in which a community grasps reality. To Sapir (1949),

Language is a guide to social reality...Human beings do not live in the objective world alone, nor alone in the world of social activity as ordinarily understood, but are very much at the mercy of the particular language which has become the medium of expression in their society. It is quite an illusion to imagine that one adjusts to reality essentially without the use of language and that language is merely an incidental means of solving specific problems of communication or reflection. The fact of the matter is that the 'real world' is to a large extent unconsciously built up on the language habits of the group...the worlds in which different societies live are distinct worlds, not merely the same world with different labels attached. (p. 162)

In spite of the tone of this passage, Sapir was not arguing for the complete determination of thought by language, and in other sections of his writings he emphasizes the interactive relationship between language and culture. Language is not only a potential determinant of such world views but is also a reflection of them. Sapir's own formulation of the issue differed from that of the German idealists in many respects, but most importantly in the implication that the truth or falsity of his position could be demonstrated empirically rather than asserted *a priori*. This led the ethnographer and linguist, Benjamin Lee Whorf, to collect evidence in support of Sapir's original formulation and thus the classic formulation of this position has now come to be known as the 'Sapir–Whorf hypothesis'.

Over the years a good deal of evidence has accumulated which is pertinent to this hypothesis. The very general form of the hypothesis has made precise predictions about the nature of the relationship between language and thought difficult. Miller & McNeil (1969) have distinguished between what they see as two versions of the basic hypothesis which they label the 'strong' and 'weak' forms. The strong form of the hypothesis emphasizes the role of language in creating cognitive categories, and is thus essentially a theory of intellectual development. The hypothesis presented in this form asserts that all cognitive behaviour, whether or not it involves a verbal component, is patterned according to the language of the actor. The weak form of the hypothesis says nothing about the existence of linguistically patterned cognitive categories. Instead it suggests that the strategy of an actor, when confronted with a non-verbal task under circumstances where his or her linguistic skills are engaged, will follow lines suggested by language. It also suggests that such linguistic skills will normally be invoked under conditions of ambiguity, arbitrariness or difficulty. In discussing the evidence relevant to the weak form of the Whorfian hypothesis Miller & McNeil (1969) suggest that a further distinction should be made between situations in which subjects perform their task when stimulation impinges directly upon them, as in tasks requiring judgements, or classifications of immediately presented stimuli, and situations in which such stimuli are not immediately present and in which subjects have to rely on memory. This latter category Miller & McNeil categorize as the 'very weak form' of the Whorfian hypothesis, and argue that language is likely to have greatest influence in this area.

Since it is normally possible to translate an utterance from one language into another, even when the languages differ markedly in lexis and syntax, there is no necessity to accept the strong form of the hypothesis. As Hockett (1954) has succinctly expressed it, languages differ amongst themselves, not so much in terms of what *can* be said in them, but rather in terms of what it is relatively *easy* to say. Consequently most studies of the relationship between language and cognition have concentrated on the facility with which distinctions can be expressed in a language, and very few have actually studied situations in which direct mutual translation equivalents are absent.

Much work on language and cognition has taken as its starting point the differences in colour vocabulary among languages. In retrospect there is a strong argument for saying that the initial concentration on colour in studying the problem of language and thought has been unfortunate. The evidence so far gives only partial support to the very weak form of the Sapir–Whorf hypothesis which asserts that under difficult and ambiguous conditions language can be used as a medium for the *memory* of colour, but that other non-linguistic perceptual mechanisms may be determinate.

It may be, however, as Cole & Scribner (1974) point out, that the influence of language is greatest in domains which are not definable in terms of physical properties, but only in terms of attributes which are culturally specified. For example, in social interaction those attributes which define categories of people (unlike those defining colours) are assigned by culture and not by nature. Similarly in the area of ideology or in theoretical work in general, concepts almost always acquire their meaning through being embedded in explanatory verbal networks, and not through definition by pointing. It is perhaps in these areas that language is more likely to play a dominant role in shaping a person's view of reality, particularly in influencing his memory and thus contributing to his understanding or misunderstanding of other cultures.

Another pertinent area of research which is less directly linked to the Whorfian hypothesis but nevertheless significant in this context derives from the writings of Bernstein. Bernstein does not accept the view that language determines culture, but instead places emphasis on changes in the social structure as major factors in shaping or changing a given culture. This is done through the influence of social structure on modes of speaking rather than on language *per se*. In this sense he differs from Whorf by asserting that 'in the context of a common language, in the sense of a general code, there will arise distinct linguistic forms, fashions of speaking, which induce in their speakers different ways of relating to object and persons' (1971). In this way Bernstein leaves open the question of whether there are features of the common culture which all members of a society share which are determined by the specific nature of the general code or language at its syntactic and morphological levels. Bernstein thus distinguishes between and emphasizes two modes of speaking in the English language, which in his earlier writings he designates 'public' and 'formal' languages and in his later work 'restricted' and 'elaborated codes'. Working class children are held to speak using a 'public language' or 'restricted code' while middle class children are held to use 'formal language' or an 'elaborated code'. Bernstein argues that the formal educational system emphasizes the 'formal language' or an 'elaborated code' and that working class children who speak in the 'public language' or 'restricted code' are thereby educationally disadvantaged.

When we consider the poor countries of the world, particularly those in Africa, we find that formal education is commonly conducted in a second or third language. In these cases we find not only differences in dialect or style, but gross differences between the languages which are used in and out of the formal educational setting. If differences in style or dialect have been shown to have educational consequences in the developed world, there is surely a strong *prima facie* case for saying that gross differences between languages would have an even greater impact.

Silvey (1964) has observed that African vernacular languages are often ill equipped to represent the abstract ideas of Western origin which figure so prominently in the formal school curriculum. One important consequence of the use of a language other than the vernacular is that concepts which are encountered only within a formal educational setting will be encountered via this other language, and could in principle be shaped by it. Furthermore it is assumed by educators that one of the primary benefits of education is that the pupil will form concepts which will be of value to him outside the formal educational setting. In order to attain this objective it is necessary that concepts acquired through the sometimes alien language used in formal education can be readily transferred to situations in which the individual uses a more familiar vernacular language.

Evidence so far adduced in support of the Whorfian hypothesis, weak as it is, leads us to question whether such transfer will always take place, particularly in the areas of role, ideology or abstract ideas, where meaning cannot be conveyed by direct appeal to sensory experience alone.

MacNamara (1970) in a provocative discussion of bilingualism and thought, points out that in the bilingual context there are three possible logical relationships between thought and language: (a) thinking may not take place in any language at all, (b) the bilingual may think in one language only and translate material in any other language into this 'thinking language', (c) the bilingual may think in one or the other language on different occasions. Although Chomsky (1968) has argued for the existence of deep universal features of language, languages differ from one another considerably in surface structure. Where concepts are learned through linguistic rather than ostensive definition and thus derive their meaning from surface properties of language, if either alternatives (b) or (c) were found to be true, then this would indicate that they could not be considered to constitute universal features readily applicable in all linguistic contexts. Moreover, if alternative (c) were true, then the acquisition by an educated elite group of knowledge in a language unintelligible to the common people could only serve to exacerbate divisions between elite and non-elite groups such as those demonstrated by Barbara Lloyd in this volume.

Throughout life a human being is forced to organize and give meaning to experience, so as to act appropriately in response to it. Different aspects of experience thus become equivalent and come to be organized in distinctive ways which have commonly been designated as concepts (e.g. see Carroll 1964). Thus English speakers organize their experience of hairy quadrupeds in terms of concepts which are labelled in English as 'dogs', 'cats' and 'horses'. Each concept commonly subsumes a good deal of variability within it, for example 'dog' includes such diverse canines as Poodles, St Bernards, Great Danes and Yorkshire Terriers, but it also contains criteria for distinguishing these from non-exemplars of the concept like Siamese Cats and Shetland Ponies. This example illustrates how concept formation does not merely consist of the formation of taxonomies, but must also include delineation of the attributes on which such taxonomies are based. Indeed a recent paper by Barrett (1978) indicates that in early language such taxonomies cannot be formed without delineations of such attributes. It is with such attributes as expressed in language that the study reported in this paper is concerned.

Much of the work in the language/cognition area has focused on single linguistic features which are present in one language and absent in another. In order to study the effect of second language learning however, it is necessary to turn attention away from individual syntactical or lexical differences and to consider more functional characteristics of the languages used in educational and non-educational contexts. Because language choice for education is based upon such factors as the availability of literature in a language rather than upon the proficiency of pupils in this language, the level of proficiency in the school language is often lower than that in the language used outside the formal school setting. The effect of lack of proficiency in the school language on the use of attributes articulated in that language is thus a very important issue about which we know very little in the bilingual context.

Aside from differences in proficiency between different languages, there is another characteristic of these languages which is important in the bilingual context. Languages used exclusively in formal educational contexts are thus more frequently employed to express the formal or technical knowledge which is purveyed in such contexts, but such languages are commonly used less for social intercourse outside the educational setting. Thus languages used frequently in formal educational contexts would be expected to enable more accurate communication to take place about attributes in these contexts, than languages used less frequently, on the grounds that such attributes should be more 'codeable' (cf. Brown & Lenneberg 1954) to both speaker and hearer. Since different topics tend to be discussed in these different settings some languages may therefore become particularly appropriate for communication and conceptualization of attributes in certain domains, while other languages become particularly appropriate for other domains. As we saw above one function of an attribute is to characterize certain examples as similar to one another and as distinguishable from others. Some attributes will enable this to be done with less ambiguity than others. Apart from this characteristic which concerns an attribute's relationship to concepts, attributes can also differ in the degree to which they are interrelated with one another in use. Some attributes may be used in a manner which suggests that they are quite independent of one another.

It was argued above that if there were to be any truth in the weak form of the Whorfian hypothesis, then we would be most likely to find it in areas where concepts derive their meaning from their embeddedness within an explanatory verbal network rather than from ostensive definition. If this verbal network is expressed in a language in which an individual has low proficiency, or in one which is socially inappropriate in a given domain then we should expect the attributes articulated in such languages to have different properties from those expressed in developed or socially appropriate languages. If an individual is asked to articulate an attribute in a language in which he is highly proficient then we should expect the embedding verbal network itself to be richer, and the individual should thus be able to articulate attributes from this network which were particularly apposite for certain concepts which fell within a domain for which this language was socially most appropriate. Were the individual to be less proficient in the language, or the language to be socially less appropriate then we should expect the attributes to be less apposite. Furthermore it would be expected that a person's proficiency in the language and its social appropriateness would also increase the strength of relationships between attributes formulated in this language. The richer the verbal network the more attributes it will contain to represent similar qualities, and the greater the degree of subtlety in meaning it should be capable of expressing. A complex verbal network should thus generate a larger number of nearly identical attributes, and the more interrelated attributes from this network will be used more often. Proficiency in a language should therefore lead to less equivocal categorizations of objects on attributes articulated in this language and should also lead to greater integration of such attributes in use. Social appropriateness of a language for a given domain would be expected to have effects similar to those of linguistic proficiency. On the other hand, if those who oppose the Whorfian hypothesis even in its weak form were correct, then the use of such attributes would be independent of the language in which they are articulated. The study reported in this paper was undertaken to test this assumption.

The pupils who were tested in this study were drawn from a large boys' boarding school in Tanzania. In this country, although many first learn one of the predominantly Bantu vernacular languages, Swahili is the official language and is widely spoken. It is the language of formal instruction in primary schools, is used for all official business, and is commonly used as the medium of social discourse outside the immediate family. By comparison English is the language of the educated elite (insofar as this term can be applied in an African socialist state) and it is learned as a second or third language while a child attends primary school. When a pupil enters the secondary school English is thus a poorly developed language, but it is nonetheless required to serve as the medium of formal instruction.

Tanzania is thus similar to the majority of other African states, and the school performance of English–Swahili bilinguals in Tanzania has relevance to many millions throughout the African continent. The use of English in the Tanzanian secondary school is normally confined to the classroom situation, while outside it, for communication with other pupils and with Tanzanian teachers Swahili is used. Thus with regard to English and Swahili these pupils are 'coordinate bilinguals' in the sense used by Lambert & Rawlings (1969).

A total of sixty pupils were tested in this study. Half of them were drawn from Form II of the school, aged upwards of 15 years, and had received about a year and a half of secondary education. The remainder were drawn from Form IV, aged upwards of 17 years, and had received about three and a half years of secondary education. It was assumed that proficiency in English, relative to Swahili, was greater in Form IV than in Form II and comparisons were based on this assumption.

The basic procedure was an adaptation of the role construct repertory test developed by George Kelly and his disciples (e.g. see Bannistair & Mair 1968, for a review). Although the test has normally been used to study personality, this procedure also provides an opportunity to study the way in which attributes are used to judge and categorize objects, and is thus particularly pertinent to the issues raised above. Topics from two realms of pupils' experience served as the object of judgement in this study, one related to the content of formal education and the other orientated toward personal relationships outside the classroom situation. Because of their prominence in the school curriculum, 'countries of the world' should form a topic to which the English language would be socially more appropriate, while 'description of classmates' was considered to be a topic for which Swahili, as the medium of social discourse, should be more appropriate. Each pupil was interviewed on one of the topics in both English and Swahili with a gap of approximately three weeks between interviews. The interviewers were students from the University of Dar es Salaam who were fluent in both languages, and the order of the interviews alternated with Swahili first on one occasion and English first on the second. Thirty-two of the pupils were interviewed about countries and twenty-eight about persons. Both groups contained equal numbers of Form II and Form IV pupils.

In the case of classmates pupils were asked to write down on cards the names of eight other pupils from the same class whom they knew well. Eight pre-selected combinations of three names each were then shown to each pupil and he was asked to say in what way a specified pair of these were similar to each other and different from the third. Eight pairs of attributes were obtained from this procedure, one attribute in each pair describing the way in which the pair were similar and the other describing the way in which the other was different (e.g. good at games, bad at games). Each attribute was written on a separate card. When this section of the interview had been completed pupils were presented with eight sheets of paper, each sheet bearing eight rows of five squares and each sheet labelled by the name of one of the eight classmates. Two cards, bearing one of the eight pairs of attributes elicited from each pupil, were placed to the left and right of each row, and the pupil asked to rate the classmate shown above each row in terms of this pair of attributes, by placing a cross in one of five squares to indicate how far he considered one attribute rather than the other characterized the classmate in question. This was repeated for all eight pairs of attributes and for all eight classmates giving a matrix of sixty-four ratings for each pupil. Different triads were used in the two interviews to prevent direct translation of attributes from one language to another. A parallel procedure was used for countries.

Since Form II pupils should be expected to show a greater language deficit in English compared with Swahili, then it follows from previous discussion that we should find these pupils making more extreme and thus less equivocal attributions to objects in Swahili than in English. In the case of Form IV pupils we should expect the differences in extremity of rating to be much less clear-cut, since the difference in proficiency in English and Swahili is much smaller for this group. Furthermore we should expect that since English is used predominantly in the classroom situation then the superiority of Form IV pupils would be most marked for topics which are dealt with in this setting, i.e. countries as opposed to classmates. For this reason results from the 'countries grids' and from the 'persons grids' were analyzed separately. Because the middle category (square 3) could imply that each of the attribute pairs applied equally well, or that neither of them applied, ratings on the five-point scale were divided up into three groups: (a) those made on either of

TABLE 9.1. *Mean difference scores for the different rating categories* (*English minus Swahili*)

|  | Form II | Form IV | $P$ |
|---|---|---|---|
| Countries |  |  |  |
| Extreme | −3·50 | +2·00 | < 0·05 |
| Intermediate | +1·94 | −2·81 | < 0·01 |
| Middle | +1·56 | +0·75 | n.s. |
| Persons |  |  |  |
| Extreme | −2·99 | −0·22 | n.s. |
| Intermediate | +5·15 | +2·14 | < 0·05 |
| Middle | −2·14 | −1·78 | n.s. |

the two extremes of the scale, (b) those made using either of the two intermediate positions, (c) those in the middle category. The mean differences in the number of ratings in each of these three categories between the Swahili and English grids are given in Table 9.1. In this table a high positive score indicates a higher frequency of ratings in English than in Swahili for a given category, while a negative score indicates a higher frequency of ratings in Swahili.

Inspection of Table 9.1 shows that when countries are the topic, language deficit does appear to influence polarization of ratings. Form II pupils make more extreme ratings in Swahili than in English, and correspondingly less intermediate ratings. Form IV pupils in contrast make more extreme ratings when they are using English than when they are using Swahili, and a correspondingly smaller number of intermediate ratings in English. Since we should expect Form IV pupils to be more proficient in English this finding is congruent with the assumption that unequivocal judgements are associated with proficiency in language in which the judgement is made, provided that this language is socially appropriate for the domain in question.

When a language is socially less appropriate, as English is when Tanzanians are asked to judge or describe people they know, we should expect to find that the effects of proficiency in that language are much less clear-cut. The results given in Table 9.1 confirm this assumption, showing that Swahili remains the superior language for such a task, although its superiority is less clear-cut for Form IV pupils than it is for Form II. In this case the differences are significant only for the intermediate category, as compared with significance for both extreme and intermediate categories in the case of countries. Combining the figures for Form II and for Form IV reveals that pupils made relatively more extreme ratings in English for countries than for persons (combined mean difference scores for countries = $-0.75$ and for persons $-1.61$) and relatively less intermediate ratings in English for countries than for persons (combined mean difference score for countries = $+0.87$ and for persons = $+3.15$). While both differences are in the expected direction only the difference for intermediate ratings achieves statistical significance ($P < 0.002$). Taken together these results indicate that language proficiency can influence clarity of categorization and that this effect is most marked when this language is socially appropriate for the domain in question.

The second dependent variable studied in this investigation was the degree of integration or strength of relationship between attributes. Attributes which are used in the same way to judge identical concepts are held to be strongly related to one another, while variation in the use of such attributes is taken as evidence of a weaker relationship between them. While the previous results indicate that language proficiency and appropriateness influence the use of single attributes, this does not necessarily imply that they have any effect on the relationships between attributes when they are used together. In order to determine these effects on the relationships between attributes, the pattern of ratings from each pair of attributes was correlated with the pattern of ratings from every other pair of attributes using a product moment correlation. The correlations were then squared to give a measure of the proportion of common variance for the Swahili and English attributes, and following previous practice the total proportion of common variance for the Swahili attributes was subtracted from the total for the English attributes. The means of these differences are shown in Table 9.2. If, as argued above, proficiency in a language was to influence the strength of relationship between attributes articulated in this language, then we should expect to find a difference in the strength of such relationships between Form II and Form IV for both countries and persons. In fact, no such significant differences were apparent as Table 9.2 shows, and we must therefore conclude that linguistic proficiency does not influence the strength of relationship between attributes, although it does influence the polarization of judgements which are made from them. Comparisons of the mean difference scores for countries and persons in Table 9.2 do, however, reveal large differences. For countries, attributes are significantly more strongly related to each other in English than in Swahili ($P < 0.01$, one tail) while for persons attributes are significantly more strongly related to each other in Swahili ($P < 0.01$, one

TABLE 9.2. *Mean integration difference scores (English minus Swahili)*

| Countries | | Persons | |
|---|---|---|---|
| Form II | Form IV | Form II | Form IV |
| +0·81 | +0·92 | −0·83 | −0·74 |

tail). If we assume that English is socially more appropriate for countries and Swahili for persons, then this result supports the assumption that attributes articulated in a socially appropriate language for a given domain are likely to be more closely related than if articulated in a socially less appropriate language.

The results from this study thus indicate that in the more complex areas of conceptualization, where attributes derive their meaning from their use in verbal networks rather than from direct sensory experience, language can influence the way in which people categorize the world for their own purposes. The medium in which attributes are articulated appears to exert an influence both in terms of the opportunity it provides for clear-cut categorizations to be made, and also in terms of the opportunities it provides for people to use attributes in interrelated ways. Both linguistic proficiency and appropriateness of language appear to influence clarity of categorization, whereas relationships between attributes in this study appear to be dependent upon appropriateness alone. These data can thus be interpreted as supportive of the hypothesis that language can influence judgement, when we are considering an area which is dominated by cultural and social factors rather than by direct sensory experience.

Aside from its theoretical importance this finding has important implications for the common practice of using a second language as the medium of instruction in schools. The necessity for such a practice is commonly dictated by the lack of suitable teaching materials in vernacular languages, and by problems of adapting a language to the expression of alien formal and sometimes quite technical material. However, one fundamental assumption in such policy is that concepts learned and articulated in one medium can be directly transferred to another medium with no loss of meaning. In MacNamara's (1970) terms it implies that for the bilingual, thinking either does not take place in any language at all, or that it takes place in one language and that material in other languages is translated into this thinking language. The results from this study suggest that concepts do not always readily transfer from one language to another in quite this way. Instead they suggest that material learned in a second language may not be directly available in the same form when an individual is forced to operate in his first language, thus further reducing the relevance of knowledge he has acquired during the process of his formal education.

In summary, therefore, the results of this study appear to confirm that when people are required to use concepts which relate to the world of social rather than physical experience, the way in which they use such concepts is influenced by the character of the language in which they are articulated. The inability of individuals to carry over concepts learned in one language into another in exactly the same form, suggests that the potentiality for the discovery of universals of human thought in these areas is likely to be limited. Insofar as such concepts derive their meaning from their position in explanatory verbal networks then they appear to be bound by the linguistic form in which they are articulated. In this sense these results provide some supportive evidence for a weak form of the Whorfian hypothesis in this area. Since formal knowledge is normally acquired and communicated by the use of language these findings also have social implications which bear upon issues of language policy, upon the possibilities of intertranslatability and upon communication between different language groups which may in future assume even greater practical importance than their not inconsiderable current theoretical interest at first implies.

### References

Bannister, D. & Mair, J. M. M. (1968) *The evaluation of personal constructs*. London: Academic Press

Barrett, M. D. (1978) 'Lexical development and overextension in child language', *Journal of Child Language* 5, no. 2, 205–19

Bernstein, B. (1971) *Class, codes and control* 1. London: Routledge & Kegan Paul

Brown, R. W. & Lenneberg, E. H. (1954) 'A study in language and cognition', *Journal of Abnormal and Social Psychology* 49, 454–62

Carroll, J. B. (1964) 'Words, meanings and concepts', *Harvard Educational Review* 34, 178–202

Chomsky, N. (1968) *Language and mind*. New York: Harcourt, Brace & World

Cole, M. & Scribner, S. (1974) *Culture and thought: a psychological introduction.* New York: Wiley

Hockett, C. F. (1954) 'Two models of grammatical description', *Word* 10, 210–33

Lambert, W. E. & Rawlings, C. (1969) 'Bilingual processing of mixed language associative networks', *Journal of Verbal Learning and Verbal Behaviour* 8, 604–9

MacNamara, J. (1970) 'Bilingualism and thought', in Alatis, J. E. (ed.) Report of 21st Annual Round Table Meeting on Linguistics and Language Studies. *Georgetown Monograph Series on Language and Linguistics* 23, 25–40

Miller, G. A. & McNeill, D. (1969) 'Psycholinguistics', in Lindzey, G. & Aronson, E. (eds.) *The handbook of social psychology* 3. Reading, Mass.: Addison-Wesley

Sapir, E. (1949) *Selected writings in language culture and personality.* Berkeley: University of California Press

Silvey, J. (1964) 'Formal and informal learning in a second language', *Proceedings of the East African Academy* 1, 57–63

Whorf, B. L. (1956) *Language, thought and reality.* Boston: MIT Press

# 10    The formation of relative clauses

*Bernard Comrie*

## Introduction •

The present paper stems from work on linguistic universals carried out in close cooperation with E. L. Keenan during the period 1971–4 and reported on in Keenan & Comrie (1977), which discusses relative clause formation in some forty languages from various typological, genetic, and geographical groupings. The present paper restricts the data to African languages, including some that are not included in Keenan & Comrie (1977). The languages treated are the following: Acholi (a Luo language of Uganda), Fula (Gombe dialect, spoken in Northern Nigeria), Hausa, Izi (a dialect of the Igbo group), Kpelle (a Mande language of Liberia and Guinea), Luganda, Malagasy (the language of the Malagasy Republic, formerly Madagascar), Swahili, Yoruba, and Zulu. Examples are for the most part taken or adapted from the sources cited in the list of references which are marked with an asterisk; a summary chart of the data is given in Table 10.1.

After a brief presentation of the relevant theoretical background in the first section, illustrative data from these ten languages will be presented in the second section followed in the final section by a discussion of some of the theoretical and methodological implications of the data and the analysis proposed here.

## Theoretical background

### Case Hierarchy

In this paper, I shall be referring throughout to the following 'syntactic relations': Subject, Direct object, Indirect object, Oblique object, Genitive. Most of these are familiar from traditional grammar, and the first four may be illustrated by the sentence: *Fred* (Subject) *sold the book* (Direct object) *to Mary* (Indirect object) *for three pounds* (Oblique object); if we replace *the book* by *Harry's book*, then we also illustrate the Genitive, namely *Harry's*. The original claim to be made concerning these syntactic relations is that they form a hierarchy (Case Hierarchy, or Accessibility Hierarchy; cf. Keenan & Comrie (1977)), as follows:

Subject – Direct object – Indirect object – Oblique object – Genitive. Thus Subject is the topmost position on the hierarchy, and Genitive the lowest. This hierarchy plays a key role in the determination of cross-language possibilities for relative clause formation.

An important claim of the present paper is that it is possible to analyze all languages in terms of these syntactic relations; although it is not necessary that every language should have every one of the five syntactic relations. In English, for instance, the presence of Indirect object as a syntactic (as opposed to a semantic) category is rather dubious, since in a sentence like *John gave the book to Mary* the so-called Indirect object *to Mary* is constructed just like any other Oblique object, with a preposition; while in the synonymous sentence *John gave Mary the book* the so-called Indirect object *Mary* is constructed just like a Direct object (cf. the passive *Mary was given the book*). In fact, in most of the African languages examined there is little or no evidence for an Indirect object position distinct from the Direct object position (exceptions are Acholi and Hausa); in Swahili, for instance, both Direct and (semantic) Indirect objects have exactly the same form. In Yoruba, moreover, there is little evidence for the position Oblique object, since most or all of what would in other languages be Oblique objects are here treated as Direct objects of verbs in a serial construction. Absence of a position is indicated by an asterisk in Table 10.1; it is possible that further investigation may show some of these assignments to be incorrect, but since this will mean replacing the asterisk by the symbol from the column to the left or right of the asterisk in Table 10.1, the general claim of this paper would remain unaffected.

### Relative clauses

For the purpose of the present paper, we may take relative clause formation as a means of taking a statement and forming from it an expression which can refer to one of the entities mentioned in the statement. Thus from the statement *people live in glass houses* we can form a noun phrase referring to the people concerned, by placing *people* first and following it with a relative pronoun to indicate the relative clause, i.e. *people who live in glass houses*. Similarly, from *I saw the man* we can move *the man* to the front to get *the man* (*whom*) *I saw*. Relative clause formation in this way destroys the structure of the original statement: neither *whom I saw* nor *I saw* is in isolation a well-formed English sentence.

In the relative clause *people who live in glass houses*, the head noun *people* is formed by moving the Subject of the sentence *people live in glass houses*, and in such cases we shall speak of relativization on the Subject. In *the man whom I saw*, from *I saw the man*, relativization is on the Direct object, since *the man* is Direct object of *I saw the man*. We are now in a position to integrate the discussion of syntactic relations into that of relative clauses. In particular, the data presented below ('Data') will serve to illustrate the hypothesis which can be stated informally as follows: in language, it is easier to relativize on positions nearer the top of the Case Hierarchy than on those lower down, i.e. the further down the Case Hierarchy we go, the harder it is to form relative clauses on that position.

## Data

### Absolute restrictions on relative clause formation

One particularly strong instance of the increase in difficulty of relative clause formation as we move down the Case Hierarchy is the following, which is illustrated and argued for in detail in Keenan & Comrie (1977): taking those strategies that can be used for relativizing on Subjects, then for any given position on the Case Hierarchy, there is some language in which it is possible to relativize on that position and on all higher positions, but not on any lower position, using the given strategy; moreover, there is no language in which it is possible to relativize on a given position but impossible to relativize on all higher positions, using the given strategy. The African languages examined present some evidence in favour of this strong claim, although for many of the positions on the Case Hierarchy they present no evidence either for or against the claim, and reference for the full justification of the claim must therefore be made to Keenan & Comrie (1977).

In Malagasy, for instance, only one position on the Case Hierarchy can be relativized on, and this is indeed the Subject position. In a sentence like (1), it is possible to relativize on the Subject to give (2), but not on the Direct object or Oblique object to give (3) or (4) (by convention, an asterisk is used to mark an ungrammatical sentence):

(1)  nividy ny  vary ho an'ny  ankizy   ny vehivavy
     bought the rice  for     the children the woman
     the woman bought the rice for the children
(2)  ny  vehivavy izay nividy  ny  vary ho an'ny  ankizy
     the woman  who bought the rice  for    the children
(3)  *ny  vary izay   nividy ho an'ny ankizy   ny vehivavy
     the rice  which bought for     the children  the woman
     the rice  which the woman bought for the children
(4)  *ny ankizy  ho an'izay nividy ny  vary ny  vehivavy
     the children for    who bought the rice  the woman
     the children for whom the woman bought the rice

Malagasy does, of course, have ways of expressing the sense of (3) and
(4), as will be shown in the section on 'Promotion' below, but not
by relativizing on a Direct or Oblique object.

   Relative clause formation in Luganda takes us one step further,
since here we can relativize on both Subjects and Direct objects, but
only on these, e.g. *ekikopo ekigudde* 'the cup which fell', cf. *ekikopo
kigudde* 'the cup fell', and *ekikopo Mukasa ky'aguze* 'the cup which
Mukasa bought', cf. *Mukasa aguze ekikopo* 'Mukasa bought the
cup'. But on an Oblique object, like *n'ekiso* 'with a knife' in (5),
relativization is not possible:

(5)  Mukasa yatta  enkoko n'    ekiso
     Mukasa killed chicken with knife
     Mukasa killed the chicken with the knife
(6)  *ekiso Mukasa kye    yatta enkoko na
     knife Mukasa which killed chicken with
     the knife which Mukasa killed the chicken with

Equally ungrammatical is *ekiso Mukasa na kye yatta enkoko* 'the
knife with which Mukasa killed the chicken'. The sense of (6) can
be expressed in Luganda, but not by relativizing on an Oblique
object; see the section on 'Promotion' below.

   All of the other African languages investigated do in fact allow
relativization on all positions on the Hierarchy, but even in these
languages we still find evidence for the Case Hierarchy, in fact for
every position on the Case Hierarchy, once we distinguish different
strategies for forming relative clauses, as will be shown in the next
section ('Pronoun-retention').

### Pronoun-retention

In English, there are some sentences where relativization on one of the noun phrases, instead of producing the expected relative clause, simply leads to an ungrammatical sentence. Thus if we start from *John knows where the road leads*, and move *the road* to the front, we get *\*the road that John knows where leads*. In fact, in English the construction represented in the above sentence is one from which a noun cannot be moved, i.e. there is a constraint on movement in such cases; for details, see Ross (1967). In fact, the structure *\*the road that John knows where leads* is not only ungrammatical in English, but likely also to be unintelligible to the native speaker of English. Some English-speakers will, however, accept a slightly modified version of this relative clause, namely *the road that John knows where it leads*, and even those speakers of English who refuse to accept this version find it readily intelligible. The difference between the unacceptable and the more acceptable versions is that the latter retains a pronoun in the position from which the noun phrase was extracted by relative clause formation, i.e. in addition to the noun phrase now at the beginning of the relative clause, there is also a pronoun in the relative clause indicating the place from which that noun phrase was moved. Note that *John knows where it leads*, unlike *\*John knows where leads*, is a perfectly good sentence of English. Thus a relative clause with pronoun-retention is more explicit than one without.

Pronoun-retention plays a rather marginal role in English, but there are many languages, including many African languages, where pronoun-retention is an integral part of one of the strategies for forming relative clauses, with no qualms or native-speaker disagreements about the grammaticality of the relative clauses so formed. Since pronoun-retention is a more explicit means of forming a relative clause, in that the structure of the original proposition is less destroyed than in the case of movement without pronoun-retention, one might expect that this more explicit strategy would be used precisely in those cases where relativization is more difficult, i.e. in particular lower down the Hierarchy. In Keenan & Comrie (1977), the following hypothesis is formulated and substantiated: if a given language has relative clause formation with pronoun-retention on a given position on the Hierarchy, then if it allows relative clause formation on lower positions on the Hierarchy it will have pronoun-retention here too; and if a given language has relative clause formation without pronoun-retention on a given position on the

Hierarchy, then if it allows relative clause formation on higher positions on the Hierarchy it will have relative clause formation without pronoun-retention here too. Both parts of this statement are necessary, since some languages have optional pronoun-retention for certain positions on the Hierarchy. Thus in Hausa, relative clauses formed on an Indirect object may have pronoun-retention (e.g. *yàròn dà sukà gayà masà*, literally 'child who they said to-him', i.e. 'the child whom they told'), but may also be formed without pronoun-retention (e.g. in the same meaning, *yàròn dà sukà gayà wà*, literally 'child who they said to'). Thus Hausa has pronoun-retention when relativization is on Indirect objects, and must therefore have it on all lower positions (in fact, it is obligatory on all lower positions). Equally, Hausa has relativization on Indirect object without pronoun-retention, and must therefore have the same on all higher positions, which is again true. Below, I examine each of the syntactic positions on the Hierarchy in turn, giving for each relevant position a language which provides evidence from the behaviour of pronoun-retention justifying setting up that syntactic relation as a separate position, in that for each position below Subject there is some language that either allows pronoun-retention on that position but does not allow it on higher positions, or requires pronoun-retention on that position but does not require it on higher positions. The data are summarized in Table 10.1.

*Subject.* None of the languages examined requires or allows pronoun-retention when relativizing on a Subject, not surprisingly so given the hypothesis of this section and the claim that Subject is the highest position. At first sight, this claim may well arouse incredulity, since Hausa, Kpelle, and Yoruba are usually analyzed as languages requiring pronoun-retention with relativization on Subject (and, for Hausa and Yoruba, not allowing it when relativizing on Direct object), as in (7) (Hausa), (8) (Kpelle), and (9) (Yoruba):

(7) dōkìn dà      ya mutù
    horse which it died
    the horse which died

(In Hausa, a noun before the relative particle *dà* takes the suffix *-n* or *-r* according to gender, which shortens a final long vowel. Different tenses, moods, etc., are expressed in Hausa by slight changes in the Subject pronoun, rather than in the verb.)

(8) ǹɛnîɨ̄    è   pà   là    -ɨ̄
    the-woman she come with-it that-one
    the woman who brought it

(9) àgbɛ̀  t'   ó   rà   á
    farmer who he buy it
    the farmer who bought it

Neither *dōkìn dà mutù* nor *ǹɛnîɨ̄ pà làī*, nor *àgbɛ̀ tí rà á* is possible.

Taking the Hausa example first, we find that if we examine the sentence from which this relative clause is formed, the appropriate sentence is *dōkì yā mutù*, literally 'horse it died', i.e. 'the horse died'; one cannot say simply *dōkì mutù*. The noun which is moved to the front of the relative clause is *dōkì*, and this gives quite automatically *dōkìn dà ya mutù*, and not *dōkìn dà mutù*. In other words, the Subject pronoun that appears in the relative clause *dōkìn dà ya mutù* is not an instance of pronoun-retention, since it is not a pronoun standing in the place of the moved noun phrase, but rather a pronoun whose presence is required quite independently of whether or not there is any movement, for instance even in the simplex sentence *dōkì yā mutù*. As such, this pronoun functions very much like verb-agreement in European languages: in English *the postman comes on Fridays*, the suffix *-s* on *comes* serves, in fact redundantly, to show that the Subject is third person singular, and when the same suffix is required in a relative clause (*the postman who comes on Fridays*), no-one would think of calling this an instance of pronoun-retention. The same is true of Spanish *-e* in *el cartero viene los viernes, el cartero que viene los viernes*, although this *-e* is not always so completely redundant as English *-s*, since *viene* on its own can mean 'he comes'. With this one might compare the Subject prefix in Swahili, e.g. *mwanamume a-me-fika* 'man he-has arrived', i.e. 'the man has arrived', which may occur (and in this tense-form must occur) in addition to the Subject noun, as also in the relative clause *mwanamume ambaye amefika* 'the man who has arrived'. Thus we shall speak of pronoun-retention only where we have a pronoun in the relative clause which would not be permitted in the sentence from which the relative clause is derived: those English-speakers who accept *the road that John knows where it leads* do not allow *John knows where the road it leads*.

Kpelle behaves essentially like Hausa here, as can be seen from comparing the relative clause *ǹɛnîɨ̄ è pà làī* 'the woman who brought it' with the sentence *ǹɛnîɨ̄ è pà là* (not *ǹɛnîɨ̄ pà là*) 'the woman brought it', literally 'the woman she brought it'.

Yoruba might still seem problematical, since in the Yoruba simplex sentence there is apparently no Subject pronoun in addition to the Subject noun, e.g. *àgbẹ̌ rà á* 'the farmer bought it', and not \**àgbẹ̀ ó rà á*. However this remains true only so long as we neglect the essential problem of tone in Yoruba. The third person singular pronoun has high tone, *ó*. The word for 'farmer' normally has low tone on the last vowel, *àgbẹ̀*, but when it immediately precedes the verb of which it is Subject this low tone is modified to a tone rising from low to high, *àgbẹ̌*; for full details of such tone modifications, see Rowlands (1969, 34–5). This final rise to high tone requires explanation, and an obvious explanation would be the following: the third person singular pronoun in Yoruba has two forms, both of which have high tone, but one of which also contains the segment *o* (which then bears the high tone), while the other contains no segments, but is realized by a modification of the preceding tone to high (or a glide to high). Thus we would claim that in *àgbẹ̌ rà á* 'the farmer bought it', there is a Subject pronoun, realized as a glide to high tone on the last syllable of the preceding word, citation form *àgbẹ̀*. The general rule in Yoruba is thus that the presence of a Subject pronoun is required even in a simplex sentence, i.e. in the relative clause we do not have an instance of pronoun-retention; when the pronoun immediately follows the Subject, it is realized as high tone alone, otherwise as the segment *ó* with high tone. Incidentally, when the verb is negative, there is no modification of the final vowel of an immediately preceding Subject, e.g. *àgbẹ̀ kò rà á* 'the farmer didn't buy it'. Particularly strong confirmation for the present analysis would be provided if the equivalent relative clause did not have the Subject pronoun *ó*; and this in fact turns out to be the case: *àgbẹ̀ tí kò rà á* 'the farmer who didn't buy it', and not \**àgbẹ̀ t'ó kò rà á* (cf. \**àgbẹ̌ kò rà á*).

*Direct object.* Pronoun-retention when a Direct object is relativized on is found consistently in Kpelle, of the languages examined. A third person singular Direct object pronoun in Kpelle appears as a low tone onset to the verb, which with verbs beginning in *y-* (e.g. *yà* 'buy') is realized as a low tone prefix *ǹ*:

(10) ŋá m̀ɔ̀lɔ̀ŋ   yà
    I   the-rice bought
    I bought the rice

(11) ŋá ǹyà
    I   it-bought
    I bought it

The equivalent relative clause has *ǹyà*, incorporating the pronoun, not *yà*:

(12) m̄ɔ́lɔŋ  ŋá ǹyà    -ī
the-rice I  it-bought that-one
the rice that I bought

Some African languages, in particular Bantu languages like Swahili and Zulu, allow Object pronouns (in fact prefixed to the verb) even in the presence of an Object noun phrase in a simplex sentence, so that such Object prefixes occurring in relative clauses are not instances of pronoun-retention, by the same argument as was used with regard to Subject pronouns in the previous section on 'Subject'. Thus Swahili has *Hamisi a-me-m-piga mwanamume*, literally 'Hamisi he-has-him-hit-man', i.e. 'Hamisi has hit the man', therefore the Object pronoun prefix which occurs equally in relative clauses is an instance of verb-agreement, rather than of pronoun-retention.

Genuine pronoun-retention with direct objects is, however, found in some instances in Zulu, namely where the Object prefix slot on the verb is already filled by some other Object prefix (e.g. an Object prefix indicating a (semantic) Indirect object). Thus the Zulu version of 'the story which you were telling to me' is:

(13) indaba obewungitshela yona
story  you-told-me    it

i.e. more literally 'the story that you told me it', with retention of the full pronoun *yona* 'it'.

According to Schachter (1973, 23), pronoun-retention is possible in some dialects of Hausa when relativizing on a Direct object.

*Indirect object.* As noted in the section on 'Case Hierarchy' above, only Acholi and Hausa of the languages examined here provide evidence for a separate Indirect object position. In both languages, pronoun-retention is optional here; in Hausa (at least, most dialects of Hausa), pronoun-retention is impossible on higher positions on the Hierarchy, and obligatory on lower positions, and optional for Indirect object, so Hausa provides clear evidence of the relevance of Indirect object on the Case Hierarchy, distinct from both higher positions (like Direct object) and lower positions (like Oblique object). Indirect object nouns are indicated in Hausa by the preposition *wa*; for pronouns there are special Indirect object forms, e.g. *masà* 'to him':

(14) sun  gayà wà yārò
they said to  child
they told the child
(15) sun  gayà masà
they said to-him
they told him
(16) yāròn dà    sukà gayà wà/ masà
child who they said to    to-him
the child whom they told

In Acholi, the verb form gï-mïïò means 'they gave', which with the
third person singular Object suffix -ɛ (before which the final -o is
elided) gives gï-mïï-ɛ 'they gave to him'. 'The person to whom they
gave the cow' may be either (17) (with pronoun-retention) or (18)
(no pronoun-retention):

(17) ŋaàt    ma  gì-  mïï -ɛ    dyaàŋ
person who they gave him  cow
(18) ŋaàt    ma  gì-  mïïo dyaàŋ
person who they gave  cow

*Oblique object.* When we come to Oblique object, pronoun-
retention is much more common. Excluding Luganda and Malagasy,
where relativization on this position is not possible, and Yoruba,
where Oblique object seems not to exist as a distinct position, we find
pronouns retained obligatorily in Fula, Hausa, Swahili, and Zulu (cf.
(19), from Hausa), retained optionally in Acholi ((20), (21)), and not
retained in Izi ((22)):

(19) wuƙâr dà    ya kashè ta  dà    ita
knife  which he killed her with it
the knife which which he killed her
(20) òdeéro ma    gì-  yɛɛ́kó  kí  bɛɛl
basket which they winnow with corn
the basket with which they winnow corn
(21) gìn  ma  gì-  pìṭ  -ì  kwédɛ
thing which they reared you with-it
the thing with which they reared you

(In Acholi, preposition and pronoun fuse to give combined forms like
kwédɛ 'with it'.)

(22) Mụ hụmarụ Nwibo Echiẹgụ zụtarụ eghu
    I    see      Nwibo Echiegu buy    goat
    I saw Nwibo, for whom Echiegu bought a goat

*Genitive.* Finally, with Genitives, pronoun-retention is obligatory in nearly all of the languages investigated, if relativization on Genitive is at all possible, i.e. Acholi, Fula, Hausa, Kpelle, Swahili, and Zulu. Example (23) is from Fula:

(23) suka   mo   ɓernde muudʼum yidʼi  soro
    youth who heart    his        want soro
    a youth whose heart wants *soro*

(*Soro* is the Fulani youths' test of endurance.) Only Izi apparently has only optional pronoun-retention, since Meier (1969, 44) gives versions of (24) both with and without pronoun-retention:

(24) ọphụ́    áà  wá    ísh'í (íy'á)
    the-one one split head   his
    the one whose head one splits

For all the other Genitive examples cited, however, Meier gives only the form with pronoun-retention, so there may be some more complex factors conditioning the presence versus absence of the retained pronoun *íy'á* in relative clauses. Since Genitive is the lowest position on the Hierarchy, our hypothesis would predict that pronoun-retention should be particularly common here.

### Promotion

In many languages, one very often finds systematic relations between virtually synonymous sentences where the noun phrases occurring in the different sentences occupy different syntactic relations. For instance, if we compare an active sentence and its corresponding passive in English, e.g. *John hit Mary* and *Mary was hit by John*, we find essentially the same meaning expressed in both sentences, although in the first *John* is subject and *Mary* Direct object, while in the second *Mary* is Subject and *John* Oblique object. The interaction of promotion rules like passivization, which promote a Direct object up the Hierarchy to Subject, and constraints on relative clause formation seems *a priori* a fruitful area to investigate, since here we have a means whereby constraints against relativization on positions low on the Hierarchy can be overcome, by promoting to higher positions.

In Malagasy, in addition to the active sentence *nividy ny vary ho an'ny ankizy ny vehivavy* ( = (1)) 'the woman bought the rice for the children', there are also two passive equivalents, one the so-called true passive ((25)) promoting the Direct object to Subject, the other the so-called circumstantial voice ((26)), promoting the Oblique object to Subject:

(25) novidin'      ny      vehivavy ho an'ny ankizy   ny  vary
     was-bought (by-)the woman  for    the children the rice
     the rice was bought by the woman for the children
(26) nividianan'    ny      vehivavy ny vary ny ankizy
     was-bought-for (by-)the woman   the rice the children
     the children were bought rice by the woman

(In Malagasy, the Subject usually comes at the end of its sentence; the agent of a passive sentence, expressed in English with the preposition *by*, is tacked on immediately after the verb.) These two voices provide us with ways of, apparently, relativizing on Direct object and Oblique object respectively; since the Direct/Oblique object of the active sentence is now presented as a Subject, relativization can operate quite normally on this Subject, giving relative clauses:

(27) ny vary izay   novidin'     ny      vehivavy ho an'ny ankizy
     the rice which was-bought (by-)the woman  for    the children
(28) ny ankizy   izay nividianan'    ny      vehivavy ny vary
     the children who were-bought-for (by-)the woman   the rice
     the children who were bought the rice by the woman

It was noted in the section on 'Absolute restrictions on relative clause formation' that Luganda allows relativization only on Subject and Direct object, and therefore not on an Oblique object like *n'ekiso* 'with the knife' in *Mukasa yatta enkoko n'ekiso* ( = (5)) 'Mukasa killed the chicken with the knife'. In Luganda, however, it is possible to form prepositional (applied) verbs by adding a suffix to simple verbs, so that from *yatta* 'he killed' we can form, for instance, *yattisa* 'he killed with'; this latter form already contains the meaning of the preposition *na* (before vowels *n'*) 'with', and as such simply takes the noun phrase expressing the instrument of the action as a Direct object:

(29) Mukasa yattisa        ekiso  enkoko
     Mukasa killed-with   knife  chicken
     Mukasa killed the chicken with the knife

Since *ekiso* is now the Direct object, we should be able to relativize it, and this is in fact possible:

(30) ekiso Mukasa kye     yattisa       enkoko
     knife Mukasa which killed-with  chicken
     the knife with which Mukasa killed the chicken

In the cases discussed so far, promotion possibilities have increased in an absolute way the range of noun phrases that can be relativized on (although in all cases the general constraint on relativization of the language concerned is retained). In many cases, promotion produces not an absolute difference of this kind, but rather a more preferable construction when relativization is on a syntactic relation higher on the Hierarchy. For instance, in Zulu it is quite possible to relativize on a Genitive:

(31) umuntu onja yakhe ifile/efile
     man       dog his    is-dead
     the man whose dog is dead

But the preferred expression in such cases is to rephrase the sentence as:

(32) umuntu onenja          efileyo
     man      who-has-dog dead

Literally, this is 'the man who has a dead dog', with relativization on the Subject rather than on a Genitive. In Swahili, since it is possible to relativize directly on both Subject and Direct object, a relative clause like (33) ought to be ambiguous, meaning either 'children who love old people' (cf. *watoto wanawapenda wazee* 'children love old people') or 'children whom old people love' (cf. *wazee wanawapenda watoto* 'old people love children'):

(33) watoto wa- na-    o-        wa-  penda wazee
     children they Present Relative them love    old-people

(In Swahili, the Subject of a verb in a relative clause follows the verb.) In fact, there is an overwhelming preference to take *watoto wanaowapenda wazee* as meaning 'children who love old people', i.e. with relativization on Subject rather than on Direct object. How then do we express in Swahili the sense of 'children whom old people love'?Swahili has a passive voice, as in *watoto wanapendwa ṇa wazee* 'children are loved by old people', and since *watoto* is here Subject, we get quite naturally the unambiguous relative clause *watoto wanaopendwa na wazee* 'children who are loved by old people', with the same meaning as 'children whom old people love'.

## Language universals

In this concluding section, I want to examine briefly some of the theoretical and methodological implications of the empirical work discussed in the section on 'Data', under the following heads: (i) range of data; (ii) abstractness of analyses; (ii) explanation in universal grammar.

### Data range for language universals

*A priori*, it might seem obvious that in order to pursue the study of language universals one should ideally use as one's data base evidence from all languages, or, given the impracticality of this, from as wide-ranging a set of languages as possible. This is in fact the line taken in Keenan & Comrie (1977). However, particularly within transformational grammar, there is an authoritive view maintaining just the opposite, namely that the most fruitful approach to linguistic universals is the detailed study of a single language, which for practical considerations usually turns out to be English (see, for instance, Chomsky & Hampshire 1968; Chomsky 1972). Perhaps the most obvious defect of such an approach is that we have no check, if we restrict ourselves to just one language, on whether or not the putative universal is in fact a universal or not, and the suggested methodology in fact discourages the linguist from carrying out this check. The usual line of argument adopted by Chomsky is to find some property of English which is statable only in abstract terms and is *a priori* very unlikely, claim on the basis of its abstractness and improbability that it is unlikely that the child could actually learn this principle on the basis of the data with which he is confronted, deduce from this that the principle in question must be innate, therefore universal (given that children are capable of learning the language of any speech community). There are several gaps in this line of reasoning, the main one being perhaps that we still have little idea what kinds of abstract principle children find easy or difficult to learn.

In the section on 'Pronoun-retention' it was noted that English cannot move the noun phrase *the road* in *John knows where the road leads* to form a relative clause; on the basis of this and similar examples one can formulate the general principle that in English it is impossible to move the Subject of a subordinate clause introduced by a conjunction. This principle is not *a priori* likely (why only the Subject? why should the conjunction have any effect?), and presumes an ability to recognize certain abstract analyses of sentences (e.g. to identify a subordinate clause); thus it might seem a good candidate for being a linguistic universal. In fact, it is not, although the reason why it is not cannot be ascertained from the study of English alone. When we turn to Dutch, we find that it is possible to say *de man die ik niet weet of kam*, literally 'the man who I not know if came', i.e. '*the man that I don't know if came', precisely the structure that is forbidden in English (and this although English and Dutch are very closely related languages).

If we turn to the kind of universals that have been discussed in the present paper, then it becomes even clearer that detailed study of a single language is insufficient for the establishment of such linguistic universals. No single language provides evidence for the relevance of every single position of the Case Hierarchy, so that the only way in which such universals as the Case Constraint or the incidence of pronoun-retention can be established is on the basis of comparing data from a wide range of languages. Thus the discovery of such universals provides particularly strong justification for the view that universal grammar must have a wide data-base: there is no other way in which such universals can be discovered and/or validated.

Looking at a wide range of languages does also, from a practical methodological point of view, entail certain difficulties: the individual linguist is unlikely to be at home in all the languages he must look at, and this brings with it the danger of his being misled by appearances in some of the languages with which he is not himself familiar. But to restrict oneself to one language on this account would be to run away from the problem, not to solve it. Ideally, close cooperation between linguists interested in universals and those working in detail on individual languages is what is required.

### Abstractness of analysis

One of the key concepts in transformational grammar is that of 'deep structure', i.e. an abstract underlying level of representation distinct from the surface structure. (It should not be forgotten, however, than even surface structure involves some degree of abstract analysis: 'surface structure Subject', for instance, as used in the main sections on 'Theoretical background' and 'Data' above, is certainly not a physical property of an utterance. The difference in abstractness is one of degree.) For instance, although the active and passive sentences *John hit Mary* and *Mary was hit by John* are rather different in surface structure, they would be assigned the same or nearly the same deep structures by most transformational grammarians, something like *John Past hit Mary*. (The notion of deep structure is discussed more fully in Chomsky (1972).) Within transformationally based study of linguistic universals it is often assumed that the further one moves away from the surface structure towards the deep structure, the more the structures become universal. A by-product of this concentration on deep structure universals has been a tendency to neglect the possibility of looking for universals at levels closer to the surface structure. One danger inherent in stating universals on deep structure is that the universals thus stated are no stronger than the abstract analyses on which they depend for their statement: quite often the putative universals are empty because the abstract analyses have no empirical content, they are simply decisions by a linguist to analyze data (any data) in a given way. To take a concrete example: Lakoff (1970, 173–83) suggests that quantifiers like *many* should always be derived from deep structures where they appear as higher predicates, i.e. *many bullets hit the soldier* would derive from something like *the bullets which hit the soldier were many*. It is in fact always possible to analyze quantifiers, in English or any other language, in this way, but this is not because of any particular property of language. There are no conceivable counter-examples to this analysis of quantifiers, because the so-called hypothesis is simply a decision by a linguist that he is going to analyze all data of a certain kind in this particular way, rather than in any of a number of other conceivable ways. Unless the hypothesis can be given empirical content, it is of little interest as a potential linguistic universal.

Apart from the potential and real dangers of basing linguistic universals on deep structure, the discussion of the section on 'Data' shows that there are at least some universals that can and must be stated not on the level of deep structure, but directly in terms of surface structure categories. Possibilities for relative clause formation are determined by the syntactic relation of a noun phrase in surface structure, irrespective of its syntactic relation in deep structure. Thus in Malagasy *ny vary izay novidin'ny vehivavy ho an'ny ankizy*

( = (27)) 'the rice which was bought by the woman for the children',
the fact that relativization is possible is determined by the fact that
*ny vary* 'the rice' is surface structure Subject of *novidin'ny vehivavy
ho an'ny ankizy ny vary* ( = (25)) 'the rice was bought by the woman
for the children', and it is quite irrelevant that *ny vary* would be the
Direct object of the verb in deep structure. Thus the emphasis on
the search for deep structure universals in so much transformational
work can lead on the one hand to the statement of spurious universals,
and on the other hand lead us away from empirically significant
and testable statements about universals. This is an area where the
balance should be redressed.

## Explanation in universal grammar

One of the points emphasized over and over again by Chomsky is the
need for the linguist to distance himself from language, his object of
study: since language is so familiar to the ordinary man in everyday
life, it requires an effort to distance oneself from it sufficiently to
realize that language does in fact present an extremely complex
phenomenon requiring explanation. This point seems undeniable,
and one of the conclusions Chomsky draws from it is that the linguist
should expect to find that the general properties of language which
he uncovers will be strange, i.e. not features which one would *a priori*
think necessary or advantageous to have as part of a communication
system, and that he should concentrate on such 'strange' universals,
as those which are most likely to characterize human language as
opposed to any other arbitrary communication system.

This approach does have the disadvantage that it often leads the
linguist away from the task of seeking explanations for the linguistic
universals he discovers. In a sense, the statement of linguistic
universals becomes itself an explanatory model of language, and since
we are led to believe that linguistic universals are strange there is no
reason to suppose that they would be predictable on the basis of some
more general principle.

In the present paper I hope to have shown that there is at least one
linguistic universal, with empirical content (i.e. it could easily not
have been true), but which can find an explanation in the general
properties of a communication system which links form to meaning:
in the section on 'Pronoun-retention', I noted that pronoun-retention
is commoner the lower one goes down the Hierarchy, i.e. the more
difficult relativization becomes; and moreover that pronoun-retention
is a way of retaining in the form of a relative clause a more explicit

TABLE 10.1. *Relative clause formation in some African languages*

| | Subject | Dir. object | Ind. object | Obl. object | Genitive |
|---|---|---|---|---|---|
| Afro-Asiatic | | | | | |
| Chadic | | | | | |
| *Hausa* | − | − | ± | + | + |
| Congo-Cordofanian | | | | | |
| Niger–Congo | | | | | |
| West Atlantic | | | | | |
| *Fula* | − | − | * | + | + |
| Mande | | | | | |
| *Kpelle* | − | + | * | + | + |
| Kwa | | | | | |
| *Yoruba* | − | − | * | * | + |
| *Izi* | − | − | * | − | ± |
| Benue–Congo | | | | | |
| Bantu | | | | | |
| *Luganda* | − | − | * | 0 | 0 |
| *Swahili* | − | − | * | + | + |
| *Zulu* | − | ± | * | + | + |
| Nilo-Saharan | | | | | |
| *Acholi* | − | − | ± | ± | + |
| Austronesian | | | | | |
| *Malagasy* | − | 0 | 0 | 0 | 0 |

Notes: + indicates pronoun-retention; − indicates no pronoun-retention; ± indicates optional pronoun-retention (or pronoun-retention in some cases only); 0 means that relativization is not possible on that position; * means that the given position does not exist as a separate position in the language. The genetic classification follows Greenberg (1963).

representation of its meaning. The two factors are clearly not unrelated: it is *a priori* quite likely that the form of a construction, which has to signal the meaning of that construction, should do so in a more explicit way the more complex the structure of the form becomes.

To conclude, I would emphasize once again that work on linguistic universals depends crucially on empirical data from a wide range of languages, although one should not lose sight of the task of finding more general explanatory principles underlying the various linguistic universals. For the relative clause constructions examined in detail, African languages provide a wide range of data of just this kind, and form an important component of the data-base necessary to validation of the universals proposed.

## Acknowledgements

I am grateful to John Gay for bringing the Kpelle data to my attention, and to Ally Abdalla and Annie K. Hawkinson for help with the Swahili data. My indebtedness to Edward L. Keenan will be apparent throughout. For fuller exposition of the theoretical linguistic aspects of the problems treated here, see Keenan & Comrie (1977).

## References

*Abraham, R. C. (1959) *The language of the Hausa people*. University of London Press, 57–8

*Arnott, D. W. (1970) *The nominal and verbal systems of Fula*. Oxford: Clarendon Press, 149–51, 382

*Ashton, E. O. (1947) *Swahili grammar* (2nd edition). London: Longman, 110–14, 309–11

*Ashton, E. O., Mulira, E. M. K., Ndawula, E. G. M. & Tucker, A. N. (1954) *A Luganda grammar*. London: Longman, 136–49

Chomsky, N. (1972) *Language and mind* (enlarged edition). New York: Harcourt, Brace & World

—— & Hampshire, S. (1968) 'Noam Chomsky and Stuart Hampshire discuss the study of language', *The Listener* 79 (2,044), 687–91

*Crazzolara, J. P. (1955) *A study of the Acooli language* (2nd edition). Oxford University Press (for the International African Institute), 93–6

*Doke, C. M. (1961) *Textbook of Zulu grammar* (6th edition). Longmans (for the University of the Witwaterstrand), 311–25

Greenberg, J. H. (1963) 'The languages of Africa', *International Journal of American Linguistics* 29, no. 1, part 2

*Keenan, E. L. (1972) 'Relative clause formation in Malagasy', in Peranteau, P. M., Levi, J. N. & Phares, G. C. (eds.) *The Chicago which hunt*. Chicago: Chicago Linguistic Society, 169–89

—— & Comrie, B. (1977) 'Noun phrase accessibility and universal grammar', *Linguistic Inquiry* 8, 63–99

Lakoff, G. (1970) *Irregularity in syntax*. New York: Holt, Rinehart & Winston

Meier, P. E. (1969) 'The relative clause in Izi', *Journal of West African Languages* 6, 35–49

Ross, J. R. (1967) 'Constraints on variables in syntax', PhD dissertation, MIT (available from Indiana University Linguistics Club, Bloomington)

Rowlands, E. C. (1969) *Teach yourself Yoruba*. London: English Universities Press, 87–90

Schachter, P. (1973) 'Focus and relativization', *Language* 49, 19–46

*Welmers, W. (1971) *A first course in Kpelle*. Ibadan: Institute of African Studies, University of Ibadan, 179

# 11 Literacy and literature

*Ruth Finnegan*

Despite the title of this paper I should explain that I am not attempting a survey of the field of 'literacy and literature' nor of possible 'universals' which might be found in that field. Rather I intend to take one small corner of this vast subject, and from that select one element as a possible candidate for a 'universal' and then see if this holds up in the light of African evidence (and, to some extent, of other comparative data).

I began this work with some doubt as to just what a 'universal' might look like if we found one, and what should be considered. Nevertheless when I examined some of the publications in the field of 'oral literature' I found that there was a view being put forward about the nature and processes of oral literature and its relation to literacy and 'orality' for which the proponents in some sense claimed universal validity and world-wide applicability. This position is often called the 'Parry–Lord theory', that adopted by the 'oral-formulaic school' of analysts. Briefly, it is a theory which deals with the nature of oral poetry and oral composition, contrasting these with written productions, and showing how they are developed out of formulaic elements known to and used by all poetically sensitive members of the culture. The theory also has many connections with more widely ranging theories and assumptions about the nature of social change, particularly about how literacy affects traditional modes of thought and expression.

I shall explain the theory in more detail shortly, but first let me cite some of the statements about this theory which inclined me to treat it as relevant in a search for possible universals. In these statements, claims are being put forward that there is something truly 'universal' about the findings of Parry and Lord.

The aims of Milman Parry, who is usually regarded as the founder of this school, were quite explicitly to develop a *universal* theory applicable to 'all oral poetries'. Referring to his early intentions, he wrote that his purpose was to obtain evidence on the basis of which could be drawn a series of generalities applicable to all oral poetries, which could allow me, in the case of a poetry for which there was not enough evidence outside the poems themselves of the way in which they were made, to say whether that poetry was oral or not...A method is here involved, that which consists in *defining the characteristics of oral style*. (Parry in Parry & Lord 1954, 4)

His work was then taken up by others as providing a universal and a proven theory on which to base their own work. Thus a fairly recent book by Kailasapathy, on Tamil heroic poetry, asserts in the preface that 'Parry formulated a universal theory' (Kailasapathy 1968, ix). Rhys Carpenter states it in even stronger terms in his *Folk tale, fiction and saga in the Homeric epics* when he speaks of 'Milman Parry's ...unanswerable and unassailable proof...Its truth abides almost as surely as Euclid's demonstrations abide whether or not anyone chooses to retrace their close-knit reasoning' (1958, 6). These amount in all to fairly clear and definitive claims for the theory presented by Parry and Lord. It is seen not only as an abstract and definitional approach but also as having solid empirical backing throughout the world, with supporting evidence now offered from scholars in many specialist areas, including Scottish Gaelic poems, Anglo-American ballads, early Hebrew poetry, later classical Greek poetry, modern Cypriot Greek narrative poetry, chanted sermons in the contemporary American South, and poetry in early Tamil, Ainu, Xhosa, Old English, and a large number of mediaeval European languages.

Therefore in the findings and generalizations put forward by Parry, Lord and their followers we seem to have come upon a strong contender for a 'universal' in the field of oral literature. It is claimed as a 'universal' both in the sense of having extremely wide empirical evidence for its constant occurrence in oral contexts and for possessing a timeless quality, comparable to that of 'Euclid's demonstrations'.

### The Parry–Lord theory

I must now explain in more detail what the 'Parry–Lord' theory is, and I will follow this with a discussion of how far I think it can be regarded as a 'universal'. Perhaps it can best be understood through a quick account of how it came to be formulated and tested. Of necessity I am giving only an extremely condensed account of a subtle and complex theory. A full understanding can only be gained by consulting the works of the 'oral-formulaic' theorists themselves, particularly the early work by Milman Parry and the classic presentation in Lord's *The singer of tales* (1968a).

The first developments were concerned with the Homeric epics, the *Iliad* and *Odyssey*. The extent of repetition including stock epithets, phrases and even whole lines in these poems had long been noted. Odysseus, for instance, is repeatedly described as 'much-counselling' or 'much-enduring, goodly' whatever the context. This repetitiveness raises the question of why it should be such a marked feature of the poetic style – was it due to the traditional handing down of stock epithets which were then used automatically whether or not they were relevant to the particular point in the narrative?

Another problem – at first sight unrelated to the first – was the original composition of these poems. Was there a single author ('Homer')? or a series of authors? Was the final poem a composite, divisible into different strata or 'layers'? How could such long and elaborate poems be composed in a period before writing was widespread? Was it feasible for a minstrel to memorize the 15,000 and 12,000 lines respectively of the *Iliad* and *Odyssey*? But if they had not been committed to memory how could the poems have been transmitted without writing? Might they have actually been compositions of a literate poet?

Parry took these two problems inherent in the Homeric poems and by treating them together suggested a solution. In a series of studies (especially Parry 1930, 1932) he argued that the style of the Homeric poems was not only 'traditional' but *oral*. Rather than memorizing a fixed and final poem and performing it by rote, the oral or non-literate poet used a stock of well-known phrases and epithets to produce his verse *as he sang*. In this way his composition was not a prior activity that could either appear in fixed written form or be handed on to someone else to memorize word-for-word, but was a process which took place only in and through his performance. This repetition in the Homeric poems is simply a characteristic of 'oral style' at the moment of performance which makes possible the composition of long epics without recourse either to the medium of writing or to word-for-word memorization.

Parry's analysis of Homer was followed up and supported by work with Lord in the 1930s on oral epics in Yugoslavia. They took the imaginative step of going beyond the scholarly analysis of the texts of early Greek poetry to a living tradition of oral epic composition.

The Yugoslav study bore out Parry's ideas about the composition of the Homeric poems. There was clear evidence in the Yugoslav situation that oral poets did indeed compose long epic poems – some of them comparable in length to the Homeric poems – without the use of either writing or exact memorization. The Yugoslav poet could pour out line after line in rapid succession, not infrequently at a speed of ten to twenty metrically accurate lines in a minute, without pausing to reflect or refer to written text or notes, using his acquired store of ready-made formulae and phrases.

The fact that the oral Yugoslav minstrel drew on an accepted store of formulae did not imply any lack of individuality. By combining formulaic elements in a personal way and adding personal phrases to fit his own experience or the mood of his audience, the poet could make each performance a unique and individual act of creation. As Lord explains in *The singer of tales* the literate model of a poem as having a fixed and correct text simply does not apply with oral poetry where there is not one authentic text. Rather there are many versions, each one as authentic as any other, moulded by the individual and creative poet from a known store of formulaic phrases, lines, themes and plots.

The Yugoslav singers themselves sometimes claimed that their different renderings of the 'same' poem were word-for-word identical. But it quickly emerged that this was not true. Parry and Lord recorded a number of the Yugoslav poems on phonograph discs and were able to compare the different versions and reveal the extent of the difference between the compositions both of the same singer on different occasions, and of different singers constructing a poem on the 'same' plot. They conducted a number of experiments to see how far a singer could take a basic plot and, from his knowledge of the traditional repertoire of phrase, theme and stock setting, construct his own individual version of it. In one case, a poet sang a song not known to a second poet, who was then asked to sing his version of the song. The resulting song was very different from the first rendering, being nearly three times its length, and including personally experienced details, expanded descriptions, new episodes and changes in the order of events (see Lord 1968a, especially 102ff).

It is clear from cases like this, fully documented in the research of Parry and Lord, that neither memorization nor exact word-for-word transmission of a 'correct' text is involved in oral composition. It is 'composition-*in*-performance'. The poet creates from a store of accepted 'formulaic' elements at his disposal which he actively combines together in his own chosen order to create his own unique poem on a specific occasion. In fact, the measure of the 'orality' of the text is the number of formulaic expressions it contains.

Besides its interest as a theory explaining the particular style and process of creation behind oral poetry, the oral-formulaic theory has other qualities which commend it to scholars, particularly concerning its relevance for analyzing social change and the significant differences between 'oral' and 'literate' cultures. The theory would appear to confirm that non-literate 'primitive' communities are more 'traditional' than modern, literate ones, because they depend on oral *formulae* rather than individual and original forms of expression. Again this approach can be envisaged as providing some backing for the kind of psychological difference that some scholars have detected between 'the oral mind' and 'the literate mind'. As Lord describes in his classic statement in *The singer of tales*, there is a basic incompatibility between the two techniques of composition: 'The two techniques [oral and written] are...contradictory and mutually exclusive. Once the oral technique is lost, it is never regained. The written technique...is not compatible with the oral technique, and the two could not possibly combine' (1968a, 129). This kind of approach fits with suggestions such as those of Talcott Parsons (1964), that writing is one of the great 'evolutionary universals' which provides a watershed in social evolution, or of Marshall McLuhan (1962, 1967) (who was in fact very much influenced by Lord) that 'oral' and 'visual' culture are fundamentally different.

It is small wonder that scholars have hailed the findings of Parry and Lord and their followers, as explaining not only 'oral style' but also certain apparently universal strands in social development, which can be assumed applicable to oral cultures and oral literature even when specific evidence is lacking.

### African evidence

The formulation of the oral-formulaic theory and the discovery of much of the evidence to support it took place outside Africa and without specific reference to African examples. But this does not mean that it is irrelevant for students of Africa. The findings of Parry and Lord are in some respects directly applicable to the African context. In fact it was through my study of African oral literature that I first became aware of the work of the oral-formulaic scholars.

It could even be argued that the findings of the oral-formulaic school have *more* importance for the study of Africa than for the societies in which they were first applied. Specifically, there has until recently been a widely-accepted view that indigenous African societies were naturally – and 'universally' therefore – characterized by a peculiar reliance on 'traditional' ways. The societies were unchanging, there was little or no individual originality, and, rather than possessing literature in the sense recognized in literate societies, they instead relied on 'oral tradition', handed down from generation to generation – often expressed as from 'time immemorial' – and transmitted essentially through passive memorization by uncreative bearers of that tradition. It is true that many scholars, even in the last century, have opposed such a view. But in general terms it has been an extremely influential picture of the nature of African and other non-literate and so-called 'primitive' societies, which was widely accepted by earlier scholars in one form or another and remains even today a widely-held popular view.

But the increasing acceptance of the Parry–Lord findings has radically changed this situation. Now there is a body of theory and of evidence to which the analyst of African culture can appeal which allows him to reject this older view about 'universals' in African cultures, and to explore the possibility of the new 'universal' formulated in the Parry–Lord theory. Both recent and older analyses of African oral literature seem to fall into place against this background.

Since I have been much influenced in my own interpretations of African literature by the oral-formulaic approach, I shall begin with some reference to my own research, first fieldwork on Limba oral literature and later more general and indirect study of other African oral literature. My original work (Finnegan 1967) used the ideas developed by Parry and Lord, as the following examples will show.

During my fieldwork among the Limba people of northern Sierra Leone in the early 1960s I was frequently told by informants that I was hearing 'exactly the same story' as that recorded on some previous occasion from the same or another narrator. Similarly, people suggested that once I had recorded one version of a well-known plot, I need search no further. If my main interest had been in some other aspect of Limba culture, I would certainly have been content to accept such statements at their face value. It was reasonable to assume that the Limba knew their own literature; if they said the various versions were identical why should I doubt it?

But when I looked into the matter a little further, I found exactly the same situation as did Parry and Lord in Yugoslavia. The different versions were often *not* the same either verbally or even in the order and interrelation of episodes, the conclusion, or the general tone of the narration. I discovered that when I was told that two stories were 'the same', this statement meant something other than that the words were the same. When I asked a Limba assistant to elucidate the words I could not catch fully while trying to transcribe taped stories, he could not be made to understand that I wanted the *exact* words on the tape. As far as he was concerned any comparable phrase with roughly the same meaning would do. It was also clear from examining the 'same' stories told by different tellers that there was wide scope for individual differences and for the creative manipulation of accepted themes and episodes.

I recorded two versions, for instance, of a young girl's revenge on the man who had killed her father for a trivial offence. The detailed episodes in the two versions are different. In one, the girl consults only her mother about her plans, while in the other she consults a finch as a diviner. One version gives the names of real chiefs in real chiefdoms visited by the girl in her travels in search of her father's murderer, while in the other they are fictional characters. The details of the actual killing by the girl and discovery of the corpse give a very different atmosphere in the two reports, each perhaps equally effective in its own way. In the first story the girl then eludes her pursuer by tricking him with false 'advice' about how to kill her, and in the second she beguiles him with her beauty. One story is intended, on the face of it at least, to explain the occasional presence of women chiefs, while the other reminds the powerful not to react violently to a trivial offence.

Other examples of individual creativity and the unique nature of each performance could be given from Limba stories to show how they too involve the kind of composition-in-performance noted by Parry and Lord rather than the memorization of a word-for-word text. There seemed in general to be little or no idea of *the* correct version of any story.

The creativity and originality of Limba narrators occurs within a framework of conventional themes and language, recognized as suitable for story-telling. This can be compared with the stock of formulaic expressions described by Parry and Lord for Yugoslav epic singers. There are set formulae to introduce a story, set protagonists with familiar characterizations, set verbal forms by which to indicate location in time and space or suggest a new move in the series of episodes, and accepted terms in which the audience's responses are cast. At a higher level the story-teller may choose from basic episodes which recur in a number of stories, like the act of telling someone's secrets to a third party, of winning a wife, tricking an opponent, or joining with someone in a 'company' of either good or evil deeds. The endings which are accepted by both teller and audience as providing a suitable close to a story include the statement of a dilemma arising from the story, a moral, a joke, a reference to some recent historical event, an aetiological explanation, or merely a last move in the plot of the story which is accepted as having its own finality, like the hero winning the girl, becoming chief, or returning home and telling his parents of his adventures. One cannot predict in advance which character or which conclusion will be used by the teller to show his originality and creativity, based on his mood, and his assessment of the reactions of the audience. Thus Limba story-tellers display the same kind of emphasis on composition-in-performance as demonstrated by Parry and Lord, accompanied both by the lack of any insistence on the *correct* version and by the basic familiarity of the formulaic elements. As a Limba story-teller put it, 'I am taught by the dead [the ancestors] and my own heart.'

It is not difficult to find similar processes at work in other story-telling situations in Africa, even those reported by researchers who themselves had no direct knowledge of the oral-formulaic school's findings. An example is Junod's description of the production of Thonga stories in south-eastern Africa, based on his long experience as a missionary in the area. He speaks of the 'antiquity' of Thonga stories, an 'antiquity' which is always transformed in the narration.

First of all *words* differ. Each narrator has his own style, speaks freely and does not feel in any way bound by the expressions used by the person who taught him the tale...

The same can be said with regard to *the sequence of the episodes*: although these often form definite cycles, it is rare to hear two narrators follow exactly the same order. They arrange their material as they like, sometimes in a very awkward way...

I go further: *new elements* are also introduced, owing to the tendency of Native story-tellers always to apply circumstances of their environment to the narration...

Lastly, my experience leads me to think that, in certain cases, *the contents of the stories* themselves are changed by oral transmission, this giving birth to numerous versions of a tale, often very different from each other and sometimes hardly recognisable. (1912–13 vol. II, 198–200)

The description has a familiar ring to anyone acquainted with the oral-formulaic approach – and suggests that there is indeed something universal in the kind of findings publicized by Parry and Lord. Recent studies of African oral poetry also show the same kind of emphasis on the lack of a correct version, the relative unimportance of exact memorization, the interplay of originality and tradition, and the manipulation of known and conventional elements by the poet in his performance.

In the *nyatiti* 'lyre' songs of the East African Luo, for example, (Anyumba 1964) the poet performs most often at funerals, where there are certain stock phrases and topics which he is expected to use in his song. These include word-groups like 'asleep on its arm' or 'sealed in dust' and a series of praise names which are constructed from references to the dead man's family, his country, his clan, and his lives. Yet the song must be unique to the occasion. The singer is judged by his ability to treat particular incidents concerning the deceased, to refer to his adventures and his words in a way which conventionally and at the same time very personally epitomizes the shock and sorrow of the mourners.

Among the Hausa praise singers of Northern Nigeria (Smith 1957) there are freelance soloists who tour the area to make their living by their songs. Smith describes vividly how the poet arrives in a village, identifies the wealthy and powerful personages in the area, and then in some public place, where he can command a good audience, commences his song of praise to one of those chosen 'patrons'. There are conventional themes in such a song: references to the patron's nobility, generosity, high birth, prosperity, political connections and influence, all interspersed with repeated demands for gifts from the patron. If these are forthcoming, the song ends with thanks, but if no gifts appear the tone changes. The same themes continue to appear in the song, but this time everything is presented in a hostile light and the song details the patron's meanness, poor reputation, political disloyalty. Finally, the ultimate insult of all, the patron's servile birth is noted. Sooner or later the patron is forced to meet the poet's demands in order to maintain his local reputation.

The older picture of a static 'oral tradition' in Africa would not fit these facts. The praise singer is not transmitting inert tradition which he has learnt from rote, but creating a new poem appropriate to the occasion. The processes involved appear to fit well the findings of Parry and Lord in Yugoslavia and once again we find the typical combination of composition and performance in oral poetry.

It is not so easy to find exact analogies in Africa of the poetry of Yugoslava epic singers in that few or no detailed studies of indisputably oral epic poems from Africa have been published, though there are some possible parallels. However one comparable genre that *is* highly developed and well studied in many parts of Africa is that of praise poetry, which, like epic, is both fairly lengthy and involves some narrative element. These panegyric poems, often hundreds of lines long, display processes similar to those observed in Yugoslav epics. Opland (1971) tested the ability of a Xhosa praise poet in Southern Africa to compose on the spur of the moment by presenting him with a topic for his poem on which the poet had not previously sung. As in the case of Yugoslav singers, the Xhosa poet was able to pour forth his praises uninterruptedly and pertinently by drawing on a store of accepted formulaic expressions. Here again, some fundamental and perhaps universal process seems to be at work.

All in all it seems that the Parry–Lord theory has indeed described something 'universal' which both receives support from the African evidence and seems to be valid cross-culturally. (For some further evidence, see Finnegan 1976, 130ff and 1977, 66ff.) If so, it is of great importance for our understanding of many aspects of culture and of human behaviour, as it affects not only the process of oral composition and oral style, but also fundamental questions about the difference between the 'oral' and the 'literate' mind, and the changes involved with the increasing reliance on writing.

And yet I am doubtful about whether the theory is in fact universally valid. I intend to devote most of the remainder of this paper to explaining why, in the last analysis, I consider that the Parry–Lord theory as formulated above does not in fact stand up as a universal.

## The Parry–Lord theory reconsidered

The first point is that the oral-formulaic theory is a cluster of ideas, rather than just one clear-cut statement; some of the ideas are less acceptable than others when stated explicitly, yet the apparent attraction of the theory seems to rest on this blend of assumptions. One basic assumption in much oral-formulaic analysis is that there is something specifically 'oral' which can be distinguished in a definitive way from what is 'written' or 'literate', specifically as it affects mental patterns, literary forms, or culture. This appears in many statements by adherents of this school. Magoun, who first applied Parry's ideas in the field of Old English studies, speaks definitively of 'the two great categories of poetry', belonging to 'the oral or to the lettered tradition' (1971, 194). One encounters such examples as 'the clearly oral characteristics' of the *Song of Roland* (Nichols 1961, 9fn), 'the traditional fixed ways' of 'the society which gives birth to oral poetry' (Notopoulos 1964, 50–1), or 'the irrefutable statistical facts that distinguish the texts of Homer from those of poets known to have composed by writing' (Nagler 1967, 274). Lord himself claimed that 'the written technique is not compatible with the oral technique, and the two could not possibly combine to form another, a third, a "transitional" technique' (1968a, 129).

How much truth is there in such claims? Certainly there are differences between the kind of literature often termed 'oral' and its written counterpart, mainly in respect of the former being *performed*. But to write as if this distinction were self-evident and definitive, with a sharp break between the two, is to go beyond the evidence.

Here the African evidence is very pertinent. Although Africa has been romantically pictured as being in the untouched 'state of nature' with literacy introduced only recently, scholars now of course recognize that this is far from true. The influence of writing through Christian missionary activity goes back a long way, and Islam and Islamic literacy even further. In the Sudanic and east coast areas a *written* literary tradition has become a truly African, not just an intrusive, phenomenon and we find that oral and written literature belong to relative and overlapping rather than mutually exclusive categories. In West Africa the long Hausa *Song of Bagauda* appears in both written and unwritten form (Hiskett 1964–5); in Swahili verse there is constant interchange and influence between orally-composed and written poetry (Whiteley 1958; Harries 1962, 3–5); and in modern Somali oral literature poets make use of the radio, face-to-face delivery, and writing 'as a visual aid to their oral memory' (Mumin 1974, 3) with equal facility. It is even common for poems to be written initially but to reach their fullest actualization and main circulation when performed orally. This applies to modern political songs and hymns, Swahili and Fulani poems, and the Hausa compositions which are written, sung aloud by beggars, chanted on the streets at night, and performed over the radio (see references in Finnegan 1970, 51, 185ff, 284ff).

Evidence from other regions echoes the doubts raised by the African evidence about the distinctiveness of 'these two great categories of poetry', oral and written. An interdependence of oral and written versions can be seen in the great epic of Gesar in Tibet and Mongolia over at least three centuries (Stein 1959, ch. 3), or in Chinese mediaeval ballads (Doleželová-Velingerová & Crump 1971) as well as in more recent Anglo-American ballads or Irish street songs, and in the mediaeval and classical reliance on oral delivery of literature initially composed in writing (see e.g. Crosby 1936; Hadas 1954). In the islands of the South Pacific, it is not uncommon for some local people to possess manuscript texts, to which they refer from time to time, even of narratives, songs or proverbs which primarily circulate orally (see e.g. Burrows 1963, 409; Holmes 1969, 351; Salmond 1975, 120–1). The Pacific 'myths and legends' with their poetic inserts that have been recorded and published by many scholars, often, in practice, rely on written versions as well as on oral dictation. It is also now a widespread phenomenon for poems to be initially composed in writing, but to reach their main circulation when performed orally. This can be through feedback from written compositions into oral forms through literate poets producing texts for joint choral performances (as for example, in the composition of the traditional *imene-tuatua* songs in the modern Cook Islands, (Tongia 1977), or – very commonly indeed – for performance over the radio). It seems that a 'mixed' form of literature is perfectly feasible, and has, in fact, frequently occurred in the course of human history.

But if a mixed product turns out to be possible, perhaps this mixing does not apply to the poet himself? What of Parry and Lord's 'proof' that 'the acquisition of writing invariably destroys the powers of an oral poet' (Kirk 1965, 30)? Here there may be evidence still to be published from the Yugoslav studies of Parry and Lord; but on my reading of the available material this 'proof' seems to rest more on assertion and presupposition than on demonstration. The original recordings were themselves selective – Parry did his best to select 'genuine traditional singers'. Even with this bias, many of their famed 'oral singers of tales' were in fact literate. It is hard to find much proof for the impossibility of a literate poet composing in the oral mode.

The African evidence also seems to cast doubt on this kind of assertion. In my own fieldwork, one of the best Limba story-tellers (best in Limba eyes too) was a highly literate product of a teacher-training college. His stories seemed to show no essential difference in style, presentation and use of varying combinations of traditional elements, from the many others which I recorded from totally illiterate narrators. Similar examples can be drawn from the many magnificent oral sermons composed and delivered so regularly to African congregations by their literate pastors. Again, a recent collection of Dinka poetry from the Southern Sudan includes in the same volume not only 'traditional' ox songs, initiation songs, and war songs, but also similarly constructed modern school songs by Dinka schoolboys. I mentioned earlier the capacity of Xhosa praise poets to compose-in-performance by means of formulae. But it is also true that some of these Xhosa poets are literate, and when they produce written praise poems – about the Apollo moon landing for example – they compose in an equally formulaic style (Opland 1971).

The African evidence does not stand alone; scholars in other areas have also pointed out that the possession of literacy need not necessarily prevent a poet from composing in the formulaic manner. Benson summed it up in an influential article in the Anglo-Saxon field. 'To prove that an Old English poem is formulaic is only to prove that it is an Old English poem, and to show that such a work has a high or low percentage of formulas reveals nothing about whether or not it is a literate composition' (Benson 1966, 336).

The rigid distinction between 'oral' and 'written' literature and composition is more doubtful than one would gather from the oral-formulaic writers, though it might be possible to save the overall distinction by taking a very narrow definition of 'oral poetry' or by pushing the matter back into unseen (and unproveable) 'mental processes' or a special 'mental template', as indeed some adherents of this theory have attempted. I would contend this is either to narrow the definition in an unhelpful and ultimately unrealistic way, or to turn the whole theory into an unfalsifiable tautology. In any everyday sense of the words, I consider that the oral-formulaic writers have not produced evidence that there is a clear-cut distinction between oral and written modes of literature and of composition, and that without such evidence their theories are unconvincing.

A further difficulty relates to the whole question of what is meant by 'the formula'. The oral-formulaic theorists have produced a vast amount of quantitative evidence, such as the 100 per cent formularity of Yugoslav epic, the 80 to 90 per cent of Homer, and so on. Such 'hard' evidence makes it seem reasonable for Lord to claim that 'A pattern of 50 to 60 per cent formula or formulaic, with 10 to perhaps 25 per cent straight formula, indicates clearly literary or written composition. I am still convinced that it is possible to determine orality by quantitative formulaic analysis, by the study of formula density' (1968b, 24).

This statement sounds precise and scientific, but it overlooks the notorious controversies within the oral-formulaic school about just what a 'formula' is. Even the agreement which can be reached in a single language or poetic tradition no longer applies to a different type of linguistic form, making comparative conclusions very difficult to reach. Yet it seems to have become almost an article of faith in the oral-formulaic approach that, even if it has proved impossible so far to agree exactly on what a 'formula' is, there is *something* real there called a 'formula' about whose incidence one can in principle draw quantitative conclusions. Of course the whole basis of statistical conclusions is that you must first be clear what are the units you count and that they are indeed comparable. When this is not so, the statistics, however mathematically sophisticated, are meaningless. Rogers' comments in the Old English context are pertinent here. 'The term "formula" becomes a portmanteau, enclosing within its ample capacity many different and often undefined sorts of lexical, morphological and syntactic similarities... One is forced to suspect that the growing dogmatism about the oral-formulaic character of Old English poetry owes more to faith and presumed psychological insight than to reason' (1966, 102).

This difficulty is critical, and raises serious doubts about the scientific and quantitative basis of the oral-formulaic theory. In addition, while some of the texts in question have been very fully analyzed, those of the Homeric epics, which formed the starting-point for the whole theory, have not. As Russo notes (1976), statements about the 80 or 90 per cent formularity of Homer, presented with such apparent confidence, in practice rest on the analysis of very few lines, primarily the opening passages or preludes. From analysis of certain later passages Russo derives lower figures, much closer to those which Lord would consider a sign of *written* composition. Perhaps one case of this kind does not invalidate a general theory – but when it concerns the ground on which the theory was first erected and from which it gained much of its attraction, it certainly raises doubts.

So far I have queried the assumptions in the oral-formulaic theory that there is a clear distinction between oral and written modes and that part of this distinction lies in the use of 'formulae', units which can be both discerned and measured in oral literature. Once these assumptions are seen as doubtful some of the plausibility of the claim that this theory provides us with a possible 'universal' begins to vanish.

I have one further assumption to examine – the belief that *all* oral poetry is composed on the Yugoslav model: that is, by simultaneous composition/performance, with no separation between these two processes. Lord claims that 'for the oral poet the moment of composition is the performance...singing, performing, composing are facets of the same act', and 'we now know exactly what is meant by these terms [oral and oral poems], at least insofar as manner of composition is concerned' (1968a, 13, 141). This general position has been taken up by other adherents of the Parry–Lord theory, who believe that all oral poetry is composed on the Yugoslav analogy, *in* performance, without prior composition.

Now it is certainly true that much oral poetry *is* composed in performance, as I have shown above. But to take the further step of claiming that this is the *only* way in which oral poetry can be, and is, composed is not justified. In fact there are a number of instances, in Africa and elsewhere, where oral poetry has involved not composition-in-performance, but long-considered and deliberate composition prior to the moment of performance.

One example of this can be found in Somali poetry. (I purposely begin with this instance, for Somali poetry has been extensively studied by scholars with a deep knowledge of Somali, who are well aware of recent work on oral literature and not liable to fall into the trap of certain earlier scholars who assumed without question that memorization was the norm.) In Somali society poetic composition is a highly-admired and discussed art. Somali audiences are enthusiastic listeners, highly critical of the poems they hear. Somali poets 'rarely perform their work until composition is completely finished in private' (Johnson 1974, 12) and 'spend many hours, sometimes even days, composing their works' before they perform them (Andrzejewski & Lewis 1964, 45). Those who hear a poet's work often memorize it and repeat it to others, in each case attributing the poem by name to its author. What is involved here is prior composition, followed by memorization, rather than composition-in-performance. This is made clear in the account by Andrzejewski & Lewis (1964, 45–6), where they describe how impressed they are

by feats of memory on the part of the poetry reciters, some of whom are poets themselves. Unaided by writing they learn long poems by heart and some have repertoires which are too great to be exhausted even by several evenings of continuous recitation...The reciters are not only capable of acquiring a wide repertoire but can store it in their memories for many years, sometimes for their lifetime...

A poem passes from mouth to mouth. Between the young Somali who listens today to a poem composed fifty years ago, five hundred miles away, and its first audience there is a long chain of reciters who passed it one to another. It is only natural that in this process of transmission some distortion occurs, but comparison of different versions of the same poem usually shows a surprisingly high degree of fidelity to the original...

Among the audience there are often people who already know by heart the particular poem, having learnt it from another source. Heated disputes sometimes arise between a reciter and his audience concerning the purity of his version.

This example does not fit the Yugoslav analogy since it involves the concept of a correct and enduring text, exact memorization by reciters of a poem, and the separation of the processes of composition and performance through the practice of prior composition by Somali poets.

This is not just an exceptional case in African oral literature. Zulu memorial panegyric poems were passed down from the original poets to singers attached to local courts who then recited set texts to their audiences. As Cope explains, the singer had to 'memorize [the praises of the chief and ancestors] so perfectly that...they pour forth in a continuous stream or torrent. Although he may vary the order of the section or stanzas of the praise-poem, he may not vary the praises themselves. He commits them to memory as he hears them, even if they are meaningless to him' (1968, 27–8).

There are other recorded instances where prior composition by the oral poet is followed by careful rehearsal before public performance. Among the Ila and Tonga of Zambia, for example, individuals are often expected to sing one of their own songs on special occasions. They often take great pains to prepare these songs carefully before-hand. The songs called *impango*, which are composed and sung by women, are usually sung to praise oneself or one's lover. When a woman has a general plan for an *impango* of her own, she goes to a well-known maker of *impango* songs for help, after which she spends several days working out the tune and practising the song with female friends until they consider the *impango* perfect. When she is invited to a festival she keeps 'singing it in her heart' until at last the time comes for her to stand up and sing it in public (Jones 1943, 11–12).

Among the Dinka of the Southern Sudan too, individuals own songs which are composed not in the moment of performance but by a complex process beforehand. Here too people sometimes call on an expert to compose a song to their requirement. Deng explains: 'While an expert composes for others, people must be near him to memorize the song as it develops. The composer mumbles to himself, constructs a few lines, tells the people to "hold this" and sings the lines. As he proceeds, they follow him. When a song is completed, the expert is likely to have forgotten it, while they remember it in full' (1973, 85). The owner of the song can then perform it on occasions when it is likely to enhance his position or bring him power or, at times, just to provide entertainment. This is clearly far from the composition-in-performance situation.

Prior composition and memorization of oral poetry is not an aberrant African phenomenon, even though many more African examples can be given. There is, for example, the reflective and deeply personal process by which Eskimo poets compose. The composer of a song may 'long walk to and fro in some solitary place, arranging his words while humming a melody which he has also made up himself' (Rasmussen 1931, 321). The process resembles that followed by mediaeval Gaelic poets when they composed their poems orally in a darkened room, and were not allowed the use of writing materials until they emerged. Their completed poem was then recited by a bard (not the composer himself) who 'got it well by heart, and now pronounc'd it orderly' (quoted in Knott & Murphy 1967, 63–4). In the South Pacific, with the frequent group performance of poetry to music and dance, prior composition by a named poet followed by word-for-word memorization by the troupe is one of the commonest patterns for poetic composition (see e.g. Handy & Winne 1925, 11; Grimble 1957, 204ff; essays on Fiji in Finnegan & Pillai 1978. For further comparative examples of prior composition, see Finnegan 1977, 73ff).

It is clear from instances such as these that the composition of oral poetry takes many other forms than that followed by the Yugoslav oral poets studied by Parry and Lord. These different cases do not invalidate the findings of Parry and Lord in Yugoslavia, nor their application to parallel cases elsewhere, but they do make clear that the Yugoslav process is not the only one followed by oral poets throughout the world – not unless the term 'oral poetry' is so narrowly defined as to become unreasonably restrictive and perhaps merely tautological. The actual processes of composition in oral poetry form so important a part of the Parry–Lord theory, that doubts about the universal applicability of the Yugoslav model of oral composition inevitably raise similar doubts about the universal validity of the theory as a whole.

My conclusion is that, despite the appeal of the theory and the widespread evidence for it, it does not stand up as a 'universal'. The claims made in it are too wide, a number of dubious assumptions are made, the apparently hard evidence is far less clear than appears at first sight, and the whole complex of processes pin-pointed by Parry and Lord in Yugoslavia turns out to have limited application.

## Conclusion

Although I am quite clear in my rejection of claims to universality I still feel I cannot just dismiss the Parry–Lord theory. Why is it that *The singer of tales* is somehow clearly a classic work? Why is it that for so many students of oral literature the world has never looked quite the same after reading it? Why does one keep coming back to the Parry–Lord work?

The answers to such questions may help to offset the otherwise negative tone of this paper. Perhaps it is partly that the findings of Parry and Lord have helped to supersede earlier misleading ideas about what was 'universal' in African (or 'primitive') communities generally; and that by setting up claims for a counter-universal they at least raised doubts about previous implicitly universalistic claims. Perhaps too their work has opened up questions which, though sometimes considered earlier, were not very commonly asked in the study of oral literature and non-literate cultures: about the relation between creativity and tradition, the individual's active role in his poetic heritage, or the importance of performance and occasion as against verbally defined text. Perhaps too they have added to our understanding of a cluster of phenomena that had not been so clearly delineated for us before, phenomena which have occurred not only in Yugoslavia in the 1930s but in many other settings too. The complex of processes may not have the complete universality claimed by some adherents of the oral-formulaic school but it is nevertheless widespread and always worth looking for as one of a series of recurrent possibilities in human culture and action.

It can be illuminating too to look not just at the reasons which still make the Parry–Lord approach significant, but also at the sort of difficulties that arose in trying to assess it. A number of these difficulties are perhaps of wider relevance than just for the analysis of oral literature, for they seem to occur frequently in the search for 'universals'.

One constantly recurring problem is that of comparability across cultures. In the Parry–Lord theory, once one moved outside a single poetic tradition, the question of 'what *is* a formula' became a difficulty. For here, as so often, even when an item (or an activity or an institution) looks the same on the surface, it sometimes turns out to be different when one looks deeper, or at the local meanings and the local uses. In the context of literature and literacy, this becomes clear when one looks hard at the different *uses* made of writing or of a 'formulaic' style. Just giving it the same label from the outside does not mean it necessarily *is* the same.

Another recurrent and hoary problem is how to relate one's theories to the data. How far must one start only from the actual instances of (in this case) oral poetries? How far is it justifiable to try to impose one model on one's interpretation of the facts – as perhaps Parry and Lord did, mistakenly but in some ways most fruitfully? When looking for 'universals' how can one ever feel confident that one has looked at 'enough' of the facts – can one's sample ever be sufficient? The Parry–Lord theorists seemed to have amassed a vast amount of evidence in support of their contentions that certain processes were universal and yet the number of exceptions to composition-in-performance seems equally impressive. Perhaps after all we can never establish universals through induction and that is why we are tempted to the kind of tautologies I have suggested in some of the claims about 'the oral mind' or a 'mental template', for they at least remain true by definition. And perhaps the best we can hope for is to put forward several models of human activity each of which is illuminating in some way. Within such limitations, it may be that there is indeed something universal about the Parry–Lord theory, presenting as it does the picture of the active creating poet as against the inert transmitter of rote-memorized tradition. But here one comes back to competing views of human nature (and to controversies, among other things, in sociological theory) rather than to the empirically established generalizations that some perhaps hoped to discover through the search for 'universals'.

A final problem that kept worrying me as I thought about Parry and Lord and 'universals' is how universal a 'universal' has to be. In one sense I cannot help feeling that there *is* something universal in what Parry and Lord pointed out, and in the formulations in *The singer of tales*, but that, as I have taken pains to reiterate, this does not mean that it always occurs! Rather it is universal in the sense that it is one commonly recurring set of possibilities in human action, complemented by other possibilities which are realized in other contexts.

Perhaps the dual conclusion must be that, first, there does indeed exist a set of frequently recurring (but not totally universal or determined) processes in human action to which Parry and Lord have directed our attention, and, second, that in doing so they have developed the kind of heuristic model which enables one to ask illuminating questions and perceive possible relationships which were before obscure. These two possibilities may be what we learn from the Parry–Lord theory, even though I would reject it as universal in any law-like or deterministic sense. But even these less drastic claims for the theory are scarcely trivial. I hope that a place will be found in the analysis of 'universals' for weaker though important claims of this kind.

## References

Andrzejewski, B. W. & Lewis, I. M. (1964) *Somali poetry : an introduction.* Oxford: Clarendon Press

Anyumba, H. O. (1964) 'The nyatiti lament songs', *East Africa past and present.* Paris: Présence africaine

Benson, L. D. (1966) 'The literary character of Anglo-Saxon formulaic poetry', *Publications of the Modern Language Association* 81

Burrows, E. G. (1963) *Flower in my ear : arts and ethos of Ifaluk atoll.* Seattle: University of Washington Press

Carpenter, R. (1958) *Folk tale, fiction and saga in the Homeric epics.* Berkeley: University of California Press

Cope, T. (ed.) (1968) *Izibongo. Zulu praise-poems.* Oxford: Clarendon Press

Crosby, R. (1936) 'Oral delivery in the Middle Ages', *Speculum* 11

Deng, F. M. (1973) *The Dinka and their songs.* Oxford: Clarendon Press

Doleželová-Velingerová, M. & Crump, J. I. (trans.) (1971) *Ballad of the hidden dragon.* Oxford: Clarendon Press

Finnegan, R. (1977) *Oral poetry : its nature, significance and social context.* Cambridge University Press

—— (1976) 'What is oral literature anyway? Some comments in the light of some African and other comparative material', in Stolz, B. A. & Shannon, R. S. (1976)

—— (1970) *Oral literature in Africa.* Oxford: Clarendon Press

—— (1967) *Limba stories and story-telling.* Oxford: Clarendon Press

—— & Pillai, R. (eds.) (1978) *Essays on Pacific literature.* Suva: Fiji museum

Grimble, A. (1957) *Return to the islands.* London: John Murray

Hadas, M. (1954) *Ancilla to classical reading.* New York: Columbia University Press

Handy, E. S. C. & Winne, J. L. (1925) *Music in the Marquesas Islands.* Bernice P. Bishop Museum Bulletin 17

Harries, L. (1962) *Swahili poetry.* Oxford: Clarendon Press

Hiskett, M. (1964–5) 'The "Song of Bagauda": a Hausa king list and homily in verse', *Bulletin of School of Oriental and African Studies* 27–8

Holmes, L. D. (1969) 'Samoan oratory', *Journal of American Folklore* 82

Johnson, J. W. (1974) *Heellooy Heelleellooy. The development of the genre heello in modern Somali poetry.* Bloomington: Indiana University Publications

Jones, A. M. (1943) *African music.* Rhodes-Livingstone Museum Occasional Paper 2

Junod, H. A. (1912–13) *The life of a South African tribe* (2 vols.). Neuchatel

Kailasapathy, K. (1968) *Tamil heroic poetry.* Oxford: Clarendon Press

Kirk, G. S. (1965) *Homer and the epic.* Cambridge University Press

Knott, E. & Murphy, G. (1967) *Early Irish literature.* London: Routledge & Kegan Paul

Lord, A. B. (1968a) *The singer of tales.* New York: Atheneum. (First published 1960)

—— (1968b) 'Homer as an oral poet', *Harvard Studies in Classical Philology* 72

—— (1965) 'Oral poetry', in Preminger, A. (ed.) *Encyclopedia of poetry and poetics.* Princeton University Press

McLuhan, M. (1962) *The Gutenberg galaxy.* London: Routledge & Kegan Paul

—— (1967) *Understanding media : the extensions of man.* London: Sphere Books

Magoun, F. P. (1971) 'Oral-formulaic character of Anglo-Saxon narrative poetry', *Speculum* 28, 1953. (Reprinted in Nicholson, L. E. (ed.) *An anthology of Beowulf criticism.* University of Notre Dame Press)

Mumin, Hassan Sheikh (1974) *Shabeelnaagood : Leopard among the women. A Somali play,* Translated by Andrzejewski, B. W. Oxford University Press

Nagler, M. N. (1967) 'Towards a generative view of the oral formula', *Transactions of the American Philological Association* 98

Nichols, S. G. (1961) *Formulaic diction and thematic composition.* University of North Carolina

Notopoulos, J. A. (1964) 'Studies in early Greek oral poetry', *Harvard Studies in Classical Philology* 68

Opland, J. (1971) '"Scop" and "imbongi": Anglo-Saxon and Bantu oral poets', *English Studies in Africa* 14

Parry, M. (1930 & 1932) 'Studies in the epic technique of oral verse-making. 1. Homer and Homeric style. 2. The Homeric language as the language of an oral poetry', *Harvard Studies in Classical Philology* 41 (1930), 43 (1932)

—— & Lord, A. B. (1954) *Serbocroatian heroic songs,* I. *Novi Pazar : English translations.* Cambridge, Mass., and Belgrade: Harvard University Press and Serbian Academy of Science

Parsons, T. (1964) 'Evolutionary universals', *American Sociological Review* 29

Rasmussen, K. (1931) *The Netsilik Eskimos : social life and spiritual culture.* Report of the Fifth Thule Expedition, vol. 8, 1/2, Copenhagen

Rogers, H. L. (1966) 'The crypto-psychological character of the oral formula', *English Studies* 47

Russo, J. (1976) 'Is "oral" or "aural" composition the cause of Homer's formulaic style?', in Stolz, B. A. & Shannon, R. S. (1976)

Salmond, A. (1975) *Hui : a study of Maori ceremonial gatherings.* Wellington: Reed

Smith, M. G. (1957) 'The social functions and meaning of Hausa praise-singing', *Africa* 27

Stein, R. A. (1959) *Recherches sur l'épopée et le barde au Tibet.* Paris: Presses universitaires de France

Tongia, M. (1977) *Rarotonga songs and their functions,* Unpublished research paper, University of South Pacific, Fiji

Whiteley, W. H. (1958) *The dialects and verse of Pemba.* Kampala: East African Swahili Committee

# 12    Review and prospectus

*Jerome Bruner*

It is my privilege to attempt an overview of our proceedings. It is not an easy task, for there is a splendid variety in the material presented that almost defies summary. Let me, then, be more personal and selective in this account – one man's review.

A proper motto for any effort that brings several disciplines together is a remark of Niels Bohr: 'Let us distinguish two kinds of truths, minor truths and major truths. It can be said of minor truths that their opposites are false. But of major truths it can be said that their opposites are also true.' With an issue like 'Universals' before us, and with several disciplines participating in the discussion, it will not be easy to tell where there are contradictions, where complementarities, and where minds do not meet at all.

There are some preliminaries that need to be got through before we come to the discussion proper. They have principally to do with contrasting ways in which people pose the problem of universals. The first of these contrasts is between *process* universals and *product* universals. Linguistics provides an excellent example. If, for example, we look at the stock of world languages, we can find certain forms that are present in virtually all languages. One of these illustrates a distinction examined with such great care by the 'modern grandfather' of linguistic universals, Roman Jakobson. It is the distinction between marked and unmarked in all languages – between the ordinary, expected, conventional, regular in contrast to the unexpected, special, irregular. It is a way in which *all* languages deal with the task of alerting the attention of the recipients of messages to what needs special processing. *That* is a process universal. Languages achieve marking in different ways – although there are some very widespread means for doing so. One that is nearly universal in practice is that the marked form is realized by *adding* something (an inflectional morpheme, a prosodic feature, an affix, etc.) and practically never by leaving off something from the linguistic constituent to be marked.

256

But that is more like a procedural realization of the universal process of marking. Then as we look at particular languages we find some 'near universals' in marking procedures. *Most* languages mark the plural form and not the singular. Or, where there is difference between the two in marking, it will be the object that is marked and not the subject. Now, these latter seem to be widespread *products* of the marking process, different common ways of realizing a universal of language. Some of them may turn out to be so widespread as to mislead us into considering them universals in their own right – like the rule that we always *add* in order to mark linguistically rather than subtracting. Chomsky in his *Reflections on language* argues that there are 'natural' ways of structuring our thoughts that force us to use certain universal processes in language, like subject and predicate. But we must not take the concrete realizations of these universal processes (linguistic *products*) and confuse them with what brought them into being.

So we shall have to beware of arguments about underlying processes that are universal and their products that may not be. *All* cultures generate kinship systems. *Not* all cultures have the same form of kinship system. The preferential role of mother's brother for male ego may not be universal, but when it is fully understood it may tell us not only about kinship systems in which it occurs but about the universal process that produces kinship systems in general. And so too with marking. If we fully understand why subject takes precedence over object in marking, it may lead us to understand more fully the universal function or realization of marking. Product and process must be kept clear, yet eventually they will explicate each other.

Bernard Comrie's chapter is a striking example of a search for a process universal in language. He rejects the approach of transformational-generative grammarians who argue *a priori* that the deep structure of language consists of abstract linguistic universals – a claim that cannot in any case be put to test on concrete, particular languages. He sets out to *discover* universals in a set of African languages, and proposes that these can be found in the phenomenon of relativization: in a Case Hierarchy, relativization becomes more difficult the further down the hierarchy one goes from subject, to direct object, to indirect object, to oblique object, to genitive. Indeed, he succeeds in finding such a universal. Now comes the task of figuring out whether the universal reflects the nature of human language, human attention, or the natural order in which events are 'thought about'. It is a bold venture to figure out how such a universal ever emerged – even if it is limited to African languages.

A second contrast is between universal functional *requirements* of societies and the diverse ways in which these are met. A good example is the Parsonian list of universal functional prerequisites for an operating society. Marxist analyses also posit such universal 're-quirements' and so too Levi-Strauss with his universal systems of exchange. Such 'universals' are hypotheses about the nature of human *societies*. They are of a different order from *universals about human nature* – about human 'instincts' or 'capacities' and it creates muddle to try to derive one from the other. We will do well to avoid that trap and to consider instead the ways in which social requirements and psychological capacities interact.

Let me examine a few examples of this interaction. Take a known psychological universal: the very limited human capacity for pro-cessing information. At any given time, the human information pro-cessing system cannot process more than seven plus or minus two 'elements' of information. This is the processing limit, or channel capacity. Let us now juxtapose *this* universal with a universal cultural requirement – that a society pass on its stock of traditions and rituals, and let us concentrate on pre-literate societies. Ruth Finnegan presented a highly tempting version of the Parry–Lord principle. In an 'oral' tradition, stories and poems are not memorized by the poet but constructed in performance from a stock of what might be called formulaic patterns or routines. I think she convinced us all that this was a magnificently wrong theory, and that while there is some truth to it, that truth may obscure the many exceptions to it. The main psychological appeal of such a theory is that it suggests ways in which the enormously rich stock of tales of a culture can be made generative and combinable and still fit within the modest processing capacity of human beings. But we now learn that oral poets do not always operate in this way. Dinka poets serve not as generative performers but as 'consultants' to others who wish to *use* a poem they have commis-sioned to be composed in their favour. The poet composes for a client who then commits the poem to this own memory and then the poet advises on use. What emerges from Ruth Finnegan's presentation is that a society with an oral tradition has its own way of dealing with the limited memory capacities of individuals, and there are lots of ways of doing it. But one forgets at one's peril that though there are lots of ways of doing it, there is still the need for mnemonic economy in meeting the constraints imposed by human capacities.

A second example of the same principle was elegantly presented by Roland Fletcher, a principle of permissible variation. Let me put it formally first: culturally permitted variation in the second moment of a distribution is proportionate to the permissible magnitude of the first moment of that distribution. Put in a less formal way, the larger the architectural element that is incorporated in a residence pattern, the larger the variation that will be permitted in its size. Is this another rule of mental economy – that variation in a visual feature of a culture should be proportionate to its average magnitude?

Or take a third example, this one from Barbara Lloyd's presentation. Whenever a new system of educational qualifications is introduced into a society, the social status within that society will very quickly reflect the new qualifications but the old status system will simply maintain its form and change its criteria. Introduce new qualifications and the initial effect will be that the old status system remains with its positions defined in terms of the new qualifications. Schooling is introduced to equalize opportunities and then school grades or amounts of schooling is used to create a new basis for defining the social-class system. Is there a universal tendency in human cultures to reduce contradiction and dissonance in its use of criteria for assigning status and position? Here I find myself in deep doubt! Certainly John Gay's study of socialization among the Kpelle, where 'new' and 'old' ways produce deep conflicts both within the culture and within individuals, speaks against such a universal 'dissonance reduction' principle. Cultures obviously produce more contradiction than individuals can easily cope with and the Nigerian case does not seem to yield any special clues about universals. Nor did Dr Lloyd intend it to.

Consider now a third contrast: between what might be called *competence* universals and *performance* differences. Let me take as an example Pierre Dasen's lucid presentation of the Piagetian cross-cultural studies. The Piagetian analysis indicates that there are invariants in the order of cognitive stages of growth in children with differences only in the ages at which these stages are reached. In the Piagetian system, a first stage is based principally on a system of 'sensori-motor action' with the child lacking a full internal representation of the environment to guide his behaviour. In a second stage of 'concrete operations', the environment is now 'concretely' represented, the representation conserving a record of actual experience. In a final stage of formal operations, there is not only a representation of the world of actual events but also, by mastery of a set of transformations, of the world of *possible* events and actions. The child now can handle combinatorial manoeuvres that permit him to generate possible worlds beyond his own experience. Now, within certain limits, these stages of development are roughly universal although they show interesting systematic variations as well. Let us say, simply, that the unfolding of logical capacities is not so different from society to society. But what *is* strikingly different from society to society is the use to which mental operations are put, what is demanded of a person using his logical operations. And it starts very early. In our own society mothers' responses to infants who are moving from pre-linguistic communication to a linguistic system show striking difference depending on whether they are middle class or working class. The former take their jobs more pedagogically. When a child can *name* a thing, the middle class mother is more likely to press him to go on to say something about its state or its action as well. She is signalling to him her expectancy about *performance*. Both sets of children have the competence to talk about states and actions of things. One set is predisposed to *use* the competence more than another or to use it in one context rather than another. So though there may be universals at the competence level, at the level of performance, in the uses to which competence is put there will be wide divergence. This, in effect, is the message of Michael Cole's work. It also helps us understand John Gay's discussion on how a forest people develop 'strip maps' as a way of mentally representing their immediate environment. It requires no special competence – anybody could do it given the time and effort. But his people specialize a set of universal competencies and convert them into a highly distinctive and idiosyncratic performance.

And so it is with the problem of developmental universals. If one works at the characterization of human competence, one is much more likely to find a unity of mankind and even a unitary developmental path. If on the other hand, the search is for the patterning of competence by use, one will be struck by differences. It is surely trivial to set the one approach against the other. For what is most striking is the manner in which *universal* competences are shaped to the uses of *different* cultures.

Those are some of the general problems that found their way into my notes. But there were also certain specifics that struck me. The first one is that there seemed to be no passionate desire in either papers or discussions to establish a catalogue of universals. Nobody was bent to emerge with a tablet upon which were inscribed the universals of mankind.

Nonetheless, some quasi-universals crept through a back door surreptitiously, particularly through social ecology. Ecological niche, some speakers implied, could be taken as an almost 'direct' determinant of the nature of mind, or of the operation of mind, or of the development of mind. Dr Dasen made it seem as if space perception among Eskimos and hunter-gatherers generally was shaped by terrain and its ecological requirements. And Dr Okonji invoked the same casual explanation in accounting for field independence among hunter-gatherers. Being a hunter-gatherer *does* impose a functional requirement and *may* shape *performance*. But I doubt that it does so necessarily on a whole people. To account for perceptual or cognitive specialization on that ground alone, without further specification of the symbolical values in the culture that support and nurture them seems to me to be an oversimplification. We need careful studies of how hunter-gatherers learn to operate in the natural situations they are in. Hunter-gatherers do more than hunt and gather. We are told of their considerable leisure in recent studies. Their women do not hunt, and they raise the children, surely not entirely for the functions of hunting and gathering. Before we accept the 'universal' that cognitive functioning mirrors the ecological requirements of a society, we must examine the complex processes whereby this shaping takes place. It may well be, for example, that hunter-gatherers are not concerned with measuring out wheat, and that may account for a delay in their mastering conservation of quantity. But they certainly *are* concerned with measuring out who gets what portion of a seal to apportion it among kinsmen. Which aspect of their ecology shapes their competence into particular patterns of performance? And what of all the leisure time spent in story telling in the winter igloos? How does *that* affect cognitive development? Man does not live by hunting and gathering alone. We need more than a specification of occupation. But both Dasen and Okonji have said the same thing.

Let me mention a last issue relating to Ruth Finnegan's and John Gay's reports. It is quite apparent from both these papers that human beings are capable of organizing their knowledge in highly varied ways. One common way is by the use of category systems based on the use of fairly large sets of criterial attributes. The other is in terms of various thematic and narrative patterns. Each type has infinite variations. And any given culture uses a staggering variety of each of them. One of the ways in which a culture gains 'control' of its members is to predispose and specialize them toward certain modes of organizing in preference to others until, at the far extreme of socialization, it creates a kind of irreversible 'cultural' deformation in its members. This, in effect, is the Whorfian hypothesis put in cultural rather than linguistic terms. And it is assumed to be the basis of cultural relativism. We still know very little about the extent to which, in fact, such enculturation produces strong and irreversible differences among people. Is it the case that, for all we might have to say about cultural universals, there is also a residual relativism based upon this type of specialization in the organizing systems that people use for forming categories and explanations? Are we as a species more like hedgehogs who only know one big thing through the lens of our culture, or like foxes capable of knowing many things depending on the opportunity for encountering them?

And finally a few brief methodological points. Gustav Jahoda made the important point in his concluding remarks that the discovery of universals requires the use of multiple methods in testing for their presence. I take its meaning in this sense: any universal (cultural or psychological) can find its expression through various modes. It is not obvious how to 'find it' once it is expressed. A single research instrument looking at single phenomena is not likely to do so. There are many local realization rules through which a universal may express itself.

Secondly, as Meyer Fortes and Ruth Finnegan both remarked, universal traits are most often contextualized in broader cultural patterns. The isolation of such traits from context always risks trivializing them. You cannot talk about a mode of representation in drawing in isolation without taking into account the set of supporting cultural traits of which it is an expression. Lists of universals have the effect of isolating culture traits as if they had no such contextualization.

And finally, there emerged from the discussion an implicit conclusion: perhaps the search for universals may have the effect of making the study of culture too static. Perhaps they are better kept in the back of one's mind. When searched for too directly, the result is often a catalogue. Process gets lost. Classification becomes obsessional. Universals found their way back into studies of culture as an antidote to cultural relativism. The emphasis upon them has surely served a useful function. But one need not live on a diet of antidote alone.

# Subject index

accessibility hierarchy, 216
acculturation
  and cognitive style, 168
  and spatial skills, 146, 148
active sentence, in grammar, 225, 226, 230
adaptation (*see* Piaget's theory of cognitive development)
African literary tradition, 244
African oral literature, 238–46, 248–50
African psychology, xi, xii, xiv, xv, xix, 194
age trends
  in drawing skill, 52, 58, 59; depth perception, 33–5, 37
  and Piagetian tasks, 177, 178, 180, 181, 184–9; psychological differentiation, 164, 165, 171
agricultural societies, 11, 124, 146, 150, 153, 161, 169
  cattle raising, 148
  cultivation, 79, 124, 148
Aristotelian space conceptualization, 2, 113, 115
arithmetic series, 76, 77
art, representational
  artistic achievement, Eskimo, 147
  clay modelling, as 3-dimensional diagram, 47
  handicrafts, 47, 179
  stone carving, 147
  Tallensi art, 47
attitude delineation in concept formation, 205–12
authority patterns, 136, 168–70

belief systems
  circular, 8, 9, 12
  divergent visions of reality, 2, 6, 8, 10–14
  representation of, 129

bilingualism, 187, 205, 206, 208, 212, 213
  compound bilingualism, 187
  coordinate bilingualism, 187, 208
biological factors
  in cognitive development, 143, 179, 180; cognitive style, 166, 171; universal traits, 41
brain (human), 71, 108

Cartesian
  space conceptualization, 2
  maps, 24, 111–13
case hierarchy, 215–20, 223, 225–7, 229, 230, 257
categorization
  and cultural relativism, 261, 262
child rearing
  and cognitive development, 139, 140, 166–8, 177; cognitive style, xviii, 166–8
Chomskian theory of language
  deep structure, 113, 229–31, 257
  surface structure, 15, 113, 205, 230
  universals, 14, 15, 228–31, 257
classification, 24, 71, 95, 118–20, 129, 180, 182
  classifications of space, 72, 73
  classification tasks, 180, 182
  free classification, 182
cluster analysis, 113, 120, 121, 124–6
codified world view, 13, 14
cognitive development, 136–8, 150, 176, 177, 186, 189, 190, 193, 194
  eco-cultural adaptive model, 146, 148, 151, 153
  eco-cultural demands, 136, 146, 161, 166, 170
  measurement, 2
  (*see also* biological factors, child rearing, cultural factors, family background, social background)

263

# Author index

## DATE DUE

| | | | |
|---|---|---|---|
| | | | |
| | | | |
| | | | |
| | | | |
| | | | |
| | | | |
| | | | |
| | | | |
| | | | |
| | | | |
| | | | |
| | | | |
| | | | |
| | | | |
| | | | |
| | | | |